359.0942   001
KEMP, PETER

NINE VANGUARDS

1 250967 001 7B
SK   ZZZ

Items should be
returned to the
library from which
they were borrowed
on or before the
date stamped above
unless a renewal
has been granted.

Gloucestershire
County Library

D0184341

H.M.S. *Vanguard*, 1947

NINE VANGUARDS

by
LIEUTENANT-COMMANDER
P. K. KEMP
R.N.

With 17 Illustrations

1951
HUTCHINSON & CO. (Publishers) LTD
London   New York   Melbourne   Sydney   Cape Town

GLOUCESTERSHIRE COUNTY LIBRARY

CLASS........ 359·0942

COPY.................... C

Printed in Great Britain
by The Anchor Press, Ltd.,
Tiptree, Essex

CONTENTS

LIST OF ILLUSTRATIONS

FOREWORD

My thanks are due to Mr. Bonner-Smith, Librarian of the Admiralty; to Lieutenant-Colonel Wilkinson, Librarian of the Royal United Service Institution; and to Miss Galway, Librarian of the Navy League, for their advice and help over the history of previous *Vanguards*; to the staff of the Public Records Office and British Museum Manuscript Room for their assistance in tracing original letters and papers; to the Department of Naval Information at the Admiralty for their help and the provision of many of the facts about the ninth *Vanguard*; to Messrs. Sampson Low, Marston and Co., Ltd., the publishers, and Mr. Raymond Blackman, the editor, for permission to incorporate information published in *Jane's Fighting Ships*; to Lady Corbett and Messrs. Longmans, Green & Co. Ltd., for permission to quote a short passage from *England in the Seven Years' War*, by the late Sir Julian Corbett; to Captain E. P. Dreyer, D.S.C., R.N., late Executive Officer of H.M.S. *Vanguard*, for reading the chapters dealing with the ninth *Vanguard*; to the late Mr. Francis McMurtrie, former editor of *Jane's Fighting Ships*, for reading the historical part of the MS. and giving me much valuable advice; and to Mr. J. Hennessy, of *The Times*, for reading and correcting the MS.

P. K. K.

THE INVINCIBLE ARMADA

". . . and I name you *Vanguard*, and may God go with you always."
It was a cold, bleak November day of 1944. Her Royal Highness
Princess Elizabeth swung the bottle and Empire wine spattered on
the great ship's bows. For a moment or two the vessel hung there,
immobile, ponderous, and then, slowly, almost imperceptibly, she
started down the ways. As she gathered speed, Messrs. John Brown's
yard at Clydebank echoed with the thunder of her launching, and
echoed again with the cheers of those who watched her take the
water. And the waters of the Clyde carried across to the Scottish hills
the sounds of the sirens and whistles of the ships in port, and the hills
echoed them back again. The ninth *Vanguard* came to rest, stopped by
the drag of the launching chains, and was taken in tow by tugs to be
moored alongside in the fitting-out basin.

Those were not the only echoes heard on that day. There were
others that echoed back through the years and the centuries—*Vanguard, Vanguard, Vanguard*—growing ever fainter till they died out
and were lost in the mists of an almost forgotten day some three
hundred and sixty years ago.

On that day of 1586 there was launched a galleon of 449 tons by
dimension, though she was rated in the Navy as of 500 tons. She was
built by Matthew Baker at the Royal Yard at Woolwich, of a new, low
freeboard type, "low and snug in the water, like a galleasse", and
represented the then pinnacle of achievement in naval architecture.
She, too, was named *Vanguard*, the first of a long line of battle-scarred
ships. She mounted 32 guns—8 demi-cannons, 10 culverins, and
14 demi-culverins—and as secondary armament carried 4 light pieces
and 18 "quick-firing" periers. Her dimensions were: length 108 feet,
beam 32, depth 13, and we can judge of her importance in the fleet
by the fact that there was paid "to William Byford, upholsterer, for
the trimming of the captain's cabin and others for gentlemen in her
Highness' ship the *Vanguard*, being garnished with green cotton", the
sum of £15 8s. 8d., he "finding at his own charges all manner of
stuff and workmanship".

The year of her launching saw England standing at the cross-
roads of her maritime history. She was faced by the naval might of
Spain and the unrelenting hostility of Philip II against Queen
Elizabeth. That year, too, saw Sir Francis Drake at work with his
squadron of ships in the Spanish Indies, when he, Martin Frobisher,
and Christopher Carleill as Lieutenant-General of the land forces,
captured and sacked Santiago, San Domingo, Porto Praya, Cartagena,
and Saint Augustine. These raids have often been described as little

less than piratical banditry, though Drake was only forestalling Philip of Spain in the declaration of war. It had been an open secret throughout Europe that Philip was busily preparing an immense force for the complete destruction of England, and that the shipyards and arsenals of Spain were working at full pressure to enable his design to be carried out.

It was in these uneasy days that the first *Vanguard* saw her early spells of service. After her building and fitting-out she was sent to join Lord Howard of Effingham's fleet at the Nore, where her first tasks were to keep watch, as part of Sir Henry Palmer's blockading squadron, on the Spanish army of the Duke of Parma in the Low Countries. For Philip was planning an amphibious invasion of England, using his great fleet to force the English Channel and escort the army over to the Thames Estuary, whence they could march on London.

Drake's successes in the West Indies had hindered Philip's designs, but had by no means killed them. The moral effect when the news reached Europe was considerable and Spain's financial credit was strained almost to breaking point. The Flemish financiers would no longer agree to provide money for Parma's starving army in the Netherlands—"they are drawing their purse strings very tight", he wrote—and the lesson of Spanish vulnerability at sea was being quickly learned. Yet still the Spanish preparations went on, although in England, where it seemed to Elizabeth that she had little to fear, no very great anxiety was apparent. Besides, to keep the fleet in full commission meant a heavy outlay, and Elizabeth was almost as hard pressed for money as Philip.

It was at this moment of apparent safety, while the *Vanguard* was keeping a weary watch on the Spanish soldiers in the Low Countries, that the Babington Plot was revealed. At once England was again awake. The plan to assassinate Elizabeth and foster a rising in favour of Mary Stuart, with the support of France and Spain, aroused again all the fierce determination of Protestant England against Catholic Spain. Mary Stuart was held in close confinement and the fleet brought to a state of immediate readiness. Behind the plot could be found the duplicity of Philip by all those who needed an excuse to counsel immediate retaliation. They were many, but Elizabeth, who had no objection to letting Philip feel the sting of her lash when she could do so without direct risk of war, was still not yet prepared to go the whole way.

Yet, behind Elizabeth's reluctance, there remained a stream of reports from agents in Spain, all telling the same story of the growing rate of naval preparation and of the unconcealed destination of the great fleet when it should at last be ready. That that destination was known to be England at last forced Elizabeth into action. She decided to strike the first blow and, in the early days of 1587, signed a commission giving Drake power to sail with a squadron to Spanish waters and there "to impeach the provisions of Spain", even to the extent of "distressing the ships within the havens themselves".

Drake lost no time, knowing something of the vagaries of Elizabeth and the speed with which she could change her mind. He assembled his squadron with the utmost haste and, working desperately, got them to sea on April 1st. Even as he sailed a messenger rode into Plymouth bearing the orders which Drake had feared. But by now Drake was well out to sea and although the new orders were sent after him in a pinnace, they never reached him. Perhaps it was no more than a coincidence that the pinnace belonged to Sir William Wynter, who himself had sailed with Drake on the expedition.

Sir William Wynter, indeed, is closely bound up with the early history of the first *Vanguard*. He had been Master of Naval Ordnance and Surveyor of the Ships. Drake himself had served under him, as also had Hawkins. But by now his reputation as a great leader was in decline and both Drake and Hawkins had outstripped him in the race. Yet for all that he was still a man of parts and his counsel in the fleet was sought and valued.

Drake's expedition to Spain was crowned with success. Cadiz was attacked and thousands of tons of shipping had been sunk or burnt and a great quantity of stores, laboriously collected for the forth-coming attack on England, destroyed. From Cadiz the squadron sailed to Lagos, which was taken by assault from the land. The great castle of Sagres, guarding the town from the sea, was captured and shipping all along the coast, from Cape St. Vincent to Lisbon, was swept into Drake's net. This was followed by a cruise to the Azores in search of the yearly treasure fleet, and especially of the *San Felipe*, a Portuguese carrack known to be returning richly laden from the East Indies. On June 8th, near St. Michael's Island, a large ship was sighted. She proved to be the *San Felipe* and was captured after a short fight, "the greatest ship in all Portugal, richly laden, to our happy joy and great gladness". As cargo she carried hundreds of tons of spices and gums, many chests of china, bales of rich silks, and much gold and jewels. She also carried an even richer cargo in the shape of her papers which revealed the secrets of the Portuguese East India trade and showed the way to the British merchants of the future.

So Drake returned home, having upset Philip's plans for launching his great Armada by his attacks on Cadiz and Lagos and by the capture of the richest of his treasure ships. Yet Philip only redoubled his efforts to collect together a fleet. Out of Spain came a whole stream of reports of renewed activity to set England on her guard. There could now be no doubt whatever of Philip's intentions and even Elizabeth was resigned to eventual war.

On his return with Drake, Wynter was appointed Vice-Admiral of the Downs squadron under the command of the Lord High Admiral, Lord Howard of Effingham. Wynter flew his flag in the *Vanguard*, which spent the winter of 1587 refitting at Sheerness. In the spring of 1588 she put to sea again to rejoin Palmer's squadron off Dunkirk. She was clean and thoroughly seaworthy and Wynter could write:

> "Our ships do show themselves like gallants here. I assure you it will do a man's heart good to behold them; and would to God the Prince of Parma were upon the sea with all his forces and we in view of them."   6

On April 17th Howard received orders from the Queen to sail with the greater part of his fleet and join Drake at Plymouth, leaving in the Downs a sufficient force to maintain the watch on Parma at Dunkirk. This blockading squadron was placed under the command of Lord Henry Seymour in the *Rainbow*, with Palmer in the *Antelope* as Vice-Admiral and Wynter in the *Vanguard* as Rear-Admiral. Seymour's squadron consisted of 17 ships of the Royal Navy with a further 23 requisitioned from the Cinque Ports and the East Coast towns. It was a ridiculously large squadron for so secondary a task   7 and Howard, now in command in the West, could well have done with some of the larger ships in his own fleet which was to bear the brunt of the Armada fighting up the Channel.

May and June passed, with Wynter in the *Vanguard* keeping an eye on Parma's movements at Dunkirk and with Howard and Drake impatient for the chance of getting to grips with Philip's fleet coming up from Spain. Twice Drake prevailed on Howard to take the English fleet down to the Spanish coast, there to fall upon the Duke of Medina Sidonia's ships and destroy them before they could sail, and twice a fickle wind drove them back when they were just short of their destination. The second occasion was during the second week in July, and the wind, which turned southerly just as they were within striking distance of the Spanish ships gathered at Corunna, brought the Invincible Armada on their heels. On July 12th the British fleet had returned to Plymouth. The Armada, sailing at a more leisurely pace, was ploughing its way up the Bay of Biscay. And on the 19th Captain Fleming, of the *Golden Hind*,

> "who had been cruizing in the Chops of the Channell for discoverie, brought advice into Plymouth that he had descried the Spanish Armado neare the Lizard, making for the entrance of the Channell with a favourable gale".   8

In the running fight up the Channel, until the Armada was lying at its uneasy anchorage off Calais, the *Vanguard* took no part. She was still with Seymour's squadron watching Parma off Dunkirk. As the Armada, pursued by Howard and Drake, passed the Isle of Wight on its way up Channel, Seymour brought some of his ships back to Dover to revictual and take on board fresh water. It was here that he received the first news that the Spanish fleet had reached English waters. A caravel, despatched by Drake, told him of the encounter off Plymouth, and he immediately sent off a pinnace with orders for the remainder of his squadron to rejoin him.

"I am most glad," he wrote to Walsingham, "of this most happy beginning of victory obtained of her Majesty's enemies, but most sorry I am so tied I cannot be an actor in the play. But if the Duke [Parma] is as good as his threats, he will now show his courage."

He wrote this "from aboard the *Rainbow*, a pretty way in the sea in Dover Road" on July 25th, 1588.

The letter shows that Seymour did not as yet appreciate that the Armada was as far up Channel as was, in fact, the case (it anchored off Calais two days later, on the 27th). He still considered the main threat to England to be Parma's army, being confident enough in the quality of the English men of war to leave the fate of Medina Sidonia's ships to Howard and Drake farther west. Wynter held a slightly different view, though he too was impressed by the danger of the army's part in the joint design. With nearly fifty years of experience as a commander at sea to guide him, he was convinced that a smaller force than that actually detailed was necessary to watch Parma. He knew, too, something of the difficulties of transporting armies at sea, for in 1544 he had taken part in Henry VIII's attack on Scotland, when Leith and Edinburgh had been burnt. Then, from 236 ships, it had only been possible to land some 11,000 men. "The Prince's (Parma) forces, being no other than that which he hath in Flanders at this time, dare not come to the seas," he wrote to Walsingham, though in the same letter he added that, "in these princely actions a man cannot be too provident, and no wisdom were it to put things to an even balance, when more weight may be added".

Wynter's advice to Seymour was that the squadron should sail at least as far down Channel as Dungeness in an attempt to gather later news of the Armada and to join the main fleet. They arrived off Dungeness only to receive special orders from the Queen that Seymour was to return with his ships and lie off Dunkirk, no matter what other orders might have been received. This, coupled with a chance meeting with three or four ships from the west which reported having seen nothing of the Armada, induced Seymour to turn back and make for the Downs and revictual. Wynter, coming on board the *Rainbow* to expostulate with Seymour, protested violently at the Queen's order and they both wrote to the Council explaining that, if they were to watch Dunkirk, then Dover was the correct place to lie, since the first gale on the Flemish coast would either drive them ashore or else off their station to the eastward.

So Seymour and Wynter fumed and fretted as they ran before the wind to the Downs. Hardly had they anchored, however, than their disappointment was dramatically ended. A pinnace from Howard,

flying before the wind, brought the news that the two fleets were
between Folkestone and Boulogne and, moreover, imperative orders
from the Lord High Admiral to Seymour to sail with his squadron
and join the main fleet. Again Wynter visited his chief, this time to
urge him to ignore the Queen's order. Seymour himself needed no
such urging. His mind was quite made up. He at once signalled to
his squadron to weigh anchor and, with only three days' provisions
aboard the ships and led by the *Rainbow* and the *Vanguard*, the Downs
squadron beat out to the southward.

In the evening of the same day they came up with the rest of the
fleet under Howard and Drake anchored off Calais. As they arrived
the *Vanguard* bore away towards the Spaniards and gave their rear
ships a broadside, as though in contempt of their lack of enterprise
in permitting the junction of the two squadrons. After this little effort
the *Vanguard* returned to her station in Seymour's squadron and
anchored with the remainder.

That evening Wynter, pacing the poop of the *Vanguard*, looked
across the waters at the Spanish fleet, anchored to leeward of the
English ships, "very round and near together, not far from the shore".   1.
It was obvious to him, as it was to Howard and Drake, that Medina
Sidonia must at all costs be prevented from making contact with
Parma, and the old admiral knew the way of ensuring that.

At about nine o'clock that evening Howard sent a pinnace across
to the *Vanguard* asking Wynter to come and confer with him:

"which I did, and having viewed myself the great and hugeness of the
Spanish army,* and did not consider that it was not possible to remove
them but by a device of firing of ships, which would make them to leese
[lose] the only road which was apt and meetest to serve their purpose, as
also an occasion to put many of them in danger of firing, and at the least
to make them to leese their cables and anchors, which could not be less
than two for every ship, I thought it well to acquaint my Lord withal at
my coming to him at that time, which was about nine of the clock at
night; and his Lordship did very well like of it and said the next day his
Lordship would call a council and put the same in practice; and his
Lordship and I were reasoning of this matter in his Lordship's cabin,
there did drive with the tide aboard my Lord's ship her Majesty's ship
the *Bear* and three others, which were all tangled together, so as there
was some hurt done by breaking of yards and spoil of tackle; but a great
favour of God showed that it had not made a destruction of many [of]
our ships".   1!

One can imagine the scorn of the old seaman as he wrote these
words. The captain of the *White Bear* was Lord Sheffield, a kinsman
of Howard's, who, although a gallant fighter, was no professional
sailor. Wynter had served almost all his life at sea and he knew that

* Army and Navy were synonymous terms in 1588.

By courtesy of the National Maritime Museum

Attack of the *Vanguard* at the Armada, 1588
From a line engraving by Willmore after Sir Oswald Brierly

By courtesy of the National Maritime Museum

George Monck, 1st Earl of Albemarle
From an oil painting by Sir Peter Lely

his own ship, the *Vanguard*, was sufficiently expertly handled to make impossible such a mishap as this.

At the council of war the following day, July 28th, the idea of using fireships to dislodge the Spaniards was approved and Palmer was sent back to Dover to collect all the suitable vessels he could and prepare them for the task. As soon as he was gone it was pointed out that he could not possibly be back the same night and that the sooner the Armada was forced to sea again the better. A number of private owners of vessels in the fleet volunteered to provide their ships for the attempt, and eight were offered and prepared.

The fireships were set adrift at midnight, by which time the tide had turned and was running strongly to the eastward, directly from the English to the Spanish fleet. They performed admirably the task for which they were used, forcing the Spaniards to cut their cables and drift in confusion out to seaward. In the pitch darkness the sight of them struck terror among the Spanish vessels, so that all was panic. "They came flaring on," wrote a Spanish officer, "spurting fire and their ordnance shooting, which was a horror to see in the night."

In the first light of the following morning the English captains looked anxiously across to the Spanish anchorage to judge the success of the night's operation. Only one Spanish vessel was there and she, having lost her rudder in a collision with another ship during the night's panic, was trying to reach the shelter of the French guns in the fort at Calais. The rest of the Armada could be seen straggling away to the north-eastward, being driven ever nearer the sandbanks off the Dutch coast.

It was the moment to attack. Medina Sidonia, quite unable to rally his fleet, was attempting to form a battle line round his most leeward ships and to bring some semblance of order among his scattered vessels. Could he be prevented from joining up with the ships farthest to leeward, then there was every prospect of destroying his fleet piecemeal and making sure of a resounding victory.

Howard, unfortunately, tempted by the sight of the drifting Spanish galleon inshore, delayed for over an hour in an attempt to capture her, sending in the boats from his squadron to board her. Drake, however, in the *Revenge*, was quick enough to grasp the main chance and, crowding on all sail, closed the Armada. He was followed by Wynter in the *Vanguard*, and the two squadrons formed up for battle. They came up with Medina Sidonia at about nine o'clock in the morning off Gravelines.

"They went into a proportion of a half moon," wrote Wynter. "Their admiral and vice-admiral they went in the midst, and the greatest number of them; and there went on each side, on the wings, their galleasses, armados of Portugal, and other good ships which did seem to be of their principal shipping. My fortune was to make choice to charge their starboard wing without shooting of any ordnance until

B

we came within six score* of them, and some of our ships did follow me
. . . how they were beaten I will leave it to the report of some of the
Spaniards that leapt into the seas and [were] taken up, and are now in
the custody of some of our fleet." 14

The Battle of Gravelines, the first *Vanguard's* first engagement,
began at nine o'clock in the morning and went on almost without
respite till six o'clock in the evening. The *Vanguard* was in the thick
of the fighting, being engaged with the two galleons *San Mateo* and
San Felipe. Both were Portuguese and both were commanded by
gallant men who, by general consent of Spanish eye-witnesses, fought
more bravely and more desperately than any other Spanish captains
on that day. In the *San Felipe* was Don Francisco de Toledo.

"He," wrote Padre Geronimo de la Torre, "fought neither more nor 15
less than most valiantly, placing himself in the hottest of the fight and
fighting with twelve or fifteen galleons without help except from God."

The *San Mateo* was under the command of Don Diego Pimentel,
and the same witness reports of him that he, too, was always most
heavily engaged until his ship

"was a thing of pity to see, riddled with shot like a sieve, and had it not
been that the Duke [Medina Sidonia] afterwards sent off his divers to
her to get the water out of her she must have gone to the bottom with all
hands".

So, throughout the day, the English fleet harried and damaged
the Armada, keeping always to windward of it and shepherding it
ever nearer the dangerous Zealand banks, where the shoal water was a
prospect just as menacing as the English guns. By the evening the
Armada seemed doomed, split up into small parties and ripe for
capture. The English ships closed in for the kill and it seemed to the
terrified Spanish sailors that even God had deserted them. But just
at that moment a squall swept down, accompanied by driving rain
that made gunfire impossible. The English ships rounded up to it, the
Spaniards, too battered and weary even to exercise so elementary a
piece of seamanship, drove before it. By the time it was over three
great ships of Spain had been lost, the *Maria Juan*, the *San Mateo*,
and the *San Felipe*. The remainder were being driven ever faster on to
the sandbanks, unable to claw their way off in the face of the fierce
wind.

The English fleet, robbed of their prey by the squall, reformed
and came up again to the attack. But there was now nothing more they
could do except to watch the Spaniards driven to almost certain
destruction. There was a little desultory fire at long range, but even

* Gunnery ranges were measured in paces.

this was limited by the shortage of powder and shot. Almost all had been fired away during the nine hours of battle.

"I deliever it unto your honour," wrote Wynter, "upon the credit of a poor gentleman, that out of my ship there was shot 500 shot of demi-cannon, culverin, and demi-culverin, and when I was furthest off in discharging any of the pieces I was not out of the shot of their harquebus, and most times within speech one of another. And surely every man did well; and as I have said, no doubt the slaughter and hurt they received was great, as time will discover it; and when every man was weary with labour, and our cartridges spent, and munitions wasted*—I think in some [ships] altogether—we ceased and followed the enemy."

So the two fleets continued, the English to windward, the Spanish far down to leeward and being driven perilously nearer the Zealand sandbanks. There was no danger to England now, for they were well past Dunkirk and could never get back to make contact with Parma. Feverishly the Spanish ships took soundings—eight fathoms, seven, six, five—and still they drove on and on towards the growing peril. "It was the most fearful day in the world," wrote one of the Spanish captains, "for all the people were now in utter despair of a happy issue and stood waiting for death."

Once again the wind saved them. It backed two points to the westward and the unwieldy Spanish ships were just able to claw their way off to windward away from the sandbanks. But the wind, as it backed, freshened to a gale, driving them northward into the grey wastes of the North Sea. There was only one path for Medina Sidonia to take now, the long, stormy path that led north of Scotland and west of Ireland and so back to the shelter of Spanish harbours.

On the following morning Howard summoned a council of war on board the *Ark Royal*. Wynter was unable to attend, for he had been hurt in the thigh during the previous day's battle by the recoil of one of the *Vanguard's* guns. But Seymour was there to hear, and protest against, the decision to order his squadron back to the Downs to resume the watch on Parma.

"I find my Lord [Howard]," he wrote, "jealous and loth to have me take part of the honour of the rest that is to win, using his authority to command me to look to our English coasts that have been long threatened by the Duke of Parma. . . . I pray God my Lord Admiral do not find the lack of the *Rainbow* and that company; for I protest before God, and have witnesses for the same, I vowed I would be as near or nearer with my little ship to encounter our enemies, as any of the greatest ships in both armies."

The *Rainbow*, the *Vanguard*, and the remainder of the ships of Seymour's squadron put into Harwich, there to revictual and land

* Expended.

their sick. Up to the northward, still driven by the hard wind, straggled the Invincible Armada, with the rest of the English fleet, under Howard and Drake, shadowing it. We know from the Spanish records that Sidonia had by then already made up his mind to attempt the northern passage back to Spain, but in the minds of Howard and the other English captains were the possibilities that he might try to make a Danish port, there to refit and make another attempt to link up with Parma, or even to find temporary shelter in a Norwegian port. It was vital to Howard's future disposal of the fleet that he know the path that Sidonia was to take.

On August 2nd, in the latitude of 55° North, the English fleet, in need of fresh water and running short of food, was forced to leave the chase and bear away for the English coast. The wind then was blowing strongly from the north-west, forcing Sidonia away towards the Norwegian coast. Two days later it backed to the south-west and freshened again to a full gale. Sidonia was now able to fetch the Orkneys and put into effect his fateful decision to return to Spain round the north of Scotland. It was to cost him dear, for of the 142 vessels that had left Corunna on the great enterprise against England, but 58 returned.

The Spanish decision to take the northern route round Scotland was still not known to the English commanders, and for some days there was a spate of conjecture. Howard and Drake returned to Harwich, Seymour and Wynter to the Downs. The gale was still blowing strongly and, while crossing the Thames Estuary, the *Vanguard* sprung her mast, though it took but a single day to fit a new one in its place at Sandwich. From there the *Vanguard* stood down to Dover, where eventually the whole of the English fleet gathered. There they re-victualled, re-armed, and landed their sick, for scurvy was rife in the ships and the men were dying in large numbers.

At last definite news of the Armada was learned. The ships had been sighted between the Orkneys and the Shetlands and it was known that the danger to England was over. The Queen decided to pay the fleet off, leaving only a few ships, of which the *Vanguard* was one, to maintain the watch on Parma. The squadron was again put under the command of Sir Henry Palmer, but by the time they reached the Flemish coast, Parma had flown. The Spanish army, like the Spanish navy, had given up all hope of invading England. And when the *Vanguard* returned to England, she too was paid off and her crew disbanded.

CHAPTER II

EXPEDITION INTO SPAIN

AFTER the disastrous defeat of his "Invincible Armada", Philip set about building a second fleet with still the same object, the invasion of England, in view. This second navy was incomparably better than his first and, moreover, was built largely on English lines. At the same time he was also trying to remedy the other grave strategical mistake of his first venture, that of attempting to conduct a campaign from two widely separated bases without commanding the sea lanes between them. In this respect he was spectacularly assisted by the action of a French nobleman, the Duc de Mercoeur, who, with pretensions of setting himself up as an independent king of Brittany, permitted the Spaniards to occupy and fortify Blavet (now Port Louis in Morbihan) and to overrun the Camaret peninsula, which juts out into the sea between the Bay of Douarnenez and Brest Roads. From their position there, the Spaniards dominated the great harbour of Brest, which was thus ready to fall into their hands like an overripe plum.

The year was 1594. The prospect of an advanced Spanish naval base so near to the approaches of the English Channel caused consternation in the English court and stung Elizabeth into action. In conjunction with Henry IV of France, plans were hurriedly drafted to relieve Brest from the Spanish danger. The Queen agreed to provide a force of her ships to attack the Spanish positions from seaward and also a land force to operate in conjunction with Henry's troops. In command at sea was to be Sir Martin Frobisher, on land Sir John Norreys.

Since the year of the Armada, the *Vanguard* had spent most of her days lying in the river at Sheerness, paid off into reserve. But early in 1594, when once again the Spanish threat against England was gathering momentum, she had been brought forward, scraped and tallowed, and fitted with new cordage and sails. Her time was come again for action, and in September of that year she was selected as Frobisher's flagship for the expedition against Blavet. With her were the *Rainbow*, Captain Thomas Fenner, the *Dreadnought*, Captain Alexander Clifford, and the *Quittance*, Captain Savile.

The squadron sailed in October and on November 1st lay before Crozon, where the main Spanish fortifications had been established. A council of war between Frobisher and Norreys had resulted in a decision to attempt the Spanish positions from the landward side. As Norreys and his men attacked, the ships stood as close in as they dared and bombarded the fortifications. So fierce was the defence, however, that Norreys was forced to call on the ships for reinforcements and Frobisher himself led the seamen of the squadron in a storming attack from the shore. It was met by a fury of musket fire. One of the first to fall was Martin Frobisher, wounded by a ball in the side. He picked himself up and, rallying his English seamen, led them on in a renewed charge. The place fell after a brisk fight and the port of Brest was saved.

But Frobisher, whose wound was allowed to fester through the incompetence of the ship's doctor, had fought his last fight. He brought his squadron safely back to anchor in Plymouth Sound but, early in January 1595, he died of his wound. He had been one of the most gallant of Drake's commanders, a dour, hard man of few words, one whose chief aim throughout his fighting life was to place himself as near the enemy as possible. Perhaps it was a fitting end that at the last he should command the *Vanguard*, for her name, too, is associated so closely with war and battle.

Two years later, in 1596, the *Vanguard* was again selected for service. This time it was for the attack on Cadiz, led by the Lord High Admiral, Lord Howard of Effingham, and the Queen's new favourite, the Earl of Essex, as joint commanders. The destination of the fleet was kept a profound secret right up to the time of sailing. At one time, indeed, it seemed hardly likely that the ships would sail at all, for Elizabeth, in her prevailing mood of indecision and procrastination, could hardly be induced to sign the necessary commissions. At the last, however, after a passionate defence of the project from Essex, the commissions were signed, though they were accompanied by a strict injunction to Howard from the queen not to allow her beloved Essex to run into any danger.

The proposed attack was in the best traditions of Drake. The Spanish king, still intent on the humbling of England and its return to Catholicism, was prosecuting the land war with vigour and considerable success. On April 15th the Spanish forces under the Archduke Albert, one of the strongest and most capable of Philip's military commanders, occupied Calais. There was at once an outcry in London, and many, Howard and Essex among them, clamoured for an immediate attack on the town to wrest it back from the Spaniards. The queen, hotly pressed by her favourite, wavered, and the fate of the expedition hung in the balance. But in the end wiser counsels prevailed. Drake had taught that the successful operation of a naval base depended on the command of the sea, and the Spaniards were a long way from achieving this in the Channel. Calais, then, could safely be ignored, for although its occupation by Spain might well be a thorn in the side of France, it could not yet harm England. The correct strategical procedure, still following Drake's teachings, was to strike at the root of Philip's power—in Spain itself. Even the hot-headed Essex was brought to realize this, and we find him, within ten days of the fall of Calais, advocating the Cadiz operation to the queen with just as much fire and passion as he had previously recommended the attack on Calais.

So it was decided. Howard and Essex, who had been at Dover with their ships in readiness to launch the attack on Calais, dropped down Channel to Plymouth, where Essex had been raising a force of landsmen to accompany the ships. Lord Thomas Howard and Sir Walter Raleigh followed them ten days later with their squadrons, till there was gathered at Plymouth a fleet of 110 ships, including a Dutch squadron under the command of Jan van Duyvenvoord, Admiral of Holland. Essex's land forces, well drilled and admirably equipped, numbered some 6,500 men. Of the whole expedition Sir George Carew, a kinsman of Raleigh's and one of the military commanders, could write:

> "They are strong enough at sea to abide the proudest fleet that ever swam, and by land our army, both in numbers and gallant men, is of strength to march and retreat in safety from a more puissant enemy than we are like to find."

The expedition finally sailed on June 3rd. Howard was still in his old ship, the *Ark Royal*. Essex, joint commander with Howard, sailed in the new galleon, the *Due Repulse*, Lord Thomas Howard in the *Merhonour*, and Raleigh in the *Warspite*. The *Vanguard*, which carried Sir John Wingfield's company of soldiers, was commanded by Sir Robert Mansell.

In an attempt to escape detection and to keep the point of attack secret, the fleet set a course well out into the Atlantic. They reached the latitude of Cape St. Vincent without the slightest suspicion by the Spaniards that they had even set sail. Here they captured a number of small craft and from them learned that a considerable naval force was concentrated at Cadiz, including the West Indian *flota*, some 40 or more carracks well laden with goods for the Spanish colonies across the Atlantic. Cadiz, then, was a prize well worth the capture.

So far all had gone wonderfully well and the stage was set for a complete surprise on one of Spain's greatest naval harbours. But on June 15th, as they rounded Cape St. Vincent, they were seen from the shore. The news was spread with the utmost speed along the coast and the officers at Cadiz began to make their plans for defence. In the harbour were four great galleons of the Guard, known as the "four Apostles", twenty war galleys, three Portuguese galleons, three strongly armed Levant ships, and three frigates, as well as the 40 carracks of the *flota*.

The Spanish plan of defence, adopted after a number of orders and counter-orders, was designed to make the greatest use of the natural strength of the harbour. The town of Cadiz lies at the end of a long neck of land projecting out into the sea from the Island of Leon. The entrance to the outer harbour is guarded by Fort St. Philip, in Cadiz itself, and the Castle of Santa Catalina on the mainland opposite. The outer harbour narrows to a channel little more

than half a mile across before widening into a great bay which forms
the inner harbour, and Fort Puntal commands the channel. In the
inner harbour lies the village of Carraca, on the bank of a long creek
which connects with the sea again nine miles below Cadiz, thus
forming the Island of Leon. Two miles south of Carraca the creek
is crossed by the Punto Zuarro, a bridge which carries the main road
from the mainland to Cadiz.

In the hands of a determined defence, the place is almost impreg-
nable. But the Spanish defence was by no means determined, although
the final positions taken up gave every chance of bringing the English
attack to a halt. Don Juan Portocarrero, the Spanish commander of
the war galleys, was stationed to seaward of Fort St. Philip, there to
harry with his nimble vessels the oncoming English ships. The "four
Apostles" were drawn up across the narrow channel under the guns
of the Puntal fort, so that their broadsides faced the attacking fleet.
Behind them were the Portuguese and Levant ships and the three
frigates. The *flota* was moved for safety into the creek below Carraca,
as far up as the Punto Zuarro.

The English ships arrived off Cadiz on the morning of the 18th,
three days after having been sighted from the neighbourhood of
Cape St. Vincent. Early in the morning the *Ark Royal* had captured
an Irish bark which had just left Cadiz bound for Waterford, and
from her captain Howard learned of the preparations being made to
put the harbour in a state of defence. The news spread quickly through
the English fleet that they would need to fight before they could capture
the town.

> "When this was once bruited in the army," wrote Dr. Marbecke,
> who was Howard's doctor in the *Ark Royal*, "that there were so
> many ships, Lord God! what a sudden rejoicing there was. How every
> man skipt and leapt for joy, and how nimble was every man to see all
> things were neat, trim, and ready for the fight, fearing all the way that
> they should never be encountered or have any 'sport', as they use to
> term it."

All that day the fleet sailed slowly towards the shore, making very
slow progress in the light wind. And it was not until June 20th, at
5 a.m., that they reached a position from which they could contemplate
a landing by the soldiers against the town. A council of war was
called, and so bitter was the wrangling that it lasted most of the day.
Essex, impetuous as ever, was for making an immediate assault on a
shelving beach, known as the Caleta, right under the walls of Cadiz
itself, offering himself to lead a "folorn" of a couple of hundred men.
Howard, more cautious, was for attacking the Spanish ships first,
which still had not yet taken up their final defensive positions and were
lying outside the outer harbour strung out just to seaward of the two
forts of St. Philip and Santa Caterina. After an immense amount of

discussion Essex's plan was adopted, with Howard to land a second
and supporting force from seaward on the narrow neck of land joining
Cadiz to the Island of Leon. Raleigh was to command an inshore
squadron whose duty was to prevent the escape of any Spanish ships
from the port, while Sir Alexander Clifford, to whom was allotted
the *Vanguard*, the *Rainbow*, and half a dozen smaller vessels, was to be
responsible for preventing any attack by the 20 war galleys.

Unfortunately, before this plan could be put into operation, the
wind began to freshen. At the same time it shifted to the south-west
and kicked up a nasty sea in the Caleta. It was obvious to all but
Essex that a landing there was now impossible without very serious
casualties from drowning. Essex, however, held to his original plan
until late in the afternoon, and only with the greatest difficulty was he
eventually dissuaded from it. Howard, too, was now loth to take the
ships inside the harbour, there to run the gauntlet of the two forts.
But in the end, due largely to the labours of Raleigh, the two joint
commanders were brought to view the problem from the same angle.
The rising sea, which had by now made any landing from the seaward
side completely impossible, decided the issue. Howard gave way
and agreed to take the fleet into the harbour. Essex, when he was
told the decision, threw his hat high in the air in his excitement at the
prospect of imminent action, so that the wind took it and carried it
far into the sea.

5

The fleet weighed anchor, but the day was too far advanced for
action before night. And since no one relished the idea of a fight in
the dark, neither Spaniard nor English, the ships anchored again and
lay off the town, just inside the outer harbour, till morning. There was
only one alarm during that night, when Portocarrero's galleys threatened an attack, but they were easily beaten back by the *Vanguard*
and the *Rainbow*.

Early the following morning, as the sun rose, a curious state of
affairs was revealed. So eager had been some of the commanders to
lead the fleet into action that many ships had stolen secretly ahead
during the night to get closer to the enemy. As they now weighed
anchor every semblance of order was lost and individual vessels tried
to jockey the others out of the place of honour. Raleigh was first away
in the *Warspite*, and as he closed the four great Spanish galleons drawn
up in the narrows he anchored in mid-channel so that no other ship
could, as he thought, squeeze past him. Vere, in the *Rainbow*, who
had been engaging the galleys with the *Vanguard*, managed to get
ahead over the shoal water, so that for a time he was in the van. Next,
Lord Thomas Howard in the *Nonpareil*, to which he had removed from
the *Merhonour*, forced his way past the *Warspite* and took the lead.

Raleigh was furious and, weighing anchor, managed to drift up
the channel ahead of the *Nonpareil* again, and again anchored, once
more nearest the enemy. Next it was the turn of Essex. He barged his
way through the ships and, after an exciting few minutes when he

fouled the *Dreadnought*, dropped anchor a ship's length ahead of Raleigh. Vere in the *Rainbow*, seeing another chance to get ahead, sent off one of his boats with a hawser which he made fast to the *Warspite*, hoping to haul himself up alongside before his trick was noticed. Unfortunately for him, Raleigh discovered what was happening and ordered the rope to be cut.

As if all this were not sufficient, Howard himself, who had been busily engaged against the Cadiz forts, decided to take a hand. His own ship, the *Ark Royal*, drew too much water to have any chance getting up within range of the Spanish galleons, so he had himself rowed to the *Merhonour*, where with his own hands he laid and fired the guns.

During this time Mansell, in the *Vanguard*, was hotly engaged with the galleys, the *Rainbow* having left them to join in the race to engage the "four Apostles". The galleys lay with their sterns towards the Cadiz walls, flanking the advancing English fleet with their batteries. Mansell, in his attack, came not only under their fire, but also under that of the Cadiz forts as well. But the *Vanguard's* steady gunnery forced the galleys to give way and all but two retired to the inner harbour under the shelter of the guns of the Puntal fort. The other two, daunted by the accurate fire of the *Vanguard*, sought safety inside the town harbour where the guns of the forts could guard them. There they lay throughout the day, taking no further part in the action. With the galleys safely accounted for, the *Vanguard* joined her sisters hammering away at the four galleons anchored across the narrow channel of the Puntal.

> "The shooting of ordnance was great," wrote Vere, "and they held us good talk by reason their ships lay athwart with their broadsides towards us, and most of us right ahead, so that we could use but our chasing pieces."

It should have proved an unequal struggle, for the Spaniards had every advantage in being able to rake the English attackers. Yet such was the accuracy and power of the English gunnery that, after about three hours, the Spanish fire began to slacken and Raleigh managed to get a warp out to one of the Spanish ships, the *San Felipe*, hauling himself up alongside in an attempt to carry her by boarding. Essex and Lord Thomas Howard followed his example and the four galleons, unable to face the fury of the attack any longer, slipped their cables and tried to retire inside the inner harbour.

Almost at once all four of them took the ground. The Spanish crews gave way to panic and began desperately to abandon ship. "There could be seen tumbling into the sea," wrote Raleigh in his report, "heaps of soldiers, so thick as if coals had been poured out of a sack in many ports at once, some drowned and some sticking in the mud." Boats from the fleet raced in to capture the four galleons, but before they could reach them, two, including the *San Felipe*, had been set on fire and were burning fiercely. The other two, the *San Andreo* and the *San Mateo*, were captured intact and towed out as prizes.

There was a pause in the fighting as the two Spanish ships burned.

"The spectacle," says Raleigh, "was very lamentable on their side; for many drowned themselves, and many half burnt leapt into the water, very many hanging by the rope ends by the ship's side under the water even to their lips, many swimming with grievous wounds strucken under water and put out of their pain. And withal so huge a fire and such tearing of the ordnance in the great 'Philip' and the rest, when the fire came to them, as if any man had a desire to see Hell itself, it was there most lively figured."

So perished the *San Felipe*, the greatest ship in all Spain, and a fitting reprisal for her previous success against Sir Richard Grenville in the *Revenge* six years before.

With the end of Spanish resistance on the water, two courses were open to the attackers. One was to continue into the inner harbour and make certain of capturing the *flota*, those 40 carracks fitted out for the West Indian trade. The other was to land on the Island of Leon and capture the town of Cadiz. It was Essex who made the decision. Without waiting to consult Howard, his joint commander, he ordered his soldiers into the boats and, drawn up in an exact and precise formation, led them to the shore. It was a wonderful and awe-inspiring sight. They rowed ashore in strict silence except for the beat of drums, which gave time to the rowers. Every boat was in its station and ahead of them was Essex in his barge, flying his banner. They landed near the Puntal fort, and the meticulous exactness of their advance so terrified the Spaniards that they abandoned the fort without firing a single shot in defence.

The town was taken that night after fierce fighting and given over to the sack. Yet such was the discipline among Essex's troops that their behaviour was exemplary and all prisoners were treated with the greatest consideration.

There remained the *flota*. Negotiations were begun for its ransom and 2,000,000 ducats was offered by the Spanish merchants for the safety of the 40 vessels. But it all came to naught. The Spanish military commanders, too proud to consider the humiliation of ransoming property belonging to merchants, gave orders that the ships were to be put to the torch. It was done, and the 40 ships, valued with their cargoes at over 12,000,000 ducats, were the scene of a vast conflagration that burned for three days.

So far all had gone well. Cadiz and the Island of Leon were firmly in English hands and all the Spanish ships, except 18 of the galleys which eventually escaped out to sea, captured or destroyed. There came the question of how to exploit the success. Essex, who alone of the leaders seemed to have any conception of the strategical reasons for the expedition, argued strongly for holding Cadiz with a permanent occupation. In this he was over-ruled by the other commanders. Next he suggested a cruise to the Azores in search of the Spanish treasure fleet. Again he was over-ruled, though this time as much by a change in the wind as by the spinelessness of Howard and Raleigh. In the end, in spite of all his protestations and expostulations, the English fleet came tamely home to England. On its arrival the *Vanguard* was sent round to Chatham to pay off.

It was a sorry ending to a well-thought-out and excellently organized expedition. Essex is the only man who really came well out of the whole affair and who showed any real grasp of the possibilities of successful exploitation. But in the face of all the difficulties, largely imaginary, put in his path by Howard and Raleigh, there was nothing more he could do. Yet even the limited success achieved had its effect in Spain.

"In the court," wrote an English spy, "great rumours, mutinies, privy meetings of the grandees, deliberations either to take the Prince from his father and proclaim him king, or the King from his favourites." 10

Although a wonderful chance had been missed in not exploiting to the full the successes at Cadiz, yet indirectly it had a great effect on the war. For Philip, wounded in his pride, swore a great oath that he would have his revenge. He threw himself into the task with redoubled vigour and again he collected a fleet, a second Armada, for the invasion of England. In October, by almost superhuman efforts, over 100 vessels had been concentrated at Ferrol, where they were commanded by Don Martin de Padilla, Conde de Gadea and Adelantado of Castille.

Philip gave his orders that they were to sail against England. In vain Padilla and his fellow admirals protested, pointing out that the lateness of the season made such a venture impossible. Philip would not listen to their advice and sent a peremptory order that they were to put to sea. They sailed in the last week in October. A week later this second Armada lay in wreck and ruin round the northern coast of Spain. They had been struck by a gale and, lacking the quality of English seamanship, were scattered and lost.

The following summer the *Vanguard* was fitted out again and served in Palmer's Channel squadron, spending many days at sea in keeping a watch on Spanish movements in France and Holland. As a result she took no part in the ill-fated expedition to the Azores under Essex and Raleigh in which, mainly because of Essex's inexpert handling of the fleet, the whole of the Spanish treasure convoy was missed by no more than an hour.

In the meantime, Philip was busy with his third Armada. The great losses in the storm of the previous autumn had not made him deviate by so much as an inch from his former oath. He was obsessed by his hatred of England, draining Spain to the last ducat in her treasury and pledging her credit for years to come. His press-gangs were busy throughout the country, providing unwilling sailors. Philip himself, old and on the verge of death, yet drove his captains with the force of his indomitable hatred of Elizabeth and England, and messenger after messenger rode into Ferrol with the king's orders for the fleet to sail. Padilla, again in command, begged Philip to postpone the attempt until there was some chance of success. The ships were badly fitted and the men mutinous. But the dying king was adamant and on October 9th the third Armada of 136 ships, carrying 4,000 seamen and 9,000 soldiers, made its way clumsily out of Ferrol and set course for the English Channel. Wrote one of the English spies, reporting the sailing:

> "Surely, Sir, in mine opinion it is just to avoid the shame of tarrying in harbour, for which the Adelantado hath been sharply threatened . . . the King sent word with all fury by Martin Vincenza, a provider of victuals, that he would hang him [Padilla] at his wife's neck, if he did not put to sea out of that corner."

The *Vanguard* at this moment was in Plymouth, having put in temporarily from the Channel Guard for water. As the first news of the Spanish fleet off the Cornish coast came in, she managed to get down as far as the Sound against a contrary wind. Here she was met by the first returning ships of Essex's fleet, home from the Azores on the same southerly gale which had brought Padilla's ships up to the western mouth of the Channel. As she lay at anchor there, unable to proceed until the wind changed, the remainder of the English fleet arrived, having sailed past the Spaniards without sight or sound of them.

As in 1588, so in 1597. Again the wind freshened to a gale, this time from the eastward. The third Armada was scattered before it could even enter the Channel. One by one the ships turned and ran for home, unable to face the fury of a storm at sea. Lord Thomas Howard, with as many English ships as he could gather together, and including the *Vanguard*, sailed out to give them battle, but though he scoured the sea there was no Spaniard left for him to fight. His squadron beat back to Plymouth again in the teeth of the gale, and his despatch to the Court that the Spaniards had flown brought to England a welcome respite from danger.

It was the end of Philip's hopes and dreams. His great "Enterprise of England" had failed, and with its failure he, too, closed his eyes. Early the following year he died, unloved and unmourned, a despot who had reduced Spain from the richest country in the world to the very depths of poverty. The debts he had saddled on that unhappy country were to dog its future for centuries.

Elizabeth's war with Spain now took on a new pattern. Little need now to organize costly expeditions to Spain, there to harass and destroy shipping, for Spanish shipping now was of no danger to England. Apart from the Channel Guard and an occasional raiding squadron in search of the annual treasure fleet, the naval side of the war languished. The *Vanguard's* duties were light, although in 1600, while in the Channel Guard, she, the *Repulse*, and the *Warspite*, slipped quietly down to the Azores, under the command of Sir Richard Leveson, in the hopes of surprising the treasure fleet. It was a fruitless cruise, for a Spanish squadron had already arrived at the Azores and, in order to escape detection, Leveson had to lie in wait for the *flota* well to the westward of the islands. The English ships returned to Plymouth on October 4th, without having sighted a single Spanish vessel.   *12*

It was the *Vanguard's* last service during the war. In March of 1603 the great queen lay dead and James of Scotland had succeeded her. As King of Scotland he had been a friend of Spain, and Elizabeth's war was not at all to his liking. Almost on his succession the war came to an end, apart from a little privateering which he found it impossible to stop.

In 1615 the *Vanguard*, which had been paid off at Chatham for some years, went into drydock for extensive rebuilding. She was almost entirely reconstructed and on her completion was rated at 650 tons, with a length of 103 feet, a beam of 35, and a draught of 14. She was re-gunned at the same time and now carried 40 in place of her original 32.

It was not till five years later, in 1620, that the *Vanguard* again took the seas. This time it was as part of a punitive expedition against the Algerine pirates, who were organized by the Dey of Algiers into a remarkably efficient fighting force, often acting together in regular fleets and squadrons. On July 16th, 1617, for instance, we find Sir Ferdinando Gorges reporting that a Barbary fleet of pirates, consisting of 40 vessels manned by over 2,000 men, was at sea, while earlier in   *13*
the same year the *Dolphin* of London, sailing in the Mediterranean, had been attacked by a squadron of five pirate vessels under the command of a renegade Englishman, named Walsyngham. Though boarded   *14*
three times, she managed to beat her attackers off in the end and won clear.

The activities of these Mediterranean pirates, so crippling to the growing English trade, forced James I into action. In 1619 he made his favourite, George Villiers, Duke of Buckingham, Lord High Admiral in place of Howard, and gave orders that the nuisance was to be put down. Accordingly, early in 1620, a fleet was fitted out to launch an attack on Algiers, headquarters of the pirate fleet. It was placed under the command of Sir Robert Mansell, the *Vanguard's* captain during the attack on Cadiz, who flew his flag in the *Lion*. The Vice-Admiral was Sir Richard Hawkyns in the *Vanguard* and the

Rear-Admiral Sir Thomas Button in the *Rainbow*. Three other ships of the Royal Navy were included in the fleet, as well as 12 armed merchant vessels.

Mansell's commission was dated June 6th, 1620, but it was not until October 22nd that they sailed from Plymouth. After a leisurely passage they anchored off Algiers on December 7th, where Mansell opened negotiations with the unrepentant Dey.

It was a sad page in English naval history, this expedition against Algiers. Mansell, who had certainly handled the *Vanguard* with skill and courage at Cadiz 24 years earlier, had become cautious with the passage of the years. The only result of his parleys with the Dey was the release of 40 English slaves from the Algerine galleys, and even while his squadron lay at anchor off the entrance to the harbour a pirate fleet arrived with a number of captured ships and was permitted to enter Algiers unmolested by the English vessels.

On the 17th, after a profitless ten days of indecision, Mansell took his fleet to Malaga. During the next few months he made desultory cruises in the western Mediterranean in search of pirate ships, but with very little success. Finally, in May of 1621, goaded by orders from Buckingham, he decided to attack Algiers with fireships and fitted out a number of small vessels for the purpose. One of them, indeed, was placed under the command of that same Walsyngham, whose pirate squadron had attacked the *Dolphin* four years previously. He had, temporarily at any rate, repented of his errors and been pardoned and rewarded with a small command in the Navy.

On the last day of May the English squadron again anchored off Algiers. After one or two abortive attempts, Mansell eventually managed to mount the attack, which went in on June 3rd. So little did the pirates expect Mansell to show any sign of action that they were all ashore and the harbour almost completely undefended. Yet the attack was not pressed home and very little damage was done apart from the destruction of a few small boats. The main pirate fleet escaped all damage. Mansell, in his report, blamed the lack of success on the calm weather, an unfortunate shower of rain, and "a sally by the cowardly Turks".

The English ships sailed from Algiers the following day, returning on the 9th for a second attempt. But by now the Dey, convinced that Mansell meant business, had organized the defence. Mansell found the harbour protected by a boom and patrolled by small boats. He summoned a council of war, where it was decided that no more could be done and that all that remained was to return home to England. Monson, in his writings, has a caustic comment on the expedition: "Besides their coming and going," he wrote, "they spent not 40 days at sea, but retired into harbours where the pirates could find them, but not they the pirates."

The *Vanguard's* next appearance on the naval scene was in 1624, when a curious agreement between James and the King of France

was made. Under the arrangement between the two kings the *Vanguard*,
commanded then by Captain John Pennington, and the *Great Neptune*,
under Sir Ferdinando Gorges, were to proceed to Dieppe where they
would embark French troops, possibly for a joint action against
Genoa, though the reason for the agreement is not mentioned. But
there had been a proposal some years before of an attack on this town
by English and French forces and it would appear to be the only
possible explanation. Nothing, however, came of it and the death of
James in 1625 looked to have killed it until it was revived the following
year by Charles I.

Accordingly, on June 13th, the two ships sailed into Dieppe. Once
there, however, there was great difficulty in getting the English sailors
to allow the French to come aboard. Both Pennington and Gorges
found the prospect equally distasteful. It was a ticklish situation, since
Pennington carried an express order from the king to hand the ships
over. It was solved rather ingeniously. The two captains connived
at a mutiny in the English ships, which was carried out with gusto
during July. On the 28th of that month the *Vanguard* and the *Neptune*
returned to England, sailed by their victorious crews with the officers
safely under hatches.

But Charles would not stand for this sort of behaviour. Once again
he issued his orders to Pennington, this time that he was to hand over
the *Vanguard* in person and force the *Neptune* to obey, "even unto
sinking". And on August 3rd both ships were back at Dieppe, where
on board them was hoisted the flag of France. The French king used
them at La Rochelle to quell a civil rising, of which it was written
that, on September 5th, "as for the *Vanguard*, she mowed them down
like grass". But that was the only service performed by the ship under
her new masters, and in the summer of the following year she returned
home to Chatham.

The affair of Pennington's ships at Dieppe and La Rochelle was
one of the pegs on which was hung the subsequent declaration of
war against France in 1626. Another was the cruise, in September
1625, of Captain Sir Samuel Argell, during the course of which he
attacked French shipping and captured a number of prizes. Charles,
pressed for money as always, sold them before they had been lawfully
condemned in prize, an affront which Louis of France found it hard
to forgive. The two countries drifted into war, for no very good reason
and with little but general apathy on either side in its conduct.

In spite of the doings at La Rochelle in 1625, when the *Vanguard*
had "mowed them (the insurgents) down like grass", Louis was still
having trouble with the town and his troops were drawn up around
it conducting a regular siege. Scenting a sore point in the French
king's armour, Charles decided to fit out a fleet to bring aid to the
citizens. Buckingham, Lord High Admiral, was to be in command
of the expedition in the *Triumph*, while the *Vanguard* carried as her
captain Sir John Burgh, who combined this command with that of

By courtesy of the Museum Boymans, Rotterdam

Detail of the hull of a second-rate

Drawing by W. Van der Velde of the *Windsor Castle*, a sister ship of the *Vanguard*

By courtesy of the National Maritime Museum

The Battle of Scheveningen, 1653

From a grisaille by W. Van der Velde

the land forces. When the fleet sailed on June 27th, 1627, it consisted of nine ships of the Royal Navy, six smaller vessels, and over 50 transports carrying 3,000 men. Two months later a further fleet of transports brought another 2,500 reinforcements.

From beginning to end the expedition was a complete failure. Buckingham's initial mistake was to land on the defended island of Rhé, in the La Rochelle roadstead, instead of making his base on Oléron, a second island some three miles to the southward and with no fixed defences. He followed this with almost every error a military commander could make. For four months the English troops remained on the island, harried by the French, short of food and military stores, and decimated by disease. The ships, badly handled and with their crews mutinous, were unable even to stop the systematic reinforcement of the island by French soldiers. Finally, at the beginning of November, when Buckingham at last decided that the relief of La Rochelle was beyond his powers, more than 4,000 men had been lost through famine, pestilence, and the sword. Among them was the *Vanguard's* captain, Burgh, who had been killed in an unsuccessful attempt to storm the fort at St. Martin.

On November 11th the fleet reached home, a sorry ending to a badly planned and ill-executed attack. Charles, more pressed for money than ever, promptly disbanded it, though it was found impossible to pay off the *Vanguard's* crew as there was insufficient money in the Treasury even to settle the seamen's wages. The ship lay at her moorings at Chatham, her men on board with their pay increasing at a rate only equalled by Charles's incapacity to find the money.

It was the end of the first *Vanguard*. For 50 years she had served in the Fleet, seventeen of them in the Tudor Navy and nearly twice that period in the Stuart. During her time the British Navy had reached one of the pinnacles of its achievement in the great victory of 1588. But in her later years, under Stuart management, the Navy had sunk back into incompetence, brought about partly by the flagrant dishonesty of Admiralty officials and other officers, partly by the lack of leaders of the stamp of Drake, Hawkins, Frobisher, and Wynter.

Yet, for all the failures during her later years, she had made a sound beginning and her decks had been trodden by many gallant men. By her two great actions at Gravelines and Cadiz she had laid a worthy foundation on which the long line of future *Vanguards* could build their trail of glory.

c

CHAPTER III

LOWER DECK LIFE IN THE SEVENTEENTH CENTURY

THE second *Vanguard* rose, Phœnix-like, from the ruins of the first. In 1630 it was decided that the original ship should be dismantled and that from her timbers, those of them which were serviceable, a new and larger ship should be built. In addition to many of the first *Vanguard's* fittings, the new vessel also took her name. The second *Vanguard* was launched in 1631, a larger ship carrying 56 guns and a crew of 390 men when fully manned.

Almost as soon as she was placed in commission we find her subject to the vicissitudes of the Stuart naval administration, which had even then become a byword for inefficiency. Almost her first mention in official papers was a complaint about dishonesty in the payment of her crew:

"above 256 men on board to be paid, which no sooner were the clerks gone from on board but three score at the least left the ship, 40 whereof had never been aboard before that time they came to receive their pay."

So was the King cheated and the Navy robbed of the money to keep it afloat. Too many ships' captains were in league with their pursers to defraud the King by drawing pay and provisions for a larger number than their crew, frequently by the entering of fictitious names in the ship's muster books and by keeping on the names of men who had died. But it was not only by this method of "dead-pays" that the King's money was wasted. The administration throughout was so woefully lax and dishonest that almost every department of the Navy was equally riddled with abuses. In 1631 we find Sir William Monson, a serving admiral, "turning physician to study how to cure the malignant diseases of corruption that had crept in and infected his Majesty's whole Navy". His findings were set out in his famous "Naval Tracts" and reveal a terrible state of affairs. Another would-be reformer was John Hollond, a former Assistant Treasurer of the Navy, and there were a number of other such men who were appalled by the dishonesty and waste and ready to bear witness to the intolerable conditions.

It was the ships and men that suffered. In the *Vanguard*, for instance, through the greed of the prestmasters who were almost always prepared to accept a bribe to release promising seamen they had pressed, only 12 men out of 150 brought in were able to take the helm at sea, and less than a third had ever been to sea before. It was the same story in the other ships. In 1636 a number of captains wrote answers to a series of charges made by the Earl of Northumberland, and their replies, almost without exception, bear out the experience of the *Vanguard* in this matter.

So the story of dishonesty could go on. In addition to pressed men who were very largely useless in a man of war, the ships suffered from inferior timber and cordage, bought cheap by the Commissioners and charged to the King at the price of the best. Much of the canvas for sails was very poor in quality and in one or two cases it was even reported that ships taken into the Navy were fitted with smaller guns than had been paid for: "so their ships shall carry so many great guns more than they are able . . . they fill up their number with cuts* and murderers† for compliance with their contracts".

But the two worst abuses, and those which affected most intimately the efficiency of the Navy, were wages and food. Men were paid by ticket at the end of a commission, with a deduction for the cost of clothing they had taken up and any other debts they had incurred. In 1626 the pay of a seaman had been raised from 10s. per lunar month to 15s., subject to deductions of 6d. for the Chatham Chest, a provident institution for the payment of pensions, 4d. for the chaplain, and 2d. for the surgeon. The ticket was, in theory, convertible into cash on presentation at the Paymaster's office in London, but only too often a man was unable to get satisfaction because of lack of money to honour the tickets. There was, too, a great deal of trading in these tickets, dealers buying them from the men at a discount of 25 per cent or even more, a form of robbery that hit hard at the most poorly paid class of men. Nor were the officers in any better case, and numerous examples can be found of senior captains and admirals being owed as much as £5,000 in arrears of pay. It was little wonder that so many of them were forced into fraud and deceit to make money out of the King.

Sir Henry Mervyn, naval commander in the Narrow Seas, wrote in 1629 on the sad plight of the sailors: "His Majesty will lose the honour of his seas, the love and loyalty of his sailors, and his Royal Navy will droop." Three years later when Sir Kenelm Digby, one of the Extra Principal Officers, offered to buy Mervyn's Channel command from him, Mervyn asked £8,000 for it, made up of £5,000 arrears of pay and £3,000, the sum which he himself had paid his predecessor.

Food, too, lent itself to many abuses.

"Englishmen, and more especially seamen, love their bellies above everything else, and therefore it must always be remembered in the management of the victualling of the Navy that to make any abatement from them in the quantity or agreeableness of the victuals is to discourage and provoke them in the tenderest point, and will sooner render them

* A full-sized gun cut down.
† A small hand gun.

disgusted with the King's service than any one other hardship that can be put upon them."

This sage Pepysian advice came forty years too late for the Navy of Charles I—not that it carried very much extra weight in Pepys's day—and the Navy's food in 1630, when the second *Vanguard* was built, was notorious. From the contractor's point of view nothing was too bad for the Navy and, in addition to supplying short weight— as much on occasions as 40 lb. in a hundredweight—rotten meat and stinking fish were thrown in with the good. It was the same with the biscuits, butter, beer, and other victuals.

"In the case of pork," wrote Hollond, "the cheeks, ears, feet, and other offal of the hog, were thrown in as part of the men's allowance . . . which among other things caused that frequent running away of the seamen from the service, rather than to live upon bones and crag-ends, souse and hogs' feet, when they knew the State allowed them better meat."

The rations laid down, if monotonous, were not ungenerous.

"On Sundays and Tuesdays one pound of biscuit, one gallon of beer, and two pounds of beef with salt for each of the said days. On Mondays and Thursdays one pound of biscuit, one gallon of beer, one pound of pork with salt, and one pint of peas, and for want of pork one pound and a half of beef in lieu. On Wednesdays, Fridays, and Saturdays one pound of biscuit, one gallon of beer, one eighth part of a sized fish, half a quarter of a pound of butter, and a quarter of a pound of cheese."

But many pursers on board used to give short weight to the men, claiming the balance as a perquisite of their office, and there always remained the question of the quality of the food. The State papers of the period reveal a never-ending stream of complaints from captains of ships. In a vessel named the *Seven Brothers*, for instance, it was certified that the fish stank, in another ship the beer was so bad that it had to be thrown overboard.

"Stinking beer", "salt beer which causes sickness", "mouldy bread", are other typical complaints, while one captain explained his putting into Spithead without orders, "as the beer stinks, which has caused many men to fall sick and others to run, and the butter and other provisions are as bad as they can be". The rottenness of the food in another ship is blamed for "strange fits, like convulsions or calenture", which had afflicted the crew. In the testimonies of a number of captains to the charges made by Northumberland in 1636 are such remarks as: "the beer is naught", "the butter and cheese were naught and some of the fish thrown overboard", "the butter very bad and much beer bad, the bread did fetch the skin off men's mouths", "much of the butter, Irish, very unwholesome. About three or four hundred of cheese was putrified and rotten",

"the beef was white and blue and mouldy, not fitting to be spent but on necessity. The pickled beef was very faulty, because it was not repickled from the bloody pickle. Both the ling and haberdine (fish) were very bad, so as there was little or none of it dressed all the voyage, except the first two months, for when it was boiled the men would not eat it, but threw it overboard. The musty and floury bread caused a soreness of the mouths and throats of divers of the company."

These were hardly conditions in which the Navy of the time could flourish. As year followed year of Charles's reign and the inefficiency grew worse, so the sailors became more and more discontented. Mutinies and riots were common, some of them serious, as when the seamen of the fleet seized the Guildhall at Plymouth in 1629. It was not until 20 years later, in 1649, when the Commonwealth succeeded Charles, that any effective attempt to better conditions in the Navy was made.

It is interesting to look back at those conditions in which the men of the second *Vanguard* served. Their ships were little more than floating pest-houses, and the men on board died by scores and by hundreds. Parson Teonge, who served as a chaplain afloat during this century, has left a vivid picture on board a man of war in the diary he kept during his years of service. We see the ships overcrowded to an extent where each man was limited to fourteen inches of space on deck in which to sleep. It was impossible to walk upright between decks, the height being not more than five feet, and no light or air was admitted except through the gun ports, which were mostly closed at sea. In the bilges there swilled about a foetid mass of evil-smelling water, so that men were known to be asphyxiated by the foul stench which pervaded the ship.

As was only to be expected, all sorts of diseases flourished in these conditions. The food, through its total lack of anti-scorbutics, was highly conducive to scurvy, and an attempt to promote the cleanliness of the men by the provision of extra clothing on board,

"to avoide nastie beastlyness by continual wearing of one suit of clothes, and therebie boddilie diseases and unwholesome ill smells in every ship",

failed because of the excessive cost of the clothes provided. An entry in Teonge's diary when he was in the *Royal Oak* shows that "on March 22nd, I buried Francis Forrest, as 'tis said eaten to death with lyce". It was typical of the times.

It was the age, too, of hard and inhuman punishment, though not, perhaps, developed as far as the soulless and callous brutality which blotted the history of some ships during the succeeding century.

Teonge again provides a window through which we may look at this 17th-century discipline.

"This day," he wrote in his diary, "2 seamen, that had stolen a piece or two of beife, were thus shamed; they had their hands tyd behind them, and themselves tyd to the maine maste, each of them a piece of raw beife tyd about their necks in a coard, and the beife bobbing before them like the knott of a crevatt; and the rest of the seamen cam one by one and rubd them over the mouth with the raw beife, and in this posture they stood 2 howers."

And again:

"This morning one of our men, viz., Skinner, a knowne coockould, for goeing on shore without leave, had his legs tyd together, his hands tyd to a greate rope, and stood on the side of the ship to be hoysted up to the yarde arme, and from thence to drop down in to the water 3 times."

But the unfortunate Skinner was lucky on this occasion,

"but he lookeing so very pittifully, and also the gentlemen's intreatys to the captaine for him, who alleaged that he had injurys enough already, as haveing a wife a whore and a schold to injure him at home, ergo, had the more need to be pittyed abroad, was spared."

Other punishments were equally severe, and again Teonge describes them.

"This day," he wrote, "David Thomas, and Marlin the coock, and our master's boy, had their hand stretched out, and with their backs to the rayles, and the master's boy with his back to the maine maste, all looking on upon the other, and in each of their mouths a maudlin-spike, viz., an iron pinn clapt cloese into their mouth, and tyd behind their heads; and there they stood a whole houre, till their mouths were very bloody; an excellent cure for swearers."

On another occasion:

"Isaac Webb stood tyd to the geares (the tackles for hoisting or lowering the lower yards) an houre, and had *speculum oris* placed in his mouth, for saying to a seaman in the captaine's hiering, 'Thou lyest, like a sonn of a whore'."

Twelve days later he wrote that

"a seaman had 29 lashes with a cat of 9 tayles, and was then washt with salt water, for stealing our carpenter's mate's wive's ring."

The three main punishments of the times were known as the

capstan, the bilboes, and ducking. A contemporary writer describes them as follows.

"A capstan barr being thrust through the hole of the barrell, the offender's armes are extended to the full length, and soe made fast untoe the bar crostwise, having sometymes a basket of bulletts or some other like weighte, hanging about his necke, in which posture he continues untill he be made either to confesse some plotte or cryme whereof he is pregnantlie suspected, or that he had received such condigne sufferings as he is sentenced to undergo by command of the captaine. . . . The punishment of the bilboes is when a delinquent is putt in irons, or a kind of stocks used for that purpose, the which are more or lesse heavy and pynchynge, as the qualitie of the offense is proved against the delinquent. . . .

"The ducking att the mayne yarde arme is when a malefactor, by having a rope fastened under his armes and abowt his myddle and under his breatche, is thus hoysed up to the end of the yarde, from whence he is againe vyolentlie lett fall intoe the sea, sometymes twyse, sometymes three several tymes one after another, and if the offense be very fowle, he is also drawne under the very keele of the ship, the which is termed keelhaling; and whilst he is thus under water a great gunn is given fire right over his head; the which is done as well toe astonish him the more with the thunder thereof, which much troubleth him, as toe give warning untoe all others toe looke out, and toe beware by his harmes."

13

Other recognized punishments are described by Mr. Oppenheim in his book on the administration of the Navy.

"Prayer," he wrote, "was said twice daily—before dinner and after the psalm sung at setting the evening watch, and anyone absent was liable to twenty-four hours in irons. Swearing was punished by three knocks on the forehead with a boatswain's whistle, and smoking anywhere but on the upper deck, 'and that sparingly', by the bilboes. The thief was tied up to the capstan, 'and every man in the ship shall give him five lashes with a three-stringed whip on his bare back'. This is, I think, the first mention of any form of cat (i.e. 1627). The habitual thief was, after flogging, dragged ashore astern of a boat and ignominiously dismissed with the loss of his wages. For brawling and fighting the offender was ducked three times from the yardarm, and similarly towed ashore and discharged, while for striking an officer he was to be tried for his life by twelve men, but whether shipmates or civilians is not said. If a man slept on watch, three buckets of water were to be poured upon his head and into his sleeves; and anyone, except 'gentlemen and officers', playing cards or dice incurred four hours of manacles."

14

15

It was against this general background that we must judge the next action of the men of the *Vanguard*, when they came to choose between their loyalty to the King and their support of Parliament. The Stuart administration, not only of the Navy, but of the country as a whole, was falling into disrepute and as early as 1636 there were signs of the impending storm which was to topple Charles from his throne. And during these uneasy years the Navy had fallen into such general contempt that even the Algerine pirates kept large fleets and squadrons permanently in English waters to take their toll of merchant ships and English lives. A pirate raid on Baltimore, in Munster, resulted in the sack of the town and the carrying off of 237 British subjects into slavery. Within the space of ten days the "Turks" captured 27 vessels and over 200 men off Plymouth, while *16* in 1640 there were 60 Algerine pirate vessels operating off the south coast of England, where they carried out a raid on Penzance, again taking a number of Englishmen to man their slave galleys.

The same thing was happening on the East coast, though here it was the Dunquerquers who were active in place of the Turks. Their privateers raided Lynn and put it to the flame. Shipping, and especially *17* the coal trade, was brought to a standstill by an almost complete blockade of the coast, so that at one period in Ipswich no fewer than 58 vessels were immobilized by their actions. A special "tunnage and *18* poundage" was levied on all seaborne trade to pay the cost of protecting English vessels against this piracy but, typical of the administration, the money thus raised found its way into other pockets and nothing was done to abate the scourge.

The final tug-of-war between King and Parliament came in 1642. Parliament appointed in June of that year the Earl of Warwick as Commander-in-Chief at sea. The King retaliated by nominating Pennington, who was too staunch a Royalist for the Parliamentary stomach. The Earl of Northumberland, who had become Lord High Admiral on the assassination of Buckingham in August 1628, added his backing to the Parliamentary nominee and was promptly dismissed by Charles for his pains. The two rival Commanders-in-Chief made their way down to the fleet in the Downs and there the sailors declared for Warwick, though some of the captains were still loyal enough to Charles to accept Pennington. Few of the crews, however, that of the *Vanguard* among them, would follow their captains and the majority of the ships took sides with Parliament in the growing quarrel.

It has often been suggested that this was an act of disloyalty on the part of the Navy, whose oath of allegiance was to the King in person. But the reasons are not far to seek. The discontent in the fleet at the many abuses, so many of them apparently directed entirely against the welfare of the sailors themselves, was a powerful incentive to follow the new regime, especially as real efforts were now being made by the commissioners appointed by Parliament to remedy the worst of them. Again, one of the first acts of the Parliament had been to increase the seaman's wage from 10s. per lunar month to 15s. But behind it all, behind the supposed disloyalty, was the fact that, in choosing to follow Parliament, the Navy sincerely believed that it was helping to bring about a reconciliation between the two opposing parties of King and Parliament,

That this was so can be seen by the happenings in 1647, when Parliament was coming more and more under the sway of the Army. On October 5th of that year, Colonel Thomas Rainborow, the son of a former naval captain, was appointed to succeed Sir William Batten in command of the Winter Guard. The men of the *Constant Reformation*, his selected flagship, refused to allow him on board the ship, an action which was applauded throughout the fleet. Rainborow was notoriously hostile to Charles and his appointment, in the eyes of the sailors, smacked of political dishonesty. Batten was quickly recalled. He was greeted with every sign of joy on board and, when he declared for Charles, eleven ships followed him and sailed to Holland, there to join the squadron being formed by the Duke of York and commanded by Charles, Prince of Wales.

The *Vanguard* was not one of these eleven ships, being at the time on detached service in the Channel under Warwick. Whether she would have followed Batten had she been in the Downs when he made his decision it is impossible to say. By the time Warwick returned it was too late, for the Parliamentary hand was firmly clapped down on every remaining ship after Batten's defection. The *Vanguard* was one of the squadron which Warwick took over to Holland to blockade the Royalist ships in Hellevoetsluis. By the time of their arrival there enthusiasm for the Stuart cause was already waning and four ships managed to slip out of the harbour to join Warwick. One by one the remainder were gradually won back, or sunk while out marauding with Prince Rupert after Charles's execution.

By 1651 the English fleet was firmly in Parliament's hands. Cromwell had appointed three "Generals-at-Sea" to command the fleet, Edward Popham, Richard Deane, and Robert Blake. To these were added later George Monck, in 1652, and after Deane was killed in 1653, William Penn and Edward Montagu. These were men of the stamp of Drake and Hawkins, and once again the Navy had the leaders it needed.

CHAPTER IV

THE HONOUR OF THE FLAG

THE Commonwealth, that infant state fathered by Cromwell and his Ironsides, was soon in difficulties. Trouble with France in 1649, begun by the death sentence carried out on Charles I, deepened in the following year to what was known as "reprisals", a state of affairs which was war in all but name. In August of that year the French Ambassador in London was bluntly informed that his country must recognize the Commonwealth before any business between England and France could be transacted. But the French were not prepared to throw over so easily their conceptions of kingship and the divine right of princes, and no recognition followed. As a result, English trade suffered and orders were given to the Generals-at-Sea to molest French trade in retaliation. It had the effect of war even if it saved the nation from the odium of the word.

In the general exercise of these reprisals, Dutch shipping suffered as much as, if not more than, that of any other country. They were the great mercantile carriers of the 17th century, their ships plying from port to port with whatever cargoes they could pick up, irrespective of nationality. The new English Navigation Acts, passed in 1650 and 1651 to protect the growing English merchant fleet, forbade the importation into this country, her colonies and dependencies, of goods not the produce of the country to which the importing vessel belonged. This hit particularly hard at the Dutch carrying trade and, although not the prime cause of the war between the two countries which was to break out in 1652, was yet a contributing factor.

A second factor was what was known as the "honour of the flag". Since the days of Elizabeth the growing naval power of England had been sufficient to enforce a salute by all foreign vessels to the English flag at sea when met in English waters. This was a vague term but was held to embrace those seas of which Britain could claim to be mistress. This saluting the flag had grown to be something looked upon as an inalienable right, and the Royal Navy was jealous of the privilege. It was challenged dramatically by the Dutch.

Tromp, Lieutenant-Admiral of Holland, cruising with his fleet of 42 ships in the Channel, anchored on May 19th, 1652, off Dover. Out of the Downs came Bourne with 10 ships, while from the West came Blake, with 13. What followed is perhaps left to the description of Thomas White, of Dover, who was a spectator of the action.

"The Dutch fleet," he wrote, "weighed anchor and stood up to the coast of France with their flags up near upon two hours, and then bore up to General Blake, each ship having a man at the topmast-head as if

they intended to have struck their flags. When they came within shot of
our Admiral he made one shot at them for to strike, but they refused,
still coming towards him, whereupon he made two shot more at them,
and then the Hollanders gave him one shot, still making nearer to him,
and, coming up to him, saluted our Admiral with a whole volley of small
shot and a broadside of gunshot, and General Blake returned him the
like, and, bearing up after him, they too discharged three or four broadsides at each other, 13 of the Hollanders gave our Admiral each of them a
broadside before any of our ships came up to second him. . . ."

It developed into a full-scale battle, the Dutch losing two ships,
the *St. Laurens* and *St. Maria*, to Bourne's squadron.

Yet a third incident which hastened the coming war was the news
from Holland that they were preparing a fleet of 150 ships in addition
to those vessels already at sea, which numbered about 50. The special
ambassadors of Holland in London sent a long "proposition" to the
English Council of State, explaining that the 150 ships were needed
for the policing of the seas and protection of Dutch trade. They
followed it with another in which they dilated on the evils of war
between the two countries.

"But amongst all kinds of wars," they wrote, "one between these
nations is to be reputed most detestable and horrible. Truly, experience
teaches us that the best and strongest wine (if it be corrupted) becomes
the sourest vinegar, and indeed if two nations, having long been friends,
and being of the same religion and lovers of liberty, living as near
neighbours on the shores of the same sea, both being valiant and warlike,
clash together, what is to be expected but the ruin of both, and, as the
proverb saith, a Cadmean victory? And what else is this, then, to afflict
and depress your friends and companions in religion in order to please
our enemies, and to give occasion openly for injury to both? An author,
being none of the least among yours, hath very well compared, as one
conceives, both the nations to two earthen pots driving in the sea, with
this device, 'If we are dashed together, we shall be broken.' That honest
man certainly hit it off well, and we believe that you are of his opinion.
But if the two nations come to an agreement, good God, what store of
happiness will this bring forth!"

But the pious hopes of the three special ambassadors were not
to be. The stumbling-block to any reconciliation was those 150 ships,
and the English Council of State wrote to the ambassadors:

"The extraordinary preparation of 150 sail of men of war without any
visible occasion, but what doth now appear a just ground of jealousy in
your own judgments when your lordships pretend to excuse it . . . do find
too much cause to believe that the Lords the States General of the
United Provinces have an intention by force to usurp the known rights of
England in the Seas, to destroy the fleets that are, under God, their walls
and bulwarks, and thereby expose this Commonwealth to invasion at
their pleasure. . . ."

War was now inevitable.

Parliament at once began to bring forward as many ships as possible. The *Vanguard*, which had been laid up at the end of 1651, was recommissioned under Captain Harrison and sent to join Sir George Ayscue in the Downs. Harrison was appointed on June 3rd, and by June 28th the ship was ready in all respects for sea. It had been quick work, but the energy of the Commonwealth officers was equal to the sudden emergency. In May of 1652 the number of vessels in the fleet, of the first, second, and third rate, did not amount to more than 20, although there were several smaller ships of various sorts. By August, by means of great efforts in bringing the laid-up ships forward and by the compulsory purchase of suitable merchant craft which, although already armed with guns could be pierced to carry more, Blake was able to take the sea with a fleet of 70 vessels. Others were arriving almost daily. It was a feat which could never have been achieved under the Stuart administration.

At the same time orders were issued for the pressing of all seamen between the ages of 15 and 50 years. The proclamation setting up the pressgangs was limited to the south-eastern counties, but as in these were to be found the bulk of English seamen, the intake was considerable. In addition a large number came forward voluntarily, for conditions in the Navy were now far better than they had been in Charles's day, and the men at least knew that they would receive the pay due to them.

With Blake and Ayscue, lying in the Downs, were 55 ships of the first, second, and third rate, two fireships, two shallops, and 18 merchantmen taken up for service. On June 27th, the day before the *Vanguard* sailed down the Thames to join the fleet, Blake sailed to the northward with the intention of disturbing the Dutch herring fishery in the North Sea, and of intercepting a homeward-bound convoy expected from the East Indies. He took with him 39 of the warships, all the merchantmen, the fireships, and the shallops. Ayscue was left with 16, and the way was left open for Tromp to attack. He was at sea with a fleet of 92 sail and still smarting from the loss of his two ships in the affair off Dover. The returning Dutch ambassadors, who fell in with Tromp on their way home, were able to tell him of Blake's mission to the northward and also of Ayscue's weakness in the Downs. Tromp swooped on the Thames.

He was, however, to be disappointed. Ayscue had withdrawn his ships as near to the coast as he could, and they lay under the protection of shore guns, mounted on special platforms run out towards the sea from the castle at Deal. Tromp's attack in the face of this defence was half-hearted, especially when he found that the guns of the English ships could outrange him. A fortunate shift in the wind to the south gave him the excuse he required to break off the action and retire with his fleet. Ayscue and his squadron, which included the *Vanguard*, were saved.

Leaving Ayscue, Tromp sailed to the north in search of Blake. But he had no more fortune in these latitudes than he had had in the Downs. He was too late to prevent Blake from capturing or sinking 12 of the 13 Dutch frigates which were guarding the herring fleet and of scattering the herring busses—over 100 were taken but later allowed to go free—although he arrived in time to safeguard the convoy, which was approaching from the west. On July 26th the two fleets lay in sight of each other, but before they could engage a hard gale from the north-west drove Tromp in confusion from the fishing-grounds, leaving his ships scattered over the North Sea. It also blew the convoy safely past Blake. By the time it had blown itself out there was nothing left for Tromp to do but to return to Holland. Once again he had no successes to show and half his ships were damaged. He was a sadly discredited man and the country clamoured for his dismissal. He was relieved of his command, though later he was to come back to the Dutch Navy and win an undying fame.

With the return of Tromp, Blake sailed to the south again and rejoined Ayscue in the Downs. Harrison, captain of the *Vanguard*, was transferred to one of Blake's ships, being succeeded by Captain William Haddock. When Ayscue was ordered to the westward to take up "the guard of the Channel and those seas", Haddock in the *Vanguard* was appointed as his Vice-Admiral, with Captain Michael Packe, of the *George*, as third in command. Ayscue sailed at the beginning of August, his fleet amounting to 40 sail, made up to this number by the addition of several armed merchantmen. His squadron was based on Plymouth.

Meanwhile, in Holland, Tromp had been replaced by Michiel Adrienszoon de Ruijter, more familiarly known as de Ruyter, and the greatest seaman that Holland has ever produced. Indeed, he was also the most outstanding naval leader of the 17th century, irrespective of nationality. He had had unrivalled experience at sea, having first served as a seaman and rising by his merits. During the war against Spain he commanded the fleet in 1641 with the rank of Lieutenant-Admiraal-Generaal, the highest rank in the Dutch Navy.

On August 3rd he put to sea with orders to escort a Dutch convoy through the Channel on its way to the Mediterranean and the Dutch East Indies. He had but 17 ships and, hearing of Ayscue's squadron off Plymouth, put into Calais to await reinforcements. They arrived on August 11th, and with a further eight men of war and a number of East Indiamen, all heavily armed, he had an effective strength of 50 sail, besides several small craft. With this force he proceeded down Channel with his convoy.

Five days later he was off Plymouth. Ayscue, cruising in those waters, sighted him and pressed in to the attack.

"Yesterday," wrote an anonymous correspondent from Plymouth, "being Monday the 16 of August, he [Ayscue] discovered the Hollanders, and about one of the clock he met with a fleet of theirs, consisting of 60 sail of men of war and 25 merchants'-men. Sir George Ayscue's fleet consisted of 41, which which he charged the Hollanders' whole fleet and made a stout fight. Sir George Ayscue charged them quite through, and not being able to go to the windward of all, received 40 broadsides, and after got away. Then Sir George Ayscue charged them again, and made another furious assault. It is supposed that we have sunk their Rear-Admiral; they (if not) will have much ado to save her.

"The fight was extreme hot, but no boarding either of other. We suppose the Hollanders' loss must needs be very great, for they were extremely torn with our bullets, and we have great loss also. Captain Lisle, a precious sweet commander, is sore wounded and almost dead. Captain Packe, that excellent stout seaman, hath his leg shot off. Night approaching, the fight ceased, and in the night both fleets lay still, having both of them their lights out. . . . Our men called upon God before they engaged; the Dutch drunk soundly to make them fight; strong drink was given to their men as their custom is to raise up a courage in them to fight the more desperately." 12

Reliable details of this brush off Plymouth are lacking. Haddock, in the *Vanguard*, followed Ayscue into the thick of the fighting— "Our Admiral, Vice-Admiral, and Rear-Admiral, with about five or six others, broke through their whole fleet, so as the 25 merchantmen [de Ruyter's convoy] ran away to the coast of France"—and on the 13 second "charge" placed the *Vanguard* within half-musket shot of one of the largest of the Dutch ships, where they hammered away at each other with broadsides as fast as the guns could be loaded. But whereas the *Vanguard* and the other English ships directed their fire at the hulls of the enemy vessels, the Dutch aimed at masts and rigging to prevent pursuit of their fleet and convoy after the action.

"We shot altogether low at them," wrote a correspondent from Plymouth, "and they received many shot in their hulls. They shot high at us, aiming thereby to spoil our masts, sails, and tackles, in which most of our ships received the greatest loss, and yet our Admiral had many shot in her hull." 14

Both sides claimed the victory. Neither had lost a ship, although both claimed one as sunk, and while the Dutch vessels suffered much in their hulls, the English ships were too shattered aloft to continue the action the following day or to follow de Ruyter to the westward.

There is a suspicion that some of the converted merchant vessels did not play their full part in the action, and that there would have been a more decisive result had they done so. "Sir George Ayscue," writes the same Plymouth man, "deserves much honour for his gallantry in the late engagement on Monday last with the Dutch fleet; had some of the merchants' ships done the like, he had banged the Dutch fleet to the purpose." But it was a common failing among 1 these converted merchant vessels, as prevalent among the Dutch fleet as the English. The charge was made over and over again during the course of the war.

In the meantime Blake had been sent to the west, by orders from the Council of State, to reinforce Ayscue. He sailed on September 14th, and on his arrival took Ayscue's squadron, or those of it still able to fight after the recent engagement, under his orders. With the main fleet he anchored in Torbay, detaching Penn with 15 sail, of which one was the *Vanguard*, to cruise for de Ruyter off the coast of Devon.

By this time de Ruyter was returning. He had escorted his convoy as far as the Scillies and, after riding out a gale there, turned for home on September 12th. On the 17th, with 40 sail under his command, he sighted Penn with his 15. De Ruyter had the windward berth, and thus was able to dictate whether to fight or not. It looked to Penn, as he vainly endeavoured to bring his small squadron within range, that at any moment de Ruyter must use the wind to come down to the attack.

All that day the two fleets sailed along in sight of each other, Penn attempting to get close enough to engage, de Ruyter as equally determined to decline the battle. As darkness fell, the wind increased and the sea began to rise. Penn kept his squadron as well together as he could, ready for the inevitable attack when it should come, although in the rising sea and the darkness one or two of his ships parted company. At about midnight he saw the flash of gunfire to the southward and at once turned to close it. It was soon lost in the murk of the night and not until the following morning did he discover what had happened. Captain Sanders of the *Assurance*, closing Penn and coming aboard, reported that he had sighted a large ship in the darkness which he had engaged and chased until he had found himself in the midst of the Dutch fleet. He had lost them as they disappeared to the eastward. Penn was incredulous that the Dutch, "would have been so poor and low-spirited", but there was no doubt that de Ruyter had given him the slip during the darkness, and that he was now too far up Channel for there to be any hope of his being caught and brought to action.

It would seem that de Ruyter had here missed a fine chance of doing considerable damage to the English ships. He outnumbered them by more than two to one and, moreover, held the windward gage, so that he could choose his own moment for forcing action. But the truth is that his ships, in addition to the rough handling they had received from Ayscue in the fight off Plymouth, had been further damaged in the storm off the Scillies. They were in no shape to fight, even with such odds in their favour.

The Dutch, in the meantime, had been equipping another fleet, which was placed under the command of Witte Corneliszood de With, an admiral much in favour with the reigning political party in Holland. He had 44 sail of men of war under his command, and his orders were to join de Ruyter and, with him, seek out and destroy Blake.

He and de Ruyter met at Calais on September 22nd and, after sending home ten men of war which had been too badly damaged to fight again before refitting, weighed anchor with a total of 64 ships in search of Blake. De With had received orders to take de Ruyter under his command for this operation, although in the battle which developed a few days later when the two fleets met, de Ruyter, like de With, flew his flag at the main to denote that he had been appointed to an independent command. De With, though a competent seaman who had fought under Piet Hein, was extremely unpopular in the fleet, and there seems to have been little love between him and de Ruyter. From the Dutch point of view it was not one of their wiser appointments.

The Council of State, having knowledge of de With's presence at sea, immediately sent word to Blake and Ayscue in the west. They also had the unpleasant task of relieving Ayscue from his command, not from any want of courage or determination on his part, but apparently because they mistrusted his Royalist sympathies. And so, when on September 18th the fleet sailed eastward up Channel in search of the Dutch, the three squadrons were commanded by Blake in the centre, Penn in the van, and Bourne in the rear. They arrived in the Downs on September 25th.

Blake seems to have entered this battle in a mood of depression. As he gave the order to weigh on September 28th, he wrote to the Council: "I engage about 70 Dutch men of war which lay by Goodwin Sands, and this may possibly be the last before I seal my faithful services with my best blood." But as he sailed to the north and sighted the Dutch fleet, all the old love of battle seems to have returned and he led his squadron into the thick of the fight. Penn, leading the fleet with his squadron, sailed too near the Kentish Knock Sands and some of his ships went ashore, leaving Blake to carry the first heat of the battle alone with his squadron.

> "I commanded no guns to be fired," he wrote, "till we came very near them, so that there passed many broadsides between us and them, and by means of their tacking, the greatest part of our fleet came suddenly to be engaged, and the dispute was very hot for a short time, continuing till it was dark night."

When de With tacked, his course was south, so that Blake and he passed on opposite courses. Penn, as has been stated, was aground on the Kentish Knock, but not for long.

> "It pleased God," he wrote, "the Disposer of all things, to disappoint us, being aground upon a sand, supposed the Kentish Knock. It was reasonably smooth, and for my part, I did not feel her strike; the master and others said they did, but the man that hove the lead overboard said we had not three fathom water, by which account it was too true. The *Sovereign* was near musket shot without us, and struck several times, for hereby we were forced to tack our ship to clear us of the sand, and,

indeed, it fell out better for doing execution upon the enemy than we could have cast it ourselves; for as the Dutch fleet cleared themselves of our General, he standing to the northward and they to the southward, we fell patt to receive them, and so stayed by them till the night caused our separation."

The *Vanguard*, in the van with Penn, did not take the sand and so was able to join in the battle. She received a number of shot through her sails and rigging, but was not badly damaged. That night she lay with the rest of the fleet keeping watch on the Dutch, whose lights could be seen down to leeward.

The dawn showed that the Dutch were in no case to continue the fight. They had lost seven ships on the previous day and during the night another 20 had stolen away unwilling to face a further day of action. De With, it is true, was anxious to renew the fight, but was dissuaded at a Council of War, the odds being too great against him. So, disheartened, the Dutch fleet turned for home, chased all the way by Blake until the proximity of the Dutch sandbanks forced him to turn back for the Downs.

"I believe it will be sad news to the States," wrote one of the English officers, "and although they thought to have foundered our ships in the sands, yet blessed be God, we have gotten the victory, and they are fled home by the weeping cross. . . . I am persuaded that the Hollanders were drunk generally the most part of them; for at first they fought exceedingly desperately as ever I saw, but after some hours were never so raliant."

This recurring idea that the Dutch drank before action to keep up their courage is to be found in many contemporary reports of the period. There is nothing to confirm it from the Dutch side and was probably no more than an expression of contempt put about by the English seamen.

De With's reception on his return was an unhappy one. There was little he could do to explain the failure except to lay the blame on the defaulting Dutch captains who had deserted him during the night. His fleet had set sail in high hopes of retrieving Dutch honour at sea after Tromp's unhappy cruise. They returned beaten and discredited.

"The news is arrived here," writes a correspondent from Amsterdam, "how pitifully the Dutch fleet hath been paid by the English; for they brought such a spectacle home as makes but a sad story. No less than 2,000 wounded men are brought ashore, nine great boatfuls hither to Amsterdam, and 10 also to other towns, but especially to Zeeland; but of the number of slain there is no certainty, though it may be imagined they could be no small number, considering the miserable torn condition of their fleet."

Of the Dutch ships taken during the battle, only one, the *Mary* of 30 guns, was in a sufficiently good state to be brought in. She was refitted and eventually added to the Royal Navy. The others were too much damaged and were sunk immediately after capture. None of the English ships was lost, though the *Resolution* was "rent and torn", and had to proceed up-river for a thorough refit.

CHAPTER V

DUNGENESS AND PORTLAND

THE first result of the Battle of the Kentish Knock, so far as the Dutch were concerned, was the recall of Tromp to command their fleet. Confidence in de With was at so low an ebb that, although he was appointed to a subordinate command in Tromp's fleet, he was replaced before sailing by de Ruyter. The ships, which numbered 88, were divided into four squadrons, commanded respectively by Tromp, Johan Evertsen, de Ruyter, and Pieter Floriszoon.

In England the victory was followed by a completely false feeling of security. It was thought that the Dutch had been so completely beaten that they were unlikely to appear again in the Channel for some months. As a result of this feeling of confidence, the Council of State proceeded to give orders dispersing the fleet. Penn was detached with 20 sail to the northward to meet and escort a convoy of colliers from Newcastle to the Thames. A squadron of 12 sail was sent to Plymouth to take over the duties of the Channel Guard. Yet a third squadron of 12 sail, under the command of Captain James Peacock, was ordered to proceed to Leghorn to operate in the Mediterranean. Fortunately, the Council of State returned to its senses before this last order could be carried out, and Peacock's departure was prevented. Even with his 12 ships retained in the fleet, Blake could muster no no more than 42 sail all told in the Downs.

The first orders received by Tromp in his new command were to collect and escort through the Channel a fleet of 300 merchantmen, which had been held up in Holland ever since de With's discomfiture at the Kentish Knock. An almost equally large fleet was collecting at the Isle of Rhé, off Brest, for convoy back to Holland. Obviously, before any operation of such magnitude could be carried through in safety, Tromp would need to be assured that the Channel was free from the English fleet. So great a convoy could not be exposed to any danger of wholesale capture.

Leaving his merchantmen on the Flemish coast, Tromp sailed with his 88 ships in search of Blake. He appeared off the back of the Goodwins on November 29th, and Blake, lying in the Downs with his 42 sail, at once weighed and beat to the southward against the south-westerly wind, on a similar course to that of Tromp on the other side of the sands.

Blake has often been criticized for this move and, in truth, it hardly conforms with his usual mastery of naval tactics. He was, by his action, standing down to almost certain defeat, for he was out-numbered by more than two to one. It is often said in his defence that his prime object was the guarding of the mouth of the Thames, but that argument hardly holds water, for he was standing away from it close-hauled on the wind, whereas had the Thames been his real consideration, he could have had a following wind on a northerly course and a considerably shorter distance to cover than Tromp.

There are two possible explanations. In the uncertain light of the November day he may have thought that the vessels he sighted were the merchant fleet which Tromp had been detailed to escort. That he knew of their existence is certain, and on the 24th he wrote to the Council of State that "since evening intelligence is brought me that from off the steeple of Margate there was observed above 400 sail", from which he must have surmised that they were already at sea. A second possible cause of his decision to sail to the southward was that he had been informed by the Council of State on the 27th that the ships from Portsmouth had been ordered to join him immediately. He may have considered that his present course might well bring him up to them before the inevitable clash with Tromp occurred.

Among Blake's fleet of 42 vessels was the *Vanguard*, now under the command of Captain John Mildmay, who had joined her from the *Nonsuch* after the Battle of the Kentish Knock. He was a man much loved by the seamen and one, moreover, to whom the sound of guns was music in his ears. There could be little doubt that in the coming action the *Vanguard* would be in the thickest of it if her present captain had any say in the matter.

Shortly after the English fleet weighed the wind veered into the north-west and freshened to a gale. The two fleets, on more or less parallel courses, came down off Dover, where Blake anchored for the night in the Roads. Tromp, a few miles to leeward, sheltered under the cliffs of the South Foreland. Perhaps the thoughts of the English sailors, as they lay at uneasy anchor during the night and contemplated the odds against them, can be summed up in a letter from the fleet.

"The Lord direct us," says the writer, "both in the van and rear, else we cannot stand; and I hope we go not out in our own strength, but in the strength and power of the living God. What the event will be, the Lord knows; but without doubt it will prove a very bloody engagement, for they seem to be a very resolved and resolute enemy. The Lord purge out all Achan's wedges and Babylonish garments out of England, and I pray to God to direct the poor nation to withdraw our eyes from Tarshish, to do our Jonah's work, so that truth and peace may flourish within its territories."

These pious hopes were not fulfilled. When the two fleets weighed anchor on the morning of November 30th, and stood down to the westward along the coast, Tromp was to seaward of the English fleet. As they approached Dungeness, where the land curves down to the southward, the English van was forced out towards the Dutch and the ships met in a fury of cannon fire.

The citizens of Dover, keen to see the fun, "came many of them down to the shore full of expectation and a confidence in that success which hath attended the English both by land and sea". The Governor of the Castle, indeed, hired a ship so that he might have a better view, but what he saw must have discouraged him. Of the English fleet of 42 vessels, more than half used the wind to keep out of the fight, some of them ships of the Royal Navy. It had been expected of some of the merchant captains, but hardly of the Navy.

The whole brunt of the fighting was carried by the ships in the English van, led by Blake in the *Triumph*, Lionel Lane in the *Victory*, and Mildmay in the *Vanguard*. The first shots were fired shortly before noon and the engagement continued till dark.

> "Our two ships," wrote an eyewitness, "called the *Vanguard* and *Victory*, were all the time of the fight (which lasted till moonshine), desperately engaged with 20 of the Dutch ships, two of which were Vice-Admirals, and yet at last they got off well, though much battered in their sails, yards, rigging, and hulls."

The *Triumph*, in an attempt to go to the aid of the *Garland*, which was hotly beset, had her fore-topmast shot away and her rigging badly damaged, so that for a time she was out of control. She was boarded by the Dutch, but Mildmay brought the *Vanguard* alongside and drove the enemy off. The *Vanguard* herself was boarded twice, but each time managed to clear her decks of the enemy and drive them off into the sea.

As soon as darkness fell Blake gathered together the battered remnants of his fleet and managed to bring them to Dover Roads, where he anchored for the night. The following morning he made for the Downs, reaching there shortly after noon. The English had lost two ships, the *Garland* and the *Bonaventure*, and the others which had been in the battle were all more or less gravely damaged. The Dutch loss had been one ship, which blew up accidentally when her powder caught fire. But the real result of the battle was that the Channel was now open to Tromp to pass his convoy through without hindrance, for there was no English fleet left to hinder him.

Blake himself was sadly cast down by his defeat, even though he himself had fought as gallantly as anyone. The defection of his captains was a more than sufficient excuse for his reverse, though he seems to have thought that his useful days were over.

> "In this account," he wrote in his report of the battle, "I am bound to let your Honours know in general that there was much baseness of spirit, not among the merchantmen only, but many of the State's ships, and therefore I make it my humble request that your Honours would be

pleased to send down some gentlemen to take an impartial and strict examination of the deportment of several commanders, that you may know who are to be confided in and who are not. It will then be time to take into consideration the grounds of some other errors and defects, especially the discouragements and want of seamen. . . . And I hope it will not be unseasonable for me, in behalf of myself, to desire your Honours that you would be pleased to think of giving me, your unworthy servant, a discharge from this employment, so far too great for me; especially since your Honours have added two such able gentlemen for the undertaking of that charge*; that so I may spend the remainder of my days in private retirement and in prayers to the Lord for a blessing upon you and the nation."   7

At the end of the same report, acknowledging the receipt of his commission which the Council of State had dispatched to him on the day of the battle, he wrote that he would:

"endeavour to put it in execution with all the power and faithfulness I can, until it shall please your Honours to receive it back again, which I trust will be very speedily, that so I may be freed from that trouble of spirit which lies upon me, arising from the sense of my own insufficiency and the usual effects thereof, reproach and contempt of men, and disservice of the Commonwealth, which may be the consequence of both."

The case of the reluctant captains was put before the Commissioners and five of them were committed to the Tower. Among them were Captains Young and Taylour, each in command of a Royal Navy ship and both known to be fearless in action. The other three were Captains Saltonstall, Wadsworth, and Chapman. The record of their examination has, apparently, not survived, and so we cannot know what excuse they put forward for their behaviour, but it was generally thought that they had been bribed before the battle by Royalist agents. Blake's own brother, Benjamin, another of the guilty ones, was not put on trial, but was "discharged from his present command in the fleet and not again to be employed nor go forth in the service".   8

One amusing account of the battle, which calls itself, "brief and impartial without passion of affection", relates how, on the Tuesday morning of the engagement, "the trumpets sounded, drums beat, and the voices of men disgorged in plenteous volleys of shouts gave the sure intimation of a hot conflict". After a lively description of the fighting, it reports that:

"The Butter-boxes [a contemporary nickname for the Dutch sailors] appeared again on the Wednesday in a full body, in high bravado; but it stood not with the safety or honour of our fleet to re-engage upon such desperate disadvantage. Whereupon, upon Thursday night, they landed 300 seamen between Romney and Hastings, which swept Romney Marsh of 200 head of cattle."   9

* Deane and Monck had just been appointed Generals-at-Sea.

It was only too true. With the Channel at his mercy, Tromp landed his men almost as he wished on the southern coast, helping himself to such cattle and other provisions as he could seize. The English shipping was swept into the Dutch net as Tromp proceeded with his big convoy down Channel, and he was followed by a host of Dutch privateers which preyed upon the coastwise trade until it was unsafe for any English ship to leave harbour.

The first action of the Council of State after receiving Blake's report was to confirm him in his position and to reassure him of his value to the fleet. Next they called out the militia of Hampshire, Surrey, and Kent, to defend the coast against attack, particularly the Isle of Wight, which they expected Tromp to attack. Orders were given for the immediate building of 30 new frigates and a large number of smaller craft, and two ordinances were promulgated. The first was to prevent seamen being allowed to go ashore while their ships were in harbour so that they might have no opportunity of deserting, the second to the effect that merchant skippers were not to command their ships in battle. And with it all, instructions were sent to press as many more men for the naval service as possible, so that in the next action with the Dutch there should at least be no lack of seamen, of which Blake had complained after the Battle of Dungeness.

These steps by Parliament, carried through with its usual vigour, did much to put the English fleet back on its feet again. So much so, indeed, that on February 10th, 1653, less than two months after the Battle of Dungeness, we find Penn being appointed as Vice-Admiral of a fleet of some 80 vessels. The three Generals-at-Sea, Blake, Deane, and Monck, were in joint command. Deane was content to serve in the *Triumph* with Blake as flagship of the Red squadron, but Monck, fearing perhaps that three commanders in one ship might lead to disagreements, chose instead to take command of the White squadron, selecting the *Vanguard* as his flagship. Penn automatically became Admiral of the Blue squadron, with the *Speaker* as his flagship.

This was, in many ways, a very different fleet from that with which Blake fought at Dungeness. To encourage the flow of recruits, Parliament raised the pay of able seamen, "fit for the helm and lead, top and yard", from 19s. to 24s. a month. All other seamen, boys and "gromets"* excepted, received 18s. Gromets were allowed 14s. 3d. a month and boys received 9s. 6d. New regulations for the treatment of sick and wounded were made and the vexed question of prize money was settled. A month's pay was given to all officers and men in respect of prizes already taken during the war, while in future prizes the men were to be allowed to plunder above the gun-deck, known as "pillage", and in addition to be allowed 10s. a ton on the prize's measurement and £6 13s. 4d. for every gun she carried, "to be divided according to the custom of the sea".

The results of these reforms were very soon apparent and it was

* From the Spanish *Gromete*, a first-class boy.

reported by Bourne, at the time in the *Vanguard* lying off Queenborough, that the seamen were coming forward at a satisfactory rate and that "the generality of men were found to be in a hopeful constitution and temper of spirit". Yet even this increase of pay could not attract sufficient men to man the growing navy completely, and recourse had to be made to the Army, of whom some 1,200 men were drafted, for instance, from Portsmouth on February 1st. Yet, on the whole, the Navy was in reasonably good heart and eager to revenge itself on Tromp when next the opportunity should present itself.

In the meantime, Tromp, having seen his outward-bound convoy safely away from the Island of Rhé, waited there for the homeward-bound merchantmen to collect. There were about 200 of them and by the middle of February they were ready. Tromp sailed on the 12th, so confident, it was said, that the Channel was still free from the English, that he hoisted a broom at his masthead as a sign that he swept the English sea. The first mention of this broom seems to be in a letter written from on board the *Nonsuch*, dated February 28th, ten days after the Battle of Portland. "Their gallant Mr. Tromp," says the writer, "when he was in France (we understand) wore a flag of broom, and being demanded what he meant by it, replied that he was going to sweep the narrow seas of all English men".

Another mention shortly afterwards was in the *Daily Intelligencer*, of March 9th of the same year, but it is unlikely that there is any truth behind the story. A broom hoisted at the masthead of a ship during the 17th century was a sign that the vessel was being put up for sale and the episode of Tromp's broom was probably little more than a lower-deck joke at the expense of the Dutch. The whip hoisted by Blake as a sign that he ruled the seas, as recounted by Weatherley's song, is nowhere mentioned in the official papers and was almost certainly fiction, probably no more than a bit of political doggerel to suit the spirit of the times.

The two commanders approached each other on opposite courses, Tromp sailing up Channel in complete ignorance even of the existence of a new English fleet, Blake dropping down Channel in search of his adversary. The English fleet was organized in three squadrons and the flag officers were:

RED SQUADRON:

Triumph (42)	Blake and Deane (Generals).
Fairfax (64)	John Lawson (Vice-Admiral).
Laurel (38)	Samuel Howett (Rear-Admiral).

WHITE SQUADRON:

Vanguard (40)	George Monck (General).
Rainbow (40)	James Peacock (Vice-Admiral).
Diamond (40)	Roger Martin (Rear-Admiral).

BLUE SQUADRON:

Speaker (64)	W. Penn (Admiral).
Victory (42)	Lionel Lane (Vice-Admiral).
Assistance (40)	John Bourne (Rear-Admiral).

The fleets met on February 18th, some 15 miles south of Portland. Blake, anxious not to miss Tromp, had been tacking down Channel against the light north-westerly wind, making long boards across to the coast of France. When eventually he sighted Tromp, early in the morning of the 18th, his squadron was about a mile ahead of Penn's, which in its turn was about four miles ahead of Monck's. The fleets were evenly matched, for while Tromp had twelve more ships than Blake, the English vessels were more heavily gunned.

Tromp at once charged in to the attack. Having the wind behind him, he had the opportunity, which he was not slow to grasp, of bringing the whole of his fleet of 81 ships into action against Blake's squadron, Penn and Monck still being some distance down to leeward.

"About eight o'clock," states a contemporary account from one of the men engaged in the battle, " . . . the *Triumph* engaged the enemy, the Dutch men of war bearing up on them, but the rest of our fleet endeavouring to follow, not above three or four of them could get up, because they were to leeward, so that the Generals (Blake and Deane were together in the *Triumph*) with these few were constrained to bear the first brunt, holding play with no less than thirty of the Dutch men of war, whereof seven at a time kept upon the *Triumph*, and yet they continued till two o'clock in the afternoon, being much shattered in her sails, but so tight in her hull that she never so much as pumped for it."

Monck, in the *Vanguard* away down to leeward, was impatient to get up into the fight. It was his first experience at sea and, having spent his previous service as a cavalry officer, he did not understand the long and tedious business of tacking into a head wind. It is said of him that, as he stood on the *Vanguard's* poop and watched the ships ahead of him wreathed in the smoke of gunfire, he drew his sword and ordered his squadron to charge. Whether he did so or not he certainly made every effort to get his ships into the action.

Penn arrived to help Blake shortly before noon, Monck about four hours later. And at once the *Vanguard* was in the thick of the fight, going alongside one of the Dutch ships and boarding her. Mildmay, her captain, was killed in the fighting, as also were about 30 of her ship's company. "In this fight," writes an officer of the *Eagle*, "Captain Mildmay and Captain Barker (captain of the *Prosperous*) deported themselves with singular dexterity and courage, but at last received their mortal wounds." In the *Triumph* Captain Ball was killed and Blake himself wounded in the thigh. The same correspondent in the *Eagle* wrote of her:

"the famous *Triumph* (to the perpetual eternizing of the General's fame, be it spoken) received near upon 700 shots, wherein was slain that noble and approved soldier, Captain Ball, with some others, besides many wounded. Amongst the rest the General himself received a wound upon the thigh by an unhappy splinter (but it is hoped not dangerous) which splinter took away part of General Deane's breeches, but not any part of his body at the least hurt."

The battle continued all day until, "the sable night ending the dispute", both fleets lay alongside each other with their lights burning   *15*
to lick their wounds and prepare for the following day. The English had lost but one ship, the *Samson*, and she had been sunk by her own commander, Captain Button, after her company had been taken off, as being too much damaged to be of any further value. The Dutch had lost seven or eight men of war, according to the joint report of the three Generals, and four by their own admission, though Jan Evertsen in his journal mentions seven. Blake, in spite of his wound, could be well satisfied by the day's work.

The fight was continued on the 19th and 20th. Tromp, who on the 18th had marshalled his convoy to windward of—i.e. behind— his fleet, now had them before him and adopted a crescent formation with his men of war to give them as much protection from the English as possible. The two fleets were by now south of the Isle of Wight and when, in the afternoon, the English caught up with Tromp, the battle broke out again as sharply as ever. But Tromp's defensive dispositions were too good to permit the English more than a modest success on this day and they captured but five more Dutch vessels.

The really decisive day was the 20th. Tromp's situation was becoming desperate, for his fleet was running short of powder and, moreover, he had reason to distrust the courage of some of his captains. The situation was all the more threatening because Blake and Monck had worked the English fleet to the northward of the Dutch and, with the wind freshening and veering into the north, they were in a position to make a direct attack on the precious convoy. As they closed to within pistol range, Tromp found his early misgivings only too justified. A number of the Dutch captains decided to run for it and, spreading all the sail they could, forced their way through the convoy and set a course for home at their best speed. Tromp, as was only to be expected, fought as hard and as gallantly as ever, but to little avail in the face of the determined English onslaught.

The fleets were off Beachy Head when the first broadsides were fired. It was, according to Captain Graves, who put into Dover with one of the Dutch prizes, "the hottest fight of all", and continued right across Channel to the French coast at Cap Gris Nez. Fifty of the Dutch merchantmen were taken in prize during the day's fighting and another eight men of war. The total losses over the three days, though the figures given in the various accounts do not tally, appear to be 17 men of war sunk or captured, and between 50 and 60 merchantmen taken. The English lost but the one ship mentioned above, the *Samson*.

Yet, at the very end, Tromp escaped the full fate which might have been his. As night drew on and the fleets approached the French coast, Blake gave the signal to anchor to avoid being swept on to a lee shore. The Dutch were expected to do the same. But during the night Tromp weighed and slipped round Cap Gris Nez to safety. When the English sailors looked for them in the morning to make a final attack, the sea was empty.

Casualties on both sides were heavy. An English estimate of 600 killed and wounded in their fleet is an obvious understatement, as also is a Dutch one of 1,100 on theirs. Fifteen hundred Dutch prisoners were taken and at least 2,000 men were killed, with probably twice that number wounded. A comparable figure for the English fleet would be about 1,200 killed and wounded.

One of the more interesting points which emerge from this battle, so far as the naval side of history is concerned, is that of tactics. Many histories quote the Battle of Portland as seeing the birth of the line ahead formation, but this is not borne out by any of the State papers of the immediate period. The English fleet, as was the Dutch, was organized on a squadronal basis, but there seems to be no further development of tactics than that, though each squadron was further divided into three divisions, each under its own commander. All the first-hand accounts of the battle itself suggest that the squadrons fought as they always had done, in loose groups and with no particular formation. As a general rule ships just charged—and it is a word frequently employed in contemporary descriptions of naval actions— into the fray as soon as they could come up within range.

A more important clue, perhaps, is the set of fighting instructions issued on February 10th, shortly before the battle, by the three Generals to Penn, who held his commission as Vice-Admiral, or second-in-command of the fleet. There is no mention in them of a line ahead formation. Yet they are sufficiently detailed for one to assume with some degree of confidence that had there been any intention of forming a line ahead, it would have been specifically mentioned in Penn's instructions.

Yet that the battle did produce the need for some closer control of individual ships is evident in a further set of fighting instructions from Blake, Deane, and Monck, issued to Penn after the battle, on March 29th. In these it was laid down that, on sighting the enemy, the ships of each squadron, "shall endeavour to keep in a line with their chief". It was an instruction that was to have an immense influence on the future of naval war.

After the battle the Generals returned to Portsmouth, there to land the wounded and to repair those ships damaged during the three days of fighting. Blake, whose wound was at first thought to be slight, "took a great cold which put him into some distrain", and later it was reported that he would never go to sea again, "for one of his hamstrings is broken and he has a continual rheum which falls into his eyes which almost blinds him". Fortunately it was not as bad as that, though he was a long time mending.

To the *Vanguard*, in the place of her dead captain Mildmay, was appointed Captain Joseph Jordan. On March 30th he sailed as Vice-Admiral in Penn's squadron which was sent north to the Humber to escort a convoy of colliers to London. The actions of the Dutch privateers in the North Sea, and the presence there of de With with a fleet of 40 Dutch men of war, had paralysed the coastwise trade and there was a coal famine in London. The price of coal had risen to as high as £5 a chaldron, "several brewers have left off brewing for want of firing, and most of our cooks have not wherewith to dress their meat; the cries of the poor are very lamentable for want of fuel". De With, on sighting Penn's squadron, prudently withdrew, and the *Vanguard* and her fellows had the satisfaction of escorting to the Thames the first coal received in the capital for some months.

Both sides spent these two or three months after the Battle of Portland in preparing for a resumption of the fight. The *Vanguard* was fortunate in that she had not suffered so extensively in the battle as some other ships, and so was able to keep at sea in Penn's squadron while the others were being repaired. Deane and Monck from their end, and the Navy Commissioners from theirs, worked at top pressure. One by one ships were added to the growing fleet till, by the beginning of May, over 100 were again in commission. Under the command of the two Generals, they were based in the North Sea, Yarmouth and Harwich being the main naval ports employed.

Equally active steps were being taken in Holland. Tromp, still in command, gathered his ships together as they came out of the repairers' hands. And by the beginning of May he, too, had 100 in commission. The stage was set for the next phase of the war.

CHAPTER VI

THE BIRTH OF NAVAL TACTICS

ON April 20th, 1653, Cromwell dissolved the Rump Parliament and became a virtual dictator in England. The news was received in the fleet the following day and, after much discussion between the Generals and the captains, was accepted, though with considerable distaste on the part of Monck. His reply showed that he and the other captains in harbour had resolved that, as the nation's business was of the chief importance and as it trusted its defence to the Generals-at-Sea, their duty was to continue to serve the country to the best of their ability, irrespective of the changed complexion of politics in London. But Monck thoroughly mistrusted the whole proceeding and it was, perhaps, then that there were sown those seeds of Royalism which were to blossom so whole-heartedly when the new king came into his own seven years later. For his part Deane found that the change

> "makes me question whether, in the great revolution, there be anybody takes care of us and of the naval affairs. I praise my God my trust is in Him and am not much solicitous though the world be turned upside down."

The month of May saw the fleets of England and Holland again reaching their full strength and engaging in a vain search for each other up and down the North Sea. On April 29th Tromp arrived off the Texel with 70 sail of men of war to escort the outward bound trade northabout round Scotland, only to find that the remainder of his promised ships were still not ready for sea. On the same day Monck and Deane slipped out of Portsmouth and joined forces with Penn in St. Helen's Roads, making a total fleet of just over 80 sail. Jordan, in the *Vanguard*, was appointed Vice-Admiral of the Blue squadron, with John Lawson commanding it in the *George*. The two Generals, Monck and Deane, were in the *Resolution*, a new ship carrying 88 guns, and Blake was still ashore, not yet fully recovered from his wound. Though still in pain, he could not remain a passive spectator of all this naval activity and took himself off to Chatham, there to set about collecting ships to form an additional squadron for the fleet.

A Council of War was called in the *Resolution* on the morning of May 2nd, "the result thereof to take the opportunity to fight the enemy". Accordingly, the English fleet sailed for the North Sea in search of Tromp. As they were passing Calais they stopped and questioned a ship out of Hamburg and from her captain learned that Tromp was still off the Texel. Monck and Deane wasted no time and by the 4th they, too, were off the Texel.

Tromp, according to de Ruyter's Journal, "heard sundry shots to the south of us", during the morning. It was the English who, having run across a fleet of Dutch herring busses, were busily capturing 40 or 50 of them. But Tromp, for all his frequent declarations of anxiety to meet the English fleet, was for the time being more intent on shepherding his convoy safely away and bringing home an incoming fleet of merchantmen, whom he hoped to meet near the Faroe Islands. He set a course to the northward, and as soon as Monck received information that he had gone, he followed on a similar course.

According to the *Vanguard's* log, the fleet arrived "near Fairy Isle" on May 13th, finally anchoring in Bressa Bay in the Shetlands on the following day, where they stayed long enough to duck the purser of the *Raven* "for misdemeanour". Though the Generals had their frigates out they could get no news of Tromp, and on May 18th Monck set sail again for the Texel. They missed the elusive Dutchman yet again, though the fleet plied up and down the Dutch coast for four days before finally abandoning the search and making for Yarmouth, where they anchored on the 29th.

Tromp, having successfully disposed of his two convoys and with his fleet increased to 103 sail, was now most anxious to come to grips with the English. "It behoves us," he wrote to the States-General on May 21st, "to attack the enemy the sooner the better, and on the coming battle the glory of our country will in a great measure depend". On May 26th, not finding the English in the Downs as he had hoped, he appeared off Dover and, "several balls were exchanged between the castles and our ships". The news of the Dover attack was quickly brought up to Monck and Deane at Yarmouth, and on June 1st, hearing that Tromp was at last in the neighbourhood, they moved out from Yarmouth and anchored for the night off the Gabbard sandbank.

At daylight on the 2nd, the two fleets were in sight of each other at a distance of about 12 miles. The wind was light and blowing from the north and east, and although the English vessels carried all the sail they could, it was eleven o'clock before the first gun was fired, and nearly two in the afternoon before they came to really close quarters. The Blue squadron, under Lawson, being disposed to port of the Generals and with the *Vanguard* in the lead, was the first into action, coming up with de Ruyter.

"My Admiral (the Blue) Lawson, with myself and Rear-Admiral," wrote Jordan in the *Vanguard's* log, "were closely engaged (with some others), after that, the General and Admiral of the White came to a close engagement. Sunk three or four."

Jordan's laconic words, however, tell very little of the story. Shortly after the Blue squadron had opened the engagement the wind shifted for a short time into the east, giving Tromp an advantage which he was quick to seize. He ordered his ships, "turned round to catch the wind, in order to cut off this squadron", and, coming up to de Ruyter's assistance, soon had Lawson and Jordan under a double fire.

"By that time," wrote an eye-witness in the *Resolution*, "we drew near them, and the enemy stood lashing away, yet did the *George* (Rear-Admiral Lawson) and his squadron very hotly engage the enemy for some hours; so Tromp declines engagement with our main body and flag, but bears up to relieve Ruijter that was hotly engaged by Rear-Admiral Lawson, who, with his second, came very well off and all his squadron (being the Blue), both with safety and honour."

Tromp's attempt to dispose of Lawson's squadron before the remainder of the fleet could come into action was foiled by the speed with which Monck, Deane, and Penn managed to reach the scene. As the *Resolution* came within range Deane was killed almost immediately, "shot into the body with a great shot the first broadside". Monck, who was standing alongside him, snatched off his cloak and flung it over the body of the dead man that the sailors might not see and become discouraged. He himself, still very much a landsman and still unfamiliar with the way of ships, continued alone to direct the battle.

Until darkness fell the two fleets kept hammering away at each other, with the English ships, by reason of their heavier guns and more accurate gunnery, doing the more damage. Late in the afternoon the wind had backed into the north-west, giving Monck the weather gage again, and Tromp's fleet seems to have been thrown into some confusion by the fierceness of the English attack. He attempted to draw off to leeward, but Monck would have none of it and, landsman though he was, used his favourable wind to press Tromp to the utmost.

All through the night the Dutch stood down towards their home ports, but with the English close on their heels. Tromp was making for the Wielings (Walcheren), but again a change in the wind favoured Monck and, with it now blowing hard from W.S.W., the English ships were able to prevent him getting in and drove him along the coast towards the Maas, fighting all the way. Yet another stroke of fortune came Monck's way during the chase when a group of flying Dutch ships fouled each other and fell an easy prey.

"Five of them in a huddle," wrote the captain of the *Vanguard*, "being foul together, well defended themselves, though Admiral Tromp had left them; one was a Vice-Admiral, another a Rear; at my passing a broadside into them they cried for quarter which was given. About thirteen this day were sunk and taken. The Rear-Admiral above mentioned confessed our broadside sunk him."

The running fight continued until ten o'clock that night when, in order to avoid being stranded on the coastal banks of Holland, Monck anchored the fleet. Tromp, with his lighter draft vessels, made good his escape. "The enemy will go," wrote Richard Lyons of the *Resolution*, "where we cannot follow him, like the Highlanders to the mountains."

It had been a good day for Monck.

"The second day," wrote the same correspondent as above, "we had the harvest and gleaning of the vintage, and with less loss than any heretofore. . . . Yet did God put a spirit of courage into the men and made them valiant and vigilant. The enemy lost that were sunk, taken and destroyed, both day's service, about twenty of his fleet, of whom were two vice-admirals, three rear-admirals."

It was this Battle of the Gabbard, rather than the preceding Battle of Portland, that marked an epoch in naval tactics. The line ahead formation was certainly attempted, even if only rudimentarily carried out.

"The English," wrote a Dutch eye-witness, "stayed on a tack for half an hour till they could put themselves into the order in which they meant to fight, which was in file at half-cannon shot."

In his long account of the battle, as seen from the *Resolution*, Lyons wrote that the fleet "did work together in better order and seconded one another",

while Jordan, in the *Vanguard's* log, stated on June 1st that he:

"sailed by my admiral and that part of his squadron which were headmost, stayed awhile for the General's coming up and many astern of him",

which points to some degree of definite formation before going into battle. And the comparative ease with which Monck was able to prevent Tromp escaping into the Wielings on the morning of June 3rd, is yet another indication that he had his ships well under control, such as only a proper battle formation could ensure.

Blake, dropping down to the Gunfleet with eight ships of his squadron which were ready for sea, heard the sound of gunfire and, suspecting what was happening, at once set sail to the eastward. But he was too late for the fighting and only managed to join Monck off the Texel after Tromp had taken his battered fleet through the shallows into the shelter of Dutch harbours.

It had been a notable victory, though the Dutch tried their best to minimize it and even, in one or two quarters, to claim it as a victory. Only de With, the Dutch Vice-Admiral, seems to have had the honesty

By courtesy of the National Maritime Museum

Above : A Commonwealth ship, *circa* 1653, similar to the second *Vanguard*

Below : Model of a third-rate ship of 1745, similar to the fourth *Vanguard*

By courtesy of the National Maritime Museum

By courtesy of the Parker Gallery, 2 Albemarle Street, London

Louisbourg, 1758. Cutting-out the *Prudent* and *Bienfaisant*

From an engraving by P. C. Canot after R. Paton

to come out with the blunt truth. Addressing the States-General he is reported to have said:

> "Why should I keep silence any longer? I am here before my sovereigns and am free to speak, and I can say that the English are at present masters both of us and of the seas."

16

It was no more than the truth. For the next two months, with the exception of a few days at the beginning of July, Blake and Monck conducted a close blockade of the Dutch coast, paralysing their coastal shipping and causing a good deal of hardship.

> "In the meantime," wrote one of the English agents in Holland, "we are fain to eat old pickled herrings instead of new, for which the English are cursed by the commons with bell, book, and candle."

17

In addition 400 merchantmen, bound for the Baltic, were forced by the blockade to lie for so long in their harbours, "that they have almost eat themselves out".

18

Behind the blockade, the indefatigable Tromp in the Maas and de With, at the Texel, were busy refitting their ships for the next encounter. Slowly vessels were repaired and new ones added, and by July 20th Tromp could report that he had 84, including fireships, ready for sea. On the same date de With mustered 30 sail of the line, with a few smaller craft. But before a new action against the English could be contemplated the two squadrons would need to be joined, and the closeness of Monck's blockade was making of that a difficult, if not impossible, operation.

On the English side the importance of keeping Tromp and de With apart was equally well appreciated. On June 30th sickness and damage through stress of weather forced Blake and Monck to lift the blockade temporarily for a short visit to England, leaving only four frigates behind to show themselves off the coast at intervals. The fleet crossed to Southwold where the many sick were landed including, as Monck wrote, "my partner Blake, gone sick ashore". Blake, indeed, had never really recovered from the effects of his wound in the Battle of Portland and Robert Blackborne, visiting him on July 6th,

> "found him in a very weak condition, full of pain both in his head and left side, which had put him into a fever, besides the anguish he endures by the gravel in his kidneys, insomuch as he takes no rest night or day, but continues groaning very sadly".

9

Monck was back again off the coast of Holland by July 16th, and so well had his frigates done their work that Tromp was unaware that the English fleet had gone until it was too late. Monck was complaining bitterly at this time of the condition of the victuals taken on board while in England, and asking his masters how they expected English seamen to fight on stinking fish and putrid butter. The beer came in

E

for his especial condemnation. "The captain of the *Reserve*," he wrote, "informs me that his men choose rather to drink water than beer." It was hardly surprising, for John Taylor, in a letter to the Admiralty Commissioners, says: "I spake with the brewer who said he could not mend the beer. He hath but 3s. 6d. a barrel for it. Divers of the men fall sick." At that price it was not to be expected that the beer could be up to much.

At last Tromp was ready and on July 25th he left his moorings at Walcheren with 86 sail of men of war. He was off Scheveningen on the 28th, and de With, in accordance with previous orders from Tromp, brought his squadron up to the mouth of the Texel. This movement of de With's ships put Monck on the alert, and at noon on the 29th Tromp's fleet was sighted to the southward. Monck at once gave chase, playing into Tromp's hands by leaving the Texel unguarded. It was exactly what the Dutch admiral wanted, for now de With could get out unmolested and Tromp was relying on his skill as a seaman to effect the junction just as soon as the first opportunity offered.

The opportunity came that same night. There was a partial engagement in the late afternoon, the faster English frigates reaching the Dutch rearguard by five o'clock, and the *Resolution*, supported by the *Vanguard*, by six. In the *Vanguard's* log Jordan reports that the fighting went on till nine at night, and the two fleets continued on parallel courses to the southward in the gathering darkness, the English attempting to keep in touch in order, "to give him (Tromp) a breakfast the next morning". But, unperceived by Monck, Tromp tacked during the night and by morning was between the English fleet and the Texel. The junction with de With was assured and Tromp now had 120 sail of men of war under his command.

It blew hard all the day of the 30th. Jordan wrote in his journal:

"Wind at W., blowing so hard in gusts, could hardly keep our topsails half mast high, sometimes down as low as could stand. Admiral Tromp's ship stood close after us to the Southward this morning within shot and fired several pieces till he came nigh."

Both fleets made several attempts to come to action, but every time they were prevented by the gale.

On the following day the wind moderated, blowing from the south, and by eight o'clock in the morning the battle was begun. Tromp had the advantage of the wind but Monck, from to leeward, was able by a series of tacks to break through the rear of the Dutch line, cutting off a few ships which were badly mauled by the English fleet. Three times during the morning he repeated the manœuvre, each time separating a few more ships from the main body and subjecting them to the fury of the English guns. Tromp, by judicious tacks, managed to keep the weather gage, but it was at tremendous cost to his rear ships.

In the afternoon the wind changed in Monck's favour, so that he could ease his sheets and bear down on the Dutch. "At last," wrote Jordan in the *Vanguard's* log, "God gave us the wind, upon which advantage the enemy ran and we pursued and continued the fight till eight at night." This is not quite all the story, for Evertsen and de Ruyter fought back to their utmost, as also did de With until sheer weight of numbers forced him to turn for home. But the hotness of the fight had discouraged some twenty or more of the Dutch captains and one by one they began to steal away. With the fleet weakened by such defections there could be only one ending, and it came during the afternoon when the action developed into a general chase.

There are, fortunately, a number of first-hand reports of the battle from various captains who were engaged. It was, writes one, "the most fierce and cruel fight that ever was fought", while another calls it, "a hot dispute, as never was in the world before".

"The very heavens were obscured by smoke, the air rent with the thundering noise, the sea all in a breach with the shot that fell, the ships even trembling, and we hearing everywhere messengers of death flying,"

wrote the captain of the *Tulip*, and in the same letter he reports the loss of his clerk of the cheque, killed by a round shot, "his brains spoilt my suit, all my back and hat being full of it".

As night fell, the wind began to freshen again, "veering out at the South-West and beginning to blow with dirt and rain". Monck, with many of his ships damaged, decided that he could not risk a chase in these conditions, especially as the Dutch vessels were nearing the shoals. He called his ships off and, turning, set a course for England. He could be well pleased with the way the day had gone for him. Tromp's fleet, 120 strong in the morning, "were very thin before the sun went down", while he himself had lost but two vessels, the *Oak* and the *Hunter*.

For the Dutch the day was a tragedy. To the bitterness of defeat was added the crowning calamity of the death of Tromp, killed by a musket ball during the morning engagement. His death was a crushing disaster, for his skill and heroism had endeared him to the nation, which had quickly forgotten his disgrace over the affair of the herring fleet at the beginning of the war.

"If they should cast twenty John Evertsens and twenty Ruijters into one, they could not make one Tromp,"

wrote a correspondent from Holland. He was irreplaceable, for de With, next in seniority, though he

"hath courage enough and is a good pilot, but in his commands he is not to be endured and John Evertsen will not serve under him. Also he is the more ancient captain, and if John Evertsen will not go to sea any more then neither will de Ruijter go to sea likewise."

There was no one to step into Tromp's shoes and although in de   2ς
Ruyter the Dutch had an even greater sailor than Tromp, his time was
not yet come.

As the English ships turned for home, they took stock of their
hurts. Masts, sails, and rigging were, as usual, much damaged from
the Dutch practice of firing high. In the *Vanguard*, Jordan reports
in the ship's log:

> "several ships' and frigates' masts, etc., much shattered, our ship at her
> lower mast unserviceable, divers shots under water we could not stop;
> five men slain, about fifteen wounded, three of them dismembered."   3ς

The total losses in the fleet amounted to about 900 men according
to Monck, though this is the highest estimate in any of the many
reports.

The Dutch losses were considerably higher. It is difficult to arrive
at any definite figures, since each account, even those of the Dutch
themselves, give different estimates. But it seems reasonably clear
that fifteen ships were sunk or destroyed. None were taken, for Monck
seems to have given an order before the battle that he did not want
prizes or prisoners, although a number of Dutchmen were rescued
from the water. In killed, wounded, and prisoners their losses numbered
nearly 4,500. But their fleet as a whole was so badly mauled that it
could no longer take the sea, and the maximum reported as able to
continue fighting was but 40. Monck's victory, indeed, was so decisive
that it is not surprising, shortly afterwards, to find Dutch Commissioners
in England, sent there by the States-General to discuss possible terms
of peace.

The war, indeed, dragged on till the following year though Monck,
at the Battle of the Texel, had already struck the decisive blow. Apart
from a few single ship actions, the occasional bringing in of a Dutch
prize, and a half-hearted attempt to renew the blockade of the Dutch
coast, there was no further fighting. Both countries were feeling the
financial drain of the war and both were ready for peace.

On April 5th, 1654, it was all over. Peace was signed and both
England and Holland could look to their respective trade in an attempt
to refill their treasuries. All of Cromwell's terms, which included the
full provisions of the Navigation Act and the honour of the flag, were
accepted. If it was, as the Dutch complained, a harsh treaty, it had
yet been fully earned by the five hard battles at sea. The *Vanguard*
had fought in each one of them and, indeed, taken a leading part in
them all.

With the coming of peace the Navy was paid off. For the next
six years the second *Vanguard* swung at a buoy below Rochester till
her services should again be required.

CHAPTER VII

THE NEW WAR WITH HOLLAND

In the late summer of 1658 a violent storm burst over southern England. The wind, which howled through the London streets, tore the roofs from houses, uprooted trees in the parks, and raised so fierce a tide against Old London Bridge that occupiers of the houses on the bridge fled for fear it would collapse. Through the height of the storm physicians battled their way to the Palace of Whitehall, where the Lord Protector was dying. "I saw and felt," wrote Cox, the Quaker, "a waft of death go forth against him, and when I came to him he looked like a dead man."

For all their skill, the doctors could not halt the disease which was carrying away the whole prop and support of the Commonwealth. For three days the storm raged, and for those three days Cromwell fought for his life. On September 3rd, he gave up the struggle and, as the fierce winds died away, Cromwell closed his eyes for the last time.

It was, to all intents and purposes, the end of the Commonwealth. Richard Cromwell, son of the Protector, made a half-hearted and ineffectual attempt to step into his father's shoes, but he had none of the qualities needed to lead a nation. Besides, a majority of the people were beginning to tire a little of the austerities of the interregnum. Talk in the country, talk in the City of London, talk even in Parliament, began to be of the benefits of a Restoration, and across the seas the second Charles was waiting.

It was left to the Navy, in 1660, to make the Restoration into a reality. In May of that year Monck, who after the Battle of the Texel had resumed his original career as a soldier and was now, as Lord General, the most powerful man in England, despatched Edward Montagu, in the *Naseby*, with Lawson as his Vice-Admiral, to Schevelling to bring Charles home to England. The Royal Squadron arrived with the King off Dover on May 28th. Charles's first acts when he "came home to enjoy his own again" was to raise Monck to the Dukedom of Albemarle, Montagu to the Earldom of Sandwich, and to change the name of the ship which had brought him home from *Naseby*, of unhappy Stuart memory, to *Royal Charles*. As he rode into London, with Monck beside him in his coach, a joyful populace strewed the streets with flowers, decked the houses with flags and carpets, and danced throughout the night round bonfires lit in the roadway. Four months later they were dancing round a special gibbet set up at Charing Cross, where Cromwell's "cobblers and draymen" —Axtall, Carew, Clements, Hacker, Hewson, Peters, Scot, Scroope, Cook, and Jones, the men who had condemned the first Charles to the scaffold—were hanged.

"I saw not their execution," wrote John Evelyn in his diary, "but met their quarters, mangl'd and cutt and reeking, as they were brought from the gallows in baskets on the hurdle. Oh! the miraculous providence of God."

Through the first five years of Charles's reign the *Vanguard* remained in the Medway, lying dismantled at a buoy in the river. There was as yet no call for a big Navy and Charles knew many pleasanter ways of spending his money than in keeping ships needlessly in commission. Although, as with his brother James, Duke of York and Lord High Admiral of England, Charles was a keen student of naval affairs and had a real affection for the Navy, the calls upon his purse of Mrs. Palmer, Louise de Kéroualle, "Mrs. Nelly" and the rest, effectively starved the Navy of the money it so desperately needed. For the most part Charles was content to leave the administration of the Navy to his brother, the Lord High Admiral, to the Navy Commissioners, and to his indefatigable Clerk of the Acts at the Admiralty, Samuel Pepys.

It was not long, however, before Charles was at loggerheads with the Dutch. As early as 1661 trade rivalry between the two nations, especially in the East and West Indies, was flaring up into occasional breaches of the peace. One result of this was the despatch of Captain Robert Holmes, who had served the King during the Civil War and had cruised with Prince Rupert when, in 1649, part of the fleet had gone over to the Royal cause, to the African coast. He was given command of a small squadron of four ships with the rank of Commodore and his commission instructed him to make reprisals on the Dutch. His little force was insufficient to do much damage to Dutch trading interests, though still large enough to fan the flames of Dutch exasperation. Two years later he was back on the same station with a larger force.

In January 1664 he captured the fort and island of Goeree in the Cape Verde Group, took in prize three Dutch vessels there, and reduced the trading stations at Cape Coast Castle, Ada, and Anamaboe, on the African coast. From there he crossed the Atlantic and joined forces with Sir Robert Carr's squadron. Between them they conquered Manhattan Island and New Amsterdam, which Holmes re-christened New York as a compliment to the Lord High Admiral. This was achieved in August 1664, and at the end of the year Holmes returned home, well pleased with his successes.

It was too much for the Dutch. A frigate was sent post haste to Admiral de Ruyter, who had been co-operating with an English squadron in the Mediterranean in a campaign against the Algerine pirates. It carried secret orders for him to leave the station and to make reprisals for Holmes's acts of aggression. De Ruyter, arriving on the African coast in Holmes's wake, took the English trading station of Cormantyne and recaptured Goeree. Then, still following Holmes, he too crossed the Atlantic. He scattered a fleet of English merchantmen lying under the guns of Barbados and took a number of prizes during a cruise up the American coast as high as Newfoundland. Then, still following Holmes, he turned for home.

While de Ruyter was still busy off the Newfoundland coast, Holland, pressed beyond endurance, declared war on England. The date was January 14th, 1665. Five weeks later, on February 23rd, England followed suit. Once again it was to be entirely a naval war.

As a background to this second conflict with the United Provinces it is necessary to consider the Dutch interests in trade at sea. Their merchant fleet numbered over 10,000 sail, manned by 268,000 seamen. In addition to the greater part of the European carrying trade they also had the sole right, by agreement with Philip IV, of the carriage of merchandise between America and Spain. In the East they had almost completely monopolized the trade by sea, forcing the native princes by embargoes to use only Dutch ships for their goods and prohibiting the shipping by them of their produce in the vessels of any other nation. It was becoming a stranglehold and the London merchants, touched in their tenderest parts, petitioned the King for a more active policy at sea. There was a good deal of truth in Monck's remark on the declaration of war. "What matters this or that reason?" he is reported to have asked. "What we want is more of the trade which the Dutch now have." For his own part Charles was by no means averse to a war with Holland. It would distract some of the public attention from the excesses of his expensive mistresses. Moreover, he had not forgotten those days in 1654 when he had been forced by the Dutch to leave their country and seek refuge in France. The insult still rankled.

With the formal declaration of war both countries began to fit out big fleets. The *Vanguard* was taken in hand at Chatham, hauled up, cleaned and tallowed, re-rigged, and given a new suit of sails. She was first commissioned under the command of Robert Anderson, who was promoted to captain while serving in her as First-Lieutenant, but she had a succession of captains during the year. Martin Carslake, Robert Moulton, Jonas Poole, and John Whitey all commanded her in 1665, Anderson, Poole, and Whitey dying while on board. Carslake and Moulton were appointed from her to other ships. Finally she came under the command of Thomas Whitty towards the end of the year.

The first fleet to be ready for operations was the English, with the Duke of York flying his flag in the *Royal Charles*. Pepys wrote in his diary on March 6th, that he had attended the Duke in London.

"Great preparations," he noted, "for his speedy return to sea. I saw him try on his buff-coat and hat-piece, covered with black velvet. It troubles me more to think of his venture than of anything else in the whole warr."

Under the command of the Lord High Admiral were 109 sail of men of war including frigates and hired merchantmen, and 28 fireships and ketches. In all, the fleet mounted 4,192 guns and carried on board 21,006 seamen, marines, and soldiers. Second in command was Prince Rupert, who had the White Squadron. Montagu, now Earl of Sandwich, commanded the Blue Squadron, while Penn sailed in the *Royal Charles* as Captain of the Fleet, with the rank of Vice-Admiral.

On April 21st the fleet sailed to the Dutch coast, reaching it on the 28th. It lay off the Texel and began a close blockade of the Zuider Zee, in which lay the Dutch men of war. The main object of this blockade was not only to confine the Dutch fleet but also to cut off and capture the homecoming merchantmen. A number of them were taken and duly sent back to England with prize crews on board. The Duke of York also had hopes of meeting de Ruyter, known to be returning from the American coast with his squadron, but on May 8th the fleet was "so ruffled by a storm that it was found necessary to retire towards our own shore".

This involuntary lifting of the close blockade gave the Dutch their chance and they were quick to seize it. With de Ruyter still absent the command of the fleet was given to Jacob van Wassenaer, Lord of Opdam, and commanding squadrons under him were Jan Evertsen, Egbert Cortenaer, Augustus Stellingwerf, Cornelis Tromp, the son of the great admiral, Cornelis Evertsen ("The Old"), and Volkhard Schram. Each of these had two junior admirals serving under him, so that the Dutch fleet, when it put to sea, flew no fewer than 21 admiral's flags, an extraordinary number even for those days of multiplicity of commanders. The fleet consisted of 103 sail of men of war, seven yachts and despatch vessels, 11 fireships, and 12 galliots. The total of guns was 4,869 and the ships carried 21,556 officers and men. It sailed on May 13th and cruised near the Dogger Bank where, on May 20th, it intercepted a British convoy of returning merchantmen from Hamburg and captured the lot, which varied from an English estimate of 10 to a Dutch one of 22. Whatever the number, it was a rude and unexpected blow to the English.

The news of this Dutch success caused an outcry in London, partly from the loss caused to the merchants and partly because the ships were carrying naval stores from the Baltic countries, particularly masts and tar, on which the Admiralty were counting for the fitting-out of further ships. The fleet was hurried out to sea, weighing from the Gunfleet on May 29th and reaching Solebay early in the morning of June 1st. On the same morning Opdam, with his fleet rather scattered, was six miles to the south-eastward and in sight of the English ships but, having the wind in his favour, could accept or decline action at will. Later in the day the wind shifted to the southward and the English vessels sailed slowly up the coast until, by the early morning of the 3rd, they were off Lowestoft,

The Dutch admiral, following the usual procedure of those days, called a Council of War as soon as he sighted the English fleet on the morning of June 1st. The Council came to no decision and Opdam, a cavalry leader who seems to have had little confidence in his ability to handle a fleet at sea, sent an express by a fast yacht home to Holland informing the States-General that the English fleet was in sight, but that he did not conceive it wise to attack them since the wind had now changed and would favour the Duke of York in a general action. He stood out to sea away from the coast and awaited their reply.

The yacht was sent back and reached the Dutch fleet the following day. It bore peremptory orders to Opdam to fight, "let the wind be as it would, on pain of losing your head". A second Council of War was called, and only Tromp of the assembled admirals favoured an immediate action, the others counselling a delay until conditions were more favourable. Opdam produced the written order he had received from the States-General. "I entirely agree with you," he said, "but here are my orders, and tomorrow shall see my head bound with laurel or with cypress." Even then he must have feared that it was to be the cypress, for before the engagement he sent a small vessel home loaded with all his silver plate.

On the morning of June 3rd, "about ten leagues north-east by north of L'Aystoff", the two fleets came within range. The first shots were fired at three o'clock in the morning when "there was but a faint light upon the sea". The *Vanguard*, in the Blue Squadron under Sandwich, was in the rear of the fleet at the first onslaught, when the fleets sailed past each other on opposite tacks. As they turned to re-engage the British ships went about simultaneously, so that as English and Dutch came to grips a second time, the Blue Squadron had become the van. The Dutch wore in succession, and as the result the order of their squadrons was unchanged.

At about noon, as once again the Duke of York and Opdam came within range, Sandwich led his squadron through the centre of the Dutch fleet, dividing it into two parts. His ships ran into a tremendous cannonade at close quarters, and at one period the *Vanguard* was serving her guns on both broadsides simultaneously when she was attacked by two Dutch ships at the same time. Whether or not this breaking of the line was a deliberate move on Sandwich's part is doubtful. Probably it was accidental since, from all contemporary accounts, the ships of both fleets were in great confusion, so that there were even occasions of vessels being engaged with others on their own side. But, whether accident or design, the effect was tremendous. The Dutch began to waver and when the ship's company of one of their vessels fell into panic and forced her officers to sail her out of the battle, 13 other Dutch ships followed her.

Opdam, in despair as he saw his fine fleet being thus scattered, at least decided to sell his life dearly and to die bravely. He laid his flagship, the *Eendracht*, alongside the *Royal Charles* and the two exchanged broadsides for an hour with great obstinacy, to the considerable danger of Charles's royal brother, the Lord High Admiral.

"Several persons of distinction," wrote Campbell, "were killed on board his ship, particularly the Earl of Falmouth, the King's favourite, Lord Muskerry, and Mr. Boyle, son to the Earl of Cork, with one ball, and so near the Duke, that he was covered with their blood and brains; nay, a splinter from the last-mentioned gentleman's skull razed his hand."

This personal duel came to an end shortly after one o'clock, when the *Eendracht* blew up with a terrific explosion, supposed to have been caused by Opdam's "black boy", a slave whom he had beaten soundly just before the battle, setting fire to the powder. A more likely cause would have been a burning wad among the powder barrels. But whatever the cause, Opdam and 400 men in his ship perished, only five out of the entire ship's company escaping with their lives.

During all this time the *Vanguard*, which had followed Sandwich into the breach in the Dutch centre, had been hotly engaged. There was now no semblance of order in either fleet and the battle had degenerated into a gigantic *mêlée*. The *Vanguard* was, at various times, engaged with the *Hilversum*, the *Nagelboom*, and the *Mars*, all of which were so much damaged that they were later captured and brought home as prizes.

The destruction of the *Eendracht* and the death of Opdam was the signal for the complete breakdown of Dutch resistance. Within the space of a few minutes the *Maarseveen*, the *Ter Goes*, and the *Svanenburg*, each of a different squadron, fouled each other at one end of the line and, while still locked together, were all successfully set on fire by an English fireship. At the other end of the line an almost exactly similar thing happened, when the *Prins Maurits*, *Coeverden*, *Utrecht*, and one other became tangled together, to suffer the same fate. It was too much for the Dutch. Two more of their admirals, Cortenaer and Stellingwerf, had by this time been killed, and with one accord they turned and fled.

"The whole Dutch fleet," wrote Grant, "seemed now to be one blaze of fire, and the cries of so many miserable wretches, perishing either by fire or water, seemed more dreadful than the noise of the cannon. The English gave their vanquished enemy all the assistance they could, while with continued fury they assailed the rest."

Only the young Tromp kept his head and, with the remains of his squadron, tried to cover the Dutch retreat by placing his ships between the flying Dutchmen and the pursuing English.

It had been a successful day for the Duke of York, and might well have been an even more successful night had the fleet followed up the scattered Dutch ships with real resolution. A number of accounts survive to explain the lack of proper zeal in the pursuit, each blaming a different officer according to the writer's political prejudice. Perhaps the most likely is that of Bishop Burnet:

"After the fight," he writes, "a Council of War was called to concert the method of action when they should come up with them. In that Council, Penn, who commanded under the Duke, happened to say that they must prepare for better work the next engagement. He knew well the courage of the Dutch was never so high as when they were desperate. The earl of Montagu, who was then a volunteer and one of the Duke's court, told me it was very visible that made an impression upon him, and all the Duke's domestics said he had got honour enough: why should he venture a second time? The Duchess had also given a strict charge to all the Duke's servants to do all they could to hinder him to engage too far. When matters were settled, they went to sleep, and the Duke ordered a call to be given him when they should get up with the Dutch fleet.

"It is not known what passed between the Duke and Brouncker, who was of his bed-chamber, and then in waiting; but he came to Penn, as from the Duke, and said the Duke ordered the sail to be slackened. Penn was struck with the order, but did not go about to argue the matter with the Duke himself, as he ought to have done: but obeyed it. When the Duke had slept, he, upon his waking, went out upon the quarter-deck, and seemed amazed to see the sails slackened, and that thereby all hopes of overtaking the Dutch was lost. He questioned Penn upon it. Penn put it upon Brouncker, who said nothing. The Duke denied he had given any such order; but he neither punished Brouncker for carrying it nor Penn for obeying it. He, indeed, put Brouncker out of his service; and it was said that he durst do no more. Brouncker was so much in the King's favour and in the Mistress's [the Duchess of Cleveland, then Lady Castlemaine]. Penn was more in his favour after that than ever before; which he continued to his son after him, though a Quaker: and it was thought that all that favour was to oblige him to keep the secret."

Yet, in spite of the failure by night, it had been a notable victory. Fourteen Dutch ships were brought in as prizes and four more so taken had to be abandoned because of their unseaworthy condition. Another 14 were sunk or burned. Over 4,000 men were slain and 2,300 taken prisoner. One English ship, the *Charity*, was taken by the Dutch and the losses in the English fleet were 250 killed and 340 wounded. About 200 men were taken prisoner by the Dutch.

There were wild scenes in Holland when the defeated fleet reached the shelter of their own harbours. Jan Evertsen, second in command to Opdam, was mobbed by the infuriated populace on his arrival, flung into the water, and nearly drowned. Four more captains were publicly shot at the Helder, another four had their swords broken over their heads by the common hangman, the master of Cortenaer's ship was ordered to stand on a scaffold with a halter round his neck while onlookers pelted him with eggs and rotten fruit, and two more masters were degraded and banished. Cornelis Evertsen, "the Old", brother of Jan, had been taken prisoner and so keenly did he feel the disgrace of the cowardly behaviour of some of the Dutch captains that, when brought before the Duke of York, he pointed to a bullet hole through his hat and remarked that he wished it had passed through his head.

In England, news of the victory was received with great acclamation. Bonfires were lit in the London streets, and for two days there was dancing and drinking.

"Fire, aire, earth, and water, it seems were imploy'd," wrote a contemporary poet:

> To strive for the conquest which we have injoy'd,
> No honour, or profit, or safety can spring,
> To those that do fight against God and the King,
>   The battel was hot,
>   And bloudily fought,
> The fire was like rain, and like hail was the shot,
> For in this ingagement ten thousand did bleed,
> Of Flemmings, who now are the Low-Dutch indeed.

The King alone seemed sad amongst such universal joy, grieving for the death of his favourite, the Earl of Falmouth. Clarendon, in his *Memoirs*, describes the King's grief, and at the same time indulges in a pungent criticism of the young man, who seems to have been something of a wastrel.

"The victory and triumph of that day," he wrote, "was surely very great, and a just argument of public joy: how it came to be no greater, shall be said anon; and the trouble and grief in many noble families, for the loss of so many worthy and gallant persons, could not but be very lamentable, in wives, in fathers and mothers, and the other nearest relations: but no sorrow was equal, at least, none so remarkable, as the King's was for the Earl of Falmouth. They who knew his Majesty best, and had seen how unshaken he had stood in other very terrible assaults, were amazed at the flood of tears he shed upon this occasion. The immenseness of the victory, and the consequences that might have attended it, the safety and preservation of his brother, with so much glory, on whose behalf he had had so terrible apprehensions during the three days' fight, having, by the benefit of the wind, heard the thunder of the ordnance from the beginning, even after, by the lessening of the noise, as from a greater distance, he concluded that the enemy was upon flight; yet all this, and the universal joy that he saw in the countenance of all men, for the victory and the safety of the Duke, made no impression in him towards the mitigation of his passion, for the loss of this young favourite, in whom few other men had ever observed any virtue or quality, which they did not wish their best friends without, and very many did believe that his death was a great ingredient and considerable part of the victory. He was young, and of insatiable ambition, and a little more experience might have taught him all things of which his weak parts were capable. But they who observed the strange degree of

favour he had on the sudden arrived to, even from a detestation the
King had towards him, and concluded from thence, and more from the
deep sorrow the King was possessed with for his death, to what a prodigious height he might have reached in a little time more, were not at all
troubled that he was taken out of the way."

It is probable that, had the English pressed their advantage on
the night of June 3rd, the resulting victory would have been so conclusive as to have brought about the end of the war. As it was, the
Government of the United Provinces bent all their energies to the
repairing of their shattered ships and bringing their new ones forward.
They were buoyed up by the news that the great de Ruyter was on
his way home, taking the passage north of Scotland.

News of de Ruyter's impending return was also known to England
and, using every dispatch, the English fleet was out again by July 5th.
Sandwich was in command, Charles being unwilling again to risk
the person of his brother and only heir, and Prince Rupert, to whom the
joint command with Sandwich was offered, declined the honour feeling
it too much of a slight upon his dignity to share the admiral's flag with
another. Sailing to the northward, Sandwich detached a squadron under
Sir Thomas Tiddiman to attack Dutch shipping which was sheltering
at Bergen, having received an assurance from the Danes that their
forts there would not open fire on the English attackers. The promise
was not kept and after a brisk bombardment Tiddiman's squadron
was forced to retire, having lost 500 men and the captains of six of
the vessels. Hardly was this sorry news received in England than an
even worse blow fell. De Ruyter, evading Sandwich, came safely
home to Holland. "It is told to the great disadvantage of our fleets,"
wrote Pepys, "and the praise of de Ruyter; but it cannot be helped,
nor do I know what to say to it."

So far, to the *Vanguard* ploughing those lonely wastes in the north
with Sandwich, it had been a barren cruise. Yet in the end there
were consolations. De Ruyter had sailed to Bergen to escort home
those same Dutch ships which Tiddiman had failed to damage. A
storm scattered his fleet on the way home, and although the greater
prize of de Ruyter himself escaped the English ships, four of his men
of war and 14 merchantmen were taken. Thankfully Sandwich
set his course for home, having at least something to show for his
exertions, and thankfully the nation, tortured by the great plague,
received the welcome news. For two of the merchantmen were East
India ships, and laden with extremely valuable cargoes of spices.

With the coming of winter both the English and Dutch fleets
sought the shelter of their harbours. In the *Vanguard*, as in the majority
of the other vessels in the fleet, the men were not paid off, as was the
usual custom, but kept on board throughout the winter months for fear
of the plague which, though much reduced from the heights reached
during the hot summer, was still carrying off some 400 to 500 people

each week. It meant a still greater drain on the King's resources, for the men had to be paid, and since there was no money with which to pay them, the number of tickets piled up. There was great bitterness among the ships' companies when there was the inevitable default on their tickets, a bitterness which led in some cases to open mutiny. It was this chronic financial situation, which became intensified during the following year, that was to be mainly responsible for the great disaster of 1667.

As the year drew to its close, Sandwich was superseded in command of the fleet. He was in disgrace following the plundering of the East India prizes he had captured during the summer, a disgrace that was nearly shared by Penn and the other admirals, and even by Pepys, who confesses in his diary that he had made £500 out of it. Charles brought back Monck and Prince Rupert as his chief commanders at sea and, under them, in the first months of the new year, the English ships were prepared for the actions which would face them in 1666.

On January 19th of this year the Dutch were heartened by a declaration of war on England by the King of France. Among other promises he made was one to fit out a squadron of 36 sail, besides galleys and fireships, to reinforce the Dutch fleet. The squadron was placed under the command of the Duc de Beaufort, and although it played no direct part in the coming battles, it yet had a great indirect bearing when, in May 1666, the English and Dutch fleets were again ready for action.

CHAPTER VIII

THE FOUR DAYS' BATTLE

As the spring of 1666 lengthened into summer, news of the Duc de Beaufort's French squadron trickled into England. Early in the year it was known to have left Toulon and its progress was reported by English agents from time to time as far as La Rochelle. And in May, when the Dutch fleet of 91 sail, mounting 4,716 guns and now under the command of de Ruyter, appeared in the Channel as far west as the Isle of Wight, it was seen as a move to make a junction with Beaufort's squadron. Thirty-six French ships, joined with 91 Dutch, was a fleet that even England, contemptuous as she was both of French and Dutch naval power, could not stomach in her seas with equanimity. Moreover, it was known that on board de Ruyter's flagship sailed the Grand Pensionary of Holland, John de Witte. In English eyes his presence on board spoke loudly of political motives, yet another pointer to a junction with Beaufort. In reality he was only there to see for himself that there was no repetition of the cowardice of the Dutch captains, which had so marred the battle the previous year off Lowestoft.

It was this much-feared junction of the French and Dutch which betrayed the English into a major strategical error in their dispositions at the end of May. Of the total fleet under Monck and Prince Rupert of 74 sail, anchored in the Downs on May 29th, it was decided to send Rupert with the White Squadron of 20 ships to the Isle of Wight, there to bring Beaufort's vessels to action and to oppose their joining up with de Ruyter.

The actual order for this dividing of the fleet appears to have come from the Court in London, where it is generally considered to have originated with the Lord Chancellor, Clarendon. Other sources quote the first suggestion as being proposed by Monck, who was certainly in favour of it. Ayscue, once again in favour and now second-in-command to Monck and Rupert, remonstrated to the best of his ability against this strategical blunder, but found himself up against a stone wall in Monck. To Monck's eye, trained as he was as a cavalry leader, it seemed a wise tactical move, something akin to detaching a body of horse to make a flank attack on the enemy, but it spelled disaster to the fleet. Ayscue's understanding of naval strategy was of no avail against the seniority of Monck and the impetuosity of Rupert, and on the evening of the 29th, Rupert and his 20 ships sailed on what was to prove no more than a wild-goose chase.

Two days later, on May 31st, Monck, with now but 54 ships left in his fleet, weighed and sailed to the southward from the Downs in search of the Dutch. Early on the morning of June 1st they were discovered at anchor off Dunkirk, outnumbering the English by nearly two to one. As Monck and his ships were sighted, de Ruyter gave orders to his fleet to cut their cables and his squadrons sailed out to battle.

The engagement which followed is one of the most memorable in British naval history. It was fought on both sides with desperate courage and, on the English side, against odds so formidable that ultimate defeat was virtually certain. It shows Monck, too, in a new light as a naval tactician, handling his ships, soldier though he was, with a skill as great as any contemporary admiral, the great de Ruyter himself not excepted. If this was the English Navy in adversity, its behaviour during the four days that the battle lasted was as glorious as any victory it has ever won.

Monck, realizing the odds against him, was yet quick enough to grasp one great flaw in the Dutch dispositions. Their three squadrons, under the command of Cornelis Evertsen, de Ruyter, and Tromp respectively, had become somewhat separated and, while Tromp was well down to windward, both the other squadrons had drifted a bit to leeward. Monck, seizing the opportunity given to him by having the weather gage, sailed down the Dutch line, out of range of Evertsen and de Ruyter, and thus concentrated as much of his fleet as could keep up with him against Tromp's squadron. While the fight lasted it was hot and furious and Tromp's ships were severely handled. It was, however, but a question of time before, first de Ruyter, and then Evertsen, could work their squadrons up to windward and so tip the scale heavily in favour of the Dutch. By noon they were in action and their numbers began to tell.

The *Vanguard*, commanded by Captain Thomas Whitty, was in the Blue Squadron and from the first was in the thick of the fight. As she came into action against Tromp's ships, Monck, in the Red Squadron, tacked suddenly to avoid running on to a sandbank. Tromp did the same with his squadron. This move, in which Monck lost a topmast and had to haul out of the fight until he could step another, was apparently not seen by the Blue Squadron, which stood on towards the south. Almost at once they fell in with de Ruyter, coming to the assistance of Tromp, and at the same time with the leading ships of Tromp's own squadron which, after their tack, were now standing up to the northward and to windward of Ayscue's Blue Squadron.

Sir William Berkeley, Vice-Admiral of the Blue in the *Swiftsure*, followed closely by the *Essex*, *Henry*, and *Vanguard*, found themselves surrounded by Dutch ships. Berkeley was almost at once shot in the throat, dying shortly afterwards, and the *Swiftsure* so closely beset that she was boarded and forced to surrender. The *Essex* was also taken by boarding and towed out of the battle by the exultant Dutch. The *Henry*, under the command of Sir John Harman, was attacked by fireships, but was fought with such extraordinary gallantry that the story is worth the telling in some detail.

By courtesy of the National Maritime Museum

"Quebec from the Bason", 1759

From an engraving by P. C. Canot

By courtesy of the National Maritime Museum

The fifth *Vanguard* dismasted and in tow, 1798

From an oil painting by Pocock

"Leading the van of the fleet," wrote Campbell in his biography of Harman, "he soon got into the centre of the Zealand squadron; and being in a short time completely disabled, one of the enemy's fireships grappled him on the starboard quarter: he was, however, freed by the almost incredible exertions of his boatswain, Thomas Lamming, as it is asserted by all historians; but, according to the navy list it appears he was his lieutenant, who, having in the midst of the flames, loosed the grappling-irons, swung back on board his own ship unhurt. The Dutch, bent on the destruction of this unfortunate ship, and seeing the ill success of the first, sent a second, who grappled her on the larboard side, and with greater success than the former, for the sails instantly taking fire, the crew were so terrified, that nearly fifty of them, among whom was the chaplain, jumped overboard. Sir John seeing this confusion, ran instantly with his sword drawn, among those who remained, and threatened with instant death the first man who should attempt to quit the ship or should not exert himself in quenching the flames. This spirited conduct had the effect; the crew returned to their duty and soon got the fire under, but the rigging being a good deal burnt, one of the top-sail yards fell and broke Sir John's leg.

"In the midst of this accumulated distress a third fireship prepared to grapple him, but before she could effect her purpose, four shots from the *Henry's* lower-deck guns sunk her. Evertsen, the Dutch vice-admiral, now bore up to him, and calling on him to surrender, offered him quarter. Sir John answered him bluntly, 'It has not come to that yet,' and giving him a broadside, killed the Dutch commander, which so intimidated the rest of his adversaries that they declined farther contest. The *Henry*, shattered as she was, her commander disabled and a great part of her crew killed or wounded, was nevertheless carried safely into Harwich, whence Sir John, having the next day refitted her and hoping to share in the honour of the last day's engagement, put to sea, notwithstanding his broken leg, but the action was over before he reached the fleet."

In the *Vanguard*, Whitty was killed by a chain-shot while his ship was being attacked on both sides. Her First-Lieutenant, Anthony Langston, took over the command and fought the ship so well that he managed to bring her clear of the Dutch. But she was badly shattered and had to haul out of the line to renew her rigging and plug the holes in her hull before continuing the action.

So it went on throughout the day.

"The English chief," wrote a Dutch volunteer serving in de Ruyter's ship, "still continued on the port tack, and as night fell we could see him proudly leading his line past the squadron of North Holland and Zealand [Evertsen's], which from noon up to that time had not been able to reach the enemy from their leewardly position. The affair continued until 10 p.m., friends and foes mixed together and as likely to receive injury from one as from the other. It will be remarked that the success of the day and the misfortunes of the English came from their being too much scattered, too extended in their line; but for which we could never have cut off a corner of them, as we did [*i.e.*, the *Swiftsure, Essex, Henry* and *Vanguard*]. The mistake of Monck was in not keeping his ships better together."

F

As Mahan remarks, this criticism is unjust, for in a line of 54 sail gaps were unavoidable because of the difference in sailing speeds.

At the end of the first day's fighting Monck despatched a "catch" (*i.e.* ketch) to London with a report on the proceedings and a request for immediate orders to be sent to Rupert to rejoin the fleet. At the same time he drew away to the north-westward for such repairs as were possible and called a Council of War of all his captains. It was held by the light of candles in the great cabin of the *Royal Charles*. And there, to the assembled captains, he made his famous speech which heartened them all for the next day's fighting.

> "If we had dreaded the number of the enemy," he said, "we should have fled; but though we are inferior to them in ships, we are in all things else superior. Force gives them courage. Let us, if we need it, borrow resolution from what we have formerly performed. Let the enemy feel that though our fleet be divided (referring to the absence of the White Squadron under Rupert), our spirit is entire. At the worst it will be more honourable to die bravely here on our own element than be made spectacles to the Dutch. To be overcome is the fortune of war; but to fly is the fashion of cowards. So let us teach the world that Englishmen would rather be acquainted with death than fear."

Monck's despatch to the King, received in London on the morning of the 2nd, created considerable excitement. "This," wrote Pepys, "put us at the Board into a tosse." He joined the King and the Duke of York in Greenwich Park "to hear the guns of the fleets go off" and, after a "dish of steaks" for dinner in the King's Head, went to superintend the despatch of 200 soldiers as reinforcements for the fleet. On the way he called on Mrs. Daniel, whose husband was with Monck in the *Royal Charles*, but was careful to tell her nothing of the action.

> "Very pleasant with her half an hour," he wrote, "and so away and down to Blackewall, and there saw the soldiers (who were by this time gotten most of them drunk) shipped off. But Lord! to see how the poor fellows kissed their wives and sweethearts in that simple manner at their going off, and shouted, and let off their guns, was strange sport."

On the second day Monck returned to the battle with such of his ships as he had left, 44 all told. The Dutch had 80 left, though some of them had been badly damaged by the English guns on the previous day. Although de Ruyter began the day with the advantage of the wind in his favour, Monck soon weathered him and passed down the Dutch line on an opposite course, pouring broadsides into the enemy vessels. Tromp, in the rear of the Dutch line, which considerably overlapped that of the English, tacked and managed to get to windward of the English van, but in so doing separated his squadron from the rest of the Dutch fleet. He was now in considerable danger, for once again Monck was able to concentrate his ships on Tromp's squadron, hammering them to such an extent that twice Tromp was forced to shift his flag into another ship less damaged than the one he was in.

De Ruyter was momentarily in a quandary for, according to the Dutch eye-witness mentioned above,

"at this moment two flag officers of the Dutch van kept broad off, presenting their sterns to the English. Ruyter, greatly astonished, tried to stop them, but in vain, and therefore felt obliged to imitate the manœuvre in order to keep his squadron together; but did so with some order, keeping some ships around him, and was joined by one of the van ships, disgusted with the conduct of his immediate superior. Tromp was now in great danger, separated from his own fleet by the English, and would have been destroyed but for Ruyter who, seeing the urgency of the case, hauled up for him."

Just at this moment de Ruyter was reinforced by 16 fresh ships from Holland, to bring his advantage in numbers to rather more than two to one.

In order to keep the advantage of the windward position, which he could in no circumstances afford to lose because of the fewness of his ships, Monck was forced to slacken his onslaught on Tromp as de Ruyter came up. He had already lost another four ships and although he now had a chance to inflict further damage on the Dutch through their faulty tactics, he was in no shape to take it. Reading again from the Dutch account:

"Tromp, immediately after this partial action, went on board his [de Ruyter's] flagship. The seamen cheered him, but Ruyter said, 'This is no time for rejoicing, but rather for tears.' Indeed, our position was bad, each squadron acting differently, in no line, and all the ships huddled together like a flock of sheep, so packed that the English might have surrounded all of them with their forty ships. The English were in admirable order, but did not push their advantage as they should, whatever the reason."

The reason, of course, was the crippled state of their spars and rigging.

Although Monck, during the morning's fighting, had managed to disable de Ruyter's flagship, shooting away her maintopmast and mainyard, he knew that retreat was now the only possible course if the English were to escape complete annihilation. There was still no sign of Rupert's squadron, though anxious eyes were strained towards the west, whence he was expected. Monck drew away northwestward towards the shelter of his own shores, and the Dutch pursued him through the night.

So dawned June 3rd, with Monck still retreating. But it was an

orderly withdrawal. Three English ships, badly crippled, were set
on fire and burned by Monck's orders, after their crews had been
taken off, so that they should not hinder the remainder of the fleet. The
badly damaged vessels were sent ahead and behind them Monck
mustered his sounder ships, now reduced to 16, as a protective screen.
The *Vanguard*, which had repaired the worst of her damage, was
among them. So steady and orderly was Monck's retreat that the
Dutch were completely unable to take advantage of their great superiority in numbers. Every time they threatened an attack, one or more
of the English ships turned and headed them off. The *Vanguard* was
frequently in action in this manner during the running fight of that
day but, like the remainder of the English ships, so furious were her
onslaughts that every time the Dutch were driven off before they
could come to the damaged vessels ahead.

Only one tragedy marred this remarkable day. During the early
afternoon Ayscue's flagship, the *Royal Prince*, ran aground on the
Galloper Sand. At once Tromp swooped. The *Royal Prince* was
surrounded and set on fire, and Ayscue and all her ship's company
were taken prisoner. It was a sad blow for Monck, for she was one
of the latest and largest of the English men of war.

In the late afternoon a fleet of 25 sail was sighted to the westward.
Was it Rupert, with the returning White Squadron, or was it Beaufort
with his French ships to reinforce still further the Dutch? For an hour
or more there was a doubt in Monck's mind until, at last, he could
recognize the cut of the sails as English. It was Rupert, "and with
hearty cheers that rang over the sea the retreating English hailed the
8   succouring White Squadron".

Thus reinforced, Monck again forced an action on the fourth day.
The wind had now freshened and was blowing strongly from the
south-west, so that the Dutch had the weather gage. Relying mainly
on the speed of his ships and their superior weatherliness, Monck
came up from astern, "with all sails set, the trumpets sounding, and
drums beating in every ship, the seamen waving in defiance their hats
9   and the officers their plumed beavers". Soon he was engaged all
along the line, with the Dutch to windward of him. For two hours
they fought as hotly as ever, and although most of the English ships
managed to break through the Dutch line, they found yet a second
Dutch line still to windward of them. By now all order had been lost
and, after another hour of confused close-range fighting, the few
English ships left were almost completely surrounded.

"At this moment," wrote the Dutch observer in de Ruyter's ship,
"the look-out was extraordinary, for all were separated, the English as
well as we. But luck would have it that the largest of our fractions
surrounding the admiral remained to windward, and the largest fraction
of the English, also with their admiral, remained to leeward. This was the
cause of our victory and their ruin. Our admiral had with him thirty-five

or forty ships of his own and of other squadrons, for the squadrons were scattered and order much lost. The rest of the Dutch ships had left him. ... Van Tromp with the rear squadron had fallen to leeward, and so had to keep on (to leeward of the English main body) in order to rejoin the admiral by passing round the English centre. Thus in less than no time we found ourselves in the midst of the English; who, being attacked on both sides, were thrown into confusion and saw their whole order destroyed, as well by dint of the action as by the strong wind that was blowing. This was the hottest of the fight. We saw the high admiral of England separated from his fleet, followed only by one fireship. With that he gained to windward, and passing through the North Holland squadron, placed himself again at the head of fifteen or twenty ships that rallied to him."

This was the end of the battle. Mercifully, both for English and Dutch, a thick fog came down shortly before 7 p.m. and separated the fleets. The Dutch withdrew to seaward, while Monck and Rupert limped slowly home, their ships sadly shattered, but with the spirits of the men undefeated. Still more English ships had been lost during the day's fighting, and Sir Christopher Myngs, flying his flag in the *Victory*, had been killed. Like Berkeley on the first day, he had been shot in the throat, but refusing to have his wound dressed he had stopped the flow of blood with his fingers and for another half-hour had fought his ship till he was put out of his pain by a second bullet.

"This," wrote Campbell, "was the most terrible battle fought in this, or perhaps in any other war, as the Dutch admirals themselves say." That it was an English defeat, and a considerable one, is certain and the most impartial source gives the respective losses as:

"The States lost in these actions three vice-admirals, two thousand men, and four ships. The loss of the English was five thousand killed, and three thousand prisoners; they lost besides seventeen ships, of which nine remained in the hands of the victors."

It is, perhaps, a reflection on the morals of the time that among the English casualties in the ships were a number of women. "And as for newes," wrote Pepys, "I do find great reason to think that we are beaten in every respect, and that we are the losers."

Yet, even in defeat, the conduct of Monck and his men could draw a tribute even from the enemy. De Witte, Grand Pensionary of Holland, in conversation with the then English ambassador, Sir William Temple, said this of them:

"If the English were beaten, their conduct did them more honour than all their former victories. Our own fleet could never have been brought on after the first day's fight, and I believe that none but theirs could; and all that the Dutch had discovered was, that Englishmen might be killed and English ships be burned, but that English courage was invincible."

Evelyn, writing in his diary on June 17th, had a sadder picture to show:

> "I went on shore at Sheerness, where they were building an arsenal for the Fleete, and designing a royal fort with a receptacle for greate ships to ride at anker; but here I beheld the sad spectacle, more than half that gallant bulwark of the kingdom miserably shattered, hardly a vessel intire, but appearing rather so many wrecks and hulls, so cruely had the Dutch mangl'd us. The losse of the *Prince*, that gallant vessell, had ben a loss to be universally deplor'd, none knowing for what reason we first engag'd in this ungrateful warr; we lost 9 or 10 more, and neere 600 men slaine and 1100 wounded, 2000 prisoners; to ballance which perhaps we might destroy 18 or 20 of the enemies ships, and 7 or 800 poore men. Weary of this sad sight I return'd home."

Until the full details of the battle were known, the action was treated in London as a great victory, mainly to bring credit to the King and to distract public attention from the excesses of the Court. Even Pepys, "idled away the whole night till twelve at night at the bonefire in the streets". There was dancing and drinking, letting off of muskets and fireworks, and other excitements to celebrate the supposed victory. "String up your hearts," sang the delighted citizens, "and tune your throats,

> With merry and triumphant notes,
> Send sorrow from your souls away,
> You never had more cause for joy:
> The creeple may cast away his crutch,
> And dance the downfal of the Dutch.
> Great Brittain now may take it's ease,
> King Charles is Soveraign of the seas."

The Four Days' Battle was a landmark in English naval history, for it marked quite clearly the transition from the crude tactics of the 17th century to the formal line of battle of the early part of the 18th.

> "Nothing," wrote the French naval historian de Guiche, who witnessed the battle from the Dutch fleet, "equals the beautiful order of the English at sea. Never was a line drawn straighter than that formed by their ships; thus they bring all their fire to bear upon those who draw near them. . . . They fight like a line of cavalry which is handled according to rule, and applies itself solely to force back those who oppose; whereas the Dutch advance like cavalry whose squadrons leave their ranks and come separately to the charge."

Precision in tactical moves by squadrons, and the line ahead formation, had been born in the previous decade, fathered by Blake, Deane, Monck, and Penn. In this battle it came to fruition and was practised with such skill by Monck that, in spite of the crushing superiority in numbers of de Ruyter, he was able to extricate the English fleet in some sort of order and to bring most of it home to Chatham.

The point is well accentuated by Chabaut-Arnault, one of the greatest of naval historians.

"Such," he wrote after his account of the battle, "was that bloody Battle of the Four Days, or Straits of Calais, the most memorable sea-fight of modern days; not, indeed, by its results, but by the aspect of its different phases; by the fury of the combatants; by the boldness and skill of the leaders; and by the new character which it gave to sea warfare. More than any other this fight marks clearly the passage from former methods to the tactics of the end of the seventeenth century. For the first time we can follow, as though traced upon a plan, the principal movements of the contending fleets. It seems quite clear that to the Dutch as well as to the English have been given a tactical book and a code of signals; or, at the least, written instructions, extensive and precise, to serve instead of such a code. We feel that each admiral now has his squadron in hand, and that even the commander-in-chief disposes at his will, during the fight, of the various subdivisions of his fleet. Compare this action with those of 1652, and one plain fact stares you in the face—that between the two dates naval tactics have undergone a revolution.

"Such were the changes that distinguish the war of 1665 from that of 1652. As in the latter epoch, the admiral still thinks the weather gage an advantage for his fleet; but it is no longer, from the tactical point of view, the principal, we might almost say the sole preoccupation. Now he wishes above all to keep his fleet in good order and compact as long as possible, so as to keep the power of *combining*, during the action, the movements of the different squadrons. Look at Ruyter, at the end of the Four Day's Fight; with great difficulty he has kept to windward of the English fleet; yet he does not hesitate to sacrifice this advantage in order to unite the two parts of his fleet, which are separated by the enemy. If, at the later fight off the North Foreland, great intervals exist between the Dutch squadrons, if the rear afterwards continues to withdraw from the centre, Ruyter deplores such a fault as the chief cause of his defeat. He so deplores it in his official report; he even accuses Tromp of treason and cowardice—an unjust accusation, but which none the less shows the enormous importance thenceforth attached, during action to the reunion of the fleet into a whole strictly and regularly maintained."

If in the actual fighting the English had covered themselves with glory, the fatal Stuart indifference to the Navy marred the aftermath. Men from the fleet, their wives and sweethearts, clamoured at the Pay Office in London, only to be turned away empty-handed for lack of money to honour their tickets.

"Then to the office," wrote Pepys, "the yarde being very full of women (I believe above three hundred) coming to get money for their husbands and friends that are prisoners in Holland; and they lay clamouring and swearing and cursing us, that my wife and I were afeard to send a venison-pasty that we have for supper to-night to the cook's to be baked, for fear of their offering violence to it. . . . I confess their cries were so sad for money, and laying down the condition of their families and their husbands, and what they have done and suffered for the King, and how ill they are used by us, and how well the Dutch [prisoners] are used here by the allowance of their masters, and what their husbands are offered to serve the Dutch abroad, that I do most heartily pity them, and was ready to cry to hear them."

Nor was the victualling any better. If anything it was worse, and the seamen were deserting faster than ever before to escape from the hardships of the sea service. Even those killed in the battle were buried without honour or recognition. The captains who had been slain, Whitty of the *Vanguard* among them, were hurriedly interred at Sheerness, the men's bodies were flung into the sea, and even Myngs, the admiral who had died so gallantly on board the *Victory*, was buried with only Sir W. Coventry and Pepys to mourn him.

"I into the church," wrote Pepys, " . . . and there met with Sir W. Coventry (who was there out of great generosity, and no person of quality there but he) and went with him into his coach, and being in it with him there happened this extraordinary case—one of the most romantic that ever I heard of in this life, and could not have believed, but that I did see it; which was this—About a dozen able, lusty, proper men came to the coachside with tears in their eyes, and one of them that spoke for the rest began and says to Sir W. Coventry, 'We are here a dozen of us that have long known and loved, and served our dead commander, Sir Christopher Mings, and have now done the last office of laying him in the ground. We would be glad we had any other to offer him, and in revenge of him. All we have is our lives; if you will please to get His Royal Highness to give us a fireship among us all, here is a dozen of us, out of all which choose you one to be commander, and the rest of us, whoever he is, will serve him; and, if possible, do that that shall show our memory of our dead commander, and our revenge.' Sir W. Coventry was herewith much moved (as well as I, who could hardly abstain from weeping)."

The King did not deserve to be served by such noble and gallant seamen.

In spite of the extensive damage to the English ships, the fleet was repaired and at sea again in less than two months, much to the surprise of the Dutch. Once again it was under the joint command of Monck and Prince Rupert, both in the *Royal Charles*, with Sir Thomas Allin and Sir Jeremiah Smith as admirals of the White and Blue Squadrons respectively. The Dutch, still under de Ruyter, had put to sea about a month earlier, but had achieved nothing during the four weeks in which they had had the seas to themselves. Both fleets were of equal numbers, each comprising 80 sail of men of war and about 20 fireships.

They met off the North Foreland on St. James's Day, July 25th. De Ruyter's squadrons lay to the north-east of Monck and, with the wind blowing freshly from the north and north-north-east, the weather advantage lay with the Dutch. The *Vanguard*, still under the command of the promoted Langston, was in the centre of the White Squadron which, on the day, was the van of the English fleet. The Blue Squadron, under Smith, had fallen a little behind the rest of the English ships, and although Monck, with his usual contempt for the Dutch, was for attacking the Dutch at once with the White and Red Squadrons, Rupert restrained him until Smith had closed up. It was at this time that Monck was seen to be, "charging a very little pistol and putting it into his pocket", apparently with the intention of discharging it into the powder magazine and blowing up the ship should there be any danger of her being taken by the Dutch.

"And therefore," wrote the Duke of Buckingham, who was a volunteer on board the *Royal Charles*, "Mr. Savill and I, in a laughing way, most mutinously resolved to throw him overboard in case we should ever catch him going down to the powder room."

The White Squadron began the battle at about noon, attacking the Dutch van under Jan Evertsen, brother to the Cornelis who had been killed in the Four Days Battle. So hot was the English attack that the Dutch were forced to give way before the accurate gunnery of the White Squadron and were thrown into complete confusion. The *Vanguard* ranged up alongside a Dutch ship of 70 guns and so hammered her that she had to leave the line little more than a wreck. Evertsen, his Vice-Admiral, de Vries, and his Rear-Admiral, Koenders, were all killed during this period. Evertsen's flagship, the *Zealand*, was taken and burnt and a 50-gun ship, the *Snoek*, captured.

An hour later, Monck and Rupert were in action with de Ruyter's squadron. In the rear, Tromp, "who fought like a madman rather than a wise commander", had engaged the Blue Squadron and broken through it. Though he had gained a local advantage by causing a temporary confusion among Smith's ships, he had also once again, as in the Four Days' Battle, made a serious tactical error by separating himself from the remainder of the Dutch fleet. It was an error that was to cost him dear, for this time de Ruyter, hard pressed by Monck and Rupert, was unable to come to his assistance.

It was now the crucial stage of the battle. If Tromp could fight his way back, if the Dutch van could reorganize themselves into a line, there was yet a chance that the fleet could withstand the fury of the English attack and retire in good order. But it was at this moment that the fatal irresolution of some of the Dutch captains again made de Ruyter's task impossible. One by one they stole away from the scene, crowding on sail to make the best of their way back to Holland. It was the end of de Ruyter's hopes and, with a heavy heart, he, too, turned and set a course for home. "My God!" he is reported to have said, "what an unhappy wretch I am. Among so many thousands of bullets is there not one to end my miserable life?"

In the meantime, Tromp and Smith, with their respective squadrons, had tacked and were now steering a south-westerly course away from the battle. Tromp's squadron was the strongest in the Dutch fleet, Smith's the weakest in the English, and for some time Tromp had the better of it, taking and burning the *Resolution*. Yet in the end it was Tromp who finally had to give way. On the evening of the 26th, Monck and Rupert, now far away down to leeward whither they had chased de Ruyter, saw Tromp's ships flying for the shelter of the Dutch Sandbanks with Smith hard at their heels. At 11 p.m. the whole English fleet was together again and anchored off the coast of Holland, while the Dutch ships, with over 20 less vessels and 7,000 fewer men than when they had sailed, sought the shelter of their harbours.

It had been a convincing victory and left England mistress of the seas. For a week or more the fleet remained in Dutch waters, ranging up and down, burning and destroying. A fleet of nearly 170 merchant vessels was discovered lying at anchor in the Vlie and was put to the torch by the boats of the fleet. The chief villages on the island of Ter Schelling were sacked and destroyed. These operations were carried out under the command of Sir Robert Holmes, and for years afterwards were known as, "Sir Robert Holmes, his bonefire". The total damage was estimated at £1,200,000, a prodigious loss to the Dutch.

Once again London was *en fête*, and this time with a better reason.

> The cannons from the Tower did roar,
> When this good news did come to shore,
> The bells did ring and bone-fires shine,
> And healths carrous'd in beer and wine,

wrote a contemporary poet. And round the bonfires danced a delighted populace, glad of the excuse for entertainment and merriment. "Then Butter-boxes all lament," they sang, "For now you are paid to your own content." It was a long song of many verses, and the good-humoured crowd sent it echoing round the houses.

> Prince Rupert and brave General Monck,
> So pelted Ruyter and Vantrump,
> That they were in a chafing sweat,
> And thought it safest to retreat,
> By little and little they shrank away,
> Their want of courage did them betray,
>   Then Butter-boxes all lament,
>   For now you are paid to your own content.

It was all very gay and exciting, for victories such as this brought with them the promise of peace,

On its return the fleet was laid up for the winter, since there was now no danger to be expected from the Dutch at sea. Only a few frigates were kept in commission for such convoy work as might be necessary against privateers. Most of the large ships were stripped, and among them was the *Vanguard*, moored in the river at Chatham just above Upnor Castle, where she swung idly to a buoy throughout the winter months.

But if there were no danger to be feared from de Ruyter and his ships, there was a much greater danger bred in the Navy by the chronic insolvency of the King. His sailors, acquired mainly by the brutalities of the press-gang, were no longer willing to risk their lives without reward. Every day the Pay Office was besieged by angry seamen presenting their pay tickets. But the Treasury was empty for Charles, who in September 1666 had been voted £1,800,000 by Parliament for the naval service, had spent the money partly in raising new regiments for the army and partly on his mistresses. So, driven by want of money and by the cynical indifference of the Court to their hardships, many of the English sailors, who had fought so gallantly against de Ruyter and Tromp, made their way over to Holland to take service in the Dutch navy. There they were paid not by tickets which were never honoured, but in silver dollars.

There was yet another cause of discontent in the Navy. It had become fashionable, now that the dashing Rupert was back in command, for the Court gallants to go to sea as volunteers in order to taste the thrills of naval battle. While there was nothing wrong in that, it had led gradually to an abuse that almost split the Navy into two camps. Men of rank used their influence with the King or the Duke of York to get themselves appointed as captains of ships so that they might enjoy the pay and prize money of senior officers as well as the excitement of action. They were known as "gentlemen captains", as opposed to those who had risen by merit and were called "tarpaulins". Pepys, talking with Coventry in Greenwich Park after the St. James's Day Battle, listened to a long lecture from the Admiralty Commissioner on the evils of the gentlemen.

> "He was very free with me in speaking his mind of the unruliness of them; and what a losse the King hath of his old men . . . and that there is but few old sober men in the fleete, and of these few of the Flags [i.e. admirals] that are so should die, he fears some other gentlemen captains will get in, and then what a council we shall have, God knows."

This second war against the Dutch, though successful enough at sea, had been a great disappointment to Charles. He had expected it to be a rich war, with many prizes taken from the Dutch trade. It had turned out very differently and he was being pressed for money on all sides. There had been, too, the great plague in 1665, followed by the even more disastrous fire of 1666, in which so much of the city of London was burned down. So it was with relief that Charles received the first overtures for peace from the United Provinces late in 1666. The King of Sweden was accepted by both sides as mediator and the conference, which was to settle terms of peace, was fixed to meet at Breda in May 1667.

Charles took the occasion to save his purse still further and, with the hope of a successful peace treaty, decided not to fit out the fleet for operations during 1667. It was a fateful decision, for until agreement was reached at Breda, the two countries were still at war. He was backed up in his decision by the Duke of York, and only Monck and the admirals stood out against it, pointing out the obvious dangers. They were overruled. Instead of keeping a fleet at sea, Charles decided to build a fort at Sheerness, at the mouth of the Medway, and to set up guns and a boom across the river below Chatham, where most of the first and second rates lay. It was expected that this would prove a sufficient safeguard.

These measures were approved at a Council meeting on March 24th, at which both the King and the Duke of York were present, and orders were given to begin the work. But such money as was voted for them was, almost inevitably, diverted to other uses and nothing was done.

While the English fleet was thus immobilized for lack of money, that of Holland was being fitted out apace. By May de Ruyter was at sea with a fleet of 79 sail, appearing in the Firth of Forth where he bombarded Burntisland, doing very little damage. On June 8th he was reported off Harwich. The "gentlemen" of the Court, scenting action, set off for the town in high spirits. "Lord Barkeley, the Duke of Monmouth, and with him a great many young Hectors, the Lord Chesterfield, my Lord Mandeville, and others; but to little purpose, I fear, but to debauch the country women thereabouts." Pepys was quite correct. It was to little purpose, for on the following day de Ruyter was in the King's Channel, off the mouth of the Thames, and on the 10th it was reported in London that Dutch ships were come up as high as the Nore. Pepys was set to work to gather fireships to annoy the Dutch. He went down-river to Deptford

"and pitched upon ships and set men to work; but Lord! to see how backwardly things move at this pinch, notwithstanding that by the enemy's being now come up as high as almost the Hope".

In his anxiety the King sent for Monck and, making him Lord High Constable, sent him down to Chatham to organize the defence. Monck, now grown old in the service of the country, hurried down to the Medway to do what he could. Lord Oxford was sent to raise the militia in Essex and Lord Middleton to mobilize that of Kent. In London the train bands were called out.

When Monck reached Sheerness he found all in confusion. The

great work of fortification, begun some months before, had progressed
so slowly that next to nothing had been done. Corruption, lack of
money, disorder, even mutiny, had all contributed to hinder the
work. In the fort at Sheerness not a single gun had been mounted,
nor was there a single soldier to defend the place. At Chatham there
was no ammunition for the few guns that had been set up, and of
the 1,500 men employed in the dockyard, none of whom had received
any pay for months, no more that three turned up in answer to Monck's
appeal for workers. The Lord General set to work, "with a great
many idle lords and gentlemen, with their pistols and fooleries", who,
inspired by his example, laboured in their shirt-sleeves in an attempt
to save Chatham and as many of the ships lying there as possible.

Monck acted with characteristic energy and for once the dissolute
followers of the Court justified their idle existence. Powder and shot
were obtained for the guns of Upnor Castle, a great chain was stretched
across the river as a bar to the Dutch and defended with batteries
on either shore, and seven of the King's ships—two large vessels and
five fireships—were sunk to block the channels below Gillingham.
The *Unity* was moored at the eastern end of the chain to assist in its
defence with her guns, and above her Monck stationed the *Carolus
Quintus*, the *Mathias*, and the *Monmouth*, so that their broadsides might
add to the weight of metal directed against the Dutch should they
attempt to advance so high up-river. Above them again lay the pride
of the English fleet, the *Royal Charles*, and, in order up the river, the
Royal Oak, *Loyal London*, *Old James*, *Katherine*, *Princess*, *Golden Ruyter*
(a Dutch prize), *Triumph*, *Rainbow*, *Unicorn*, *Henry*, *Hilversum*, and
Vanguard, the latter just below Rochester Bridge. Peter Pett, the
Commissioner at Chatham, was ordered by Monck to tow the *Royal
Charles*, his old flagship, further up-river, but Pett was too busy trying
to save his own personal goods to heed the order, and the great ship
remained in her place of danger.

The Dutch did little on the 11th, beyond passing an advance
squadron of four men of war, three armed yachts, and two fireships
into the mouth of the Medway. But on the 12th, when the flood tide
began to run at seven o'clock in the morning, the Dutch, led by
Captain Jan van Brakel in the *Vrede*, advanced up-river with the aid
of a fresh north-easterly breeze. Van Brakel laid the *Vrede* alongside
the *Unity* and carried her by boarding, clearing the way for an attack
on the chain by the two fireships, *Susanna* and *Pro Patria*. Amid the
thunder of the guns the *Susanna* charged the chain. It held firm and
for a moment or two it looked as though Chatham might yet be
saved.

Monck, followed by fifty of the "idle lords and gentlemen with
their fooleries", went on board the *Monmouth* determined to fight the
guns of the ship himself in defence of the English fleet. Then the *Pro
Patria* followed the *Susanna* in a second assault on the chain. There
was a minute or two of silence as she gathered way and charged the

obstruction, and English voices were heard on board the Dutch ships crying, "We did heretofore fight for tickets, now we fight for dollars." As the *Pro Patria* hit the chain it parted with a loud crash and the Dutch were through.

The *Carolus Quintus* and *Mathias* were at once set on fire by the Dutch and burnt to the water's edge. Frantic efforts were made to tow the *Monmouth* away out of danger, but she fell foul of the *Mary*, a Dutch prize which had been sunk as a blockship by Monck, and she, too, was set on fire. The *Royal Charles*, in which Monck had fought so gallantly and in which, when she was still the *Naseby*, Charles himself had been brought home as King, was captured and taken down-river as a prize of war. The *Royal Oak*, the *Loyal London*, and the *Old James* were all attacked by the Dutch, all captured, and all sunk at their moorings. Only the *Royal Oak* made any show of resistance. Douglas, her captain, fought her to the end. "It shall never be said," he cried, "that a Douglas quitted his post without orders." He died in the flames of his vessel, a gallant exception to the general behaviour of the Navy at that grave hour.

Chatham that day presented a sight that was almost unique in English naval history. To the roar of the guns were added the explosions of burning vessels as the flames reached their powder rooms, the crash of falling masts and yards, the cheers of the exultant Dutch as they passed on from success to success, the bitter taunts against the King of those English sailors who had taken service in the invading ships. The roll of drums, the calls of trumpets, the screams of burned and wounded men added to the clamour. And above it all lay a pall of smoke as the English ships burned, and the savage gleams of flaming wreckage flickered over the water.

As the news reached London there was a panic. Banks were forced to suspend payment, so great was the run on them, and fear of a Dutch invasion was so prevalent that most of the richer citizens loaded their furniture and goods on hastily bought carts and trundled it into the country. Cautious Mr. Pepys made two fair copies of his will, and sent his wife and father out of London with as much gold as they could carry, giving them instructions to bury it in the garden of his father's house in Huntingdonshire. As he hurried about his business, he could hear the sound of the guns at Chatham, a constant urge to him and to all others to work with redoubled energy in a hope of averting the threat of a Dutch descent on the capital. The King and the Duke of York, taking personal charge of the defence of London, ordered ships to be sunk in the river below Woolwich and Blackwall. So great was the panic, however, that instead of using some of the old hulks which lay alongside the wharves, the ships scuttled were four of the newest, three of them just loaded with precious stores for the Navy. Without counting the value of the four ships themselves, over £120,000 worth of naval stores were sent needlessly to the bottom.

On the night of June 12th, after the sinking of the *Royal Oak*, *Loyal London*, and *Old James*, and the capture of the *Royal Charles*, the Dutch dropped down-river again on the falling tide, well satisfied with the day's work. But on the morning of the 13th, with the rising tide carrying them back to Chatham, they were once again at their work of destruction. In an attempt to stop them, Monck ordered the sinking of two more vessels still higher up the river, the *Katherine* just above Upnor Castle and the *Vanguard* just below Rochester Bridge.

Although Monck could not know it at the time of ordering these ships to be sunk, the force of the Dutch was almost spent. They had used up all their fireships but two, and powder and shot was also running short. Arriving below Upnor Castle they finished off the work of destruction begun the previous day, setting fire to those parts of the three ships sunk which remained above water and burning them to the water's edge. They towed away the *Unity*, which they had captured before the assault on the boom, sent a landing party ashore and blew up a magazine attached to one of the batteries, and exchanged shots with Upnor Castle. But that was all. In the afternoon they dropped down-river again and on the 14th were back at the Nore. They carried out a reconnaissance of the Thames as far as the Hope, to see whether there was any possibility of sailing up the river to London, but found the defences now organized and the prospect too hazardous. So, for the rest of the month, de Ruyter remained off the mouth of the Thames, carrying out so close a blockade that the price of coal in London rose from 10s. a chaldron to £5 10s., and other goods carried by sea in a similar proportion.

There was, of course, an enquiry and a scapegoat had to be found to divert suspicion from the King. It was the unfortunate Pett, Commissioner of the Dockyard at Chatham, on whom the blame was fastened and he was brought to the Tower, "to be kept close prisoner for dangerous practices and misdemeanours". Perhaps he could have saved the *Royal Charles*, had he had her towed up-river in the beginning as he was ordered, but he was to blame no more than many another man, much less, indeed, than Charles or the Duke of York, who were responsible for the policy to have no Navy out that year. Marvell, in his satirical *Instructions to a Painter*, has a biting comment to make:

> After this loss, to relish discontent,
> Some one must be accused by Parliament;
> All our miscarriages on Pett must fall,
> His name alone seems fit to answer all.
> Whose counsel first did this mad war beget?
> Who all commands sold through the Navy? *Pett.*
> Who would not follow when the Dutch were beat?
> Who treated out the time at Bergen? *Pett.*
> Who, the Dutch fleet with storm disabled, met,
> And, rifling prizes, them neglected? *Pett.*
> Who with false news prevented the Gazette,

The fleet divided, writ for Rupert? *Pett.*
. Who all our seamen cheated of their debt?
And all our prizes who did swallow? *Pett.*
Who did advise no navy out to set?
And who the forts left unprepared? *Pett.*
Who to supply with powder did forget
Languard, Sheerness, Gravesend, and Upnor? *Pett.*
Who all our ships exposed in Chatham net?
Who should it be but the fanatick *Pett?*
Pett, the sea-architect, in making ships,
Was the first cause of all these naval slips.
Had he not built, none of these faults had been;
If no creation, there had been no sin;
But his great crime, one boat away he sent,
That lost our fleet, and did our flight prevent.

In due course almost all the ships sunk at Chatham were raised. "The bottom of the *Royal James* is got afloat and those of the *Loyal London* and *Royal Oak* soon will be," wrote John Conny from Chatham. Only the *Vanguard* remained where she was, scuttled below Rochester Bridge. It was found impossible to raise her. What was left of her above water was dismantled and her hull destroyed.

So perished the second *Vanguard.* She had added seven battle honours to the *Vanguard* roll, and in all of them had fought gallantly and hard. And even at the end of her life she had served the country well in its greatest extremity. Hers is a proud record, for in all those savage battles against the Dutch she had been in the hottest part of the fight. With her, the *Vanguard* tradition, begun in the year of the Armada, was now firmly established.

CHAPTER IX

WITH ROOKE AT LA HOGUE

ON an April day in 1678, a coach, decorated on all its panels with scenes of battles at sea, of ships lying in harbour, of vessels labouring in heavy weather, could be seen behind a team of spirited horses making its way down the Portsmouth road. In it sat Mr. Pepys, no longer Clerk of the Acts, but now Secretary of the Admiralty, no less. An older and staider Mr. Pepys, and a man whose meticulous attention to detail and whose industrious thirst for knowledge had already made him the greatest naval expert of the times. No longer did he take such delight in tumbling Doll Lane at the "Swann", in tasting the illicit pleasures of Mrs. Bagwell at his office or in her home, in taking Mrs. Knipp on his knee in a coach and "employing my hands about her person", or in enticing Pegg Pen into his closet so that he might, "*a la baiser mouche et toucher ses cosas*, upon her breast", as he had done in the second *Vanguard's* time. Those days were over now and a new dignity sat, perhaps a little pompously, on those important shoulders.

The coach rocked as it passed over the cobbled streets of Portsmouth Town and finally drew to a halt in the dockyard. Pepys was come to see for himself the progress being made on those of the famous "Thirty New Ships", which were being built at Portsmouth, the *Vanguard*, a Second rate, and the *Eagle* and *Expedition*, Third rates. All three were being constructed by Mr. Daniel Furzar, and the new *Vanguard* was a ship of 1,357 tons, carrying 90 guns and a complement of 640 men. Her length was 126 feet, her beam 45 feet, and her draught of water 20 feet. She was a three-decker, with her lowest tier of guns raised to 4 feet 6 inches above her waterline after the new French fashion, so that the ports could be opened and the guns used even in a moderate sea. Under the old pattern, the lowest tier could only be employed on calm days, for they were so little above the waterline that any appreciable movement of the seas brought water pouring in cascades through the open gunports.

The third *Vanguard*, in one way, owed more than this arrangement of her guns to the French. The order for her building, and for another 29 ships, had been pressed through Parliament by Pepys, against considerable opposition, largely because of the big increases being made in the French Navy at that time under the vigorous policy of Colbert. "Our neighbour's strength," had said Pepys in his speech, "is now greater than ours, and they will still be building, so that we are as well to overtake them for the time past as to keep pace with them in the present building." The Dutch, too, were adding to their

Navy by new construction, yet another spur used on a reluctant Parliament to vote the necessary money. The argument had dragged on from year to year since 1675, and it had taken two whole years to convince Parliament of the country's need for these additional vessels.

In the meantime, since the unhappy end of the second *Vanguard* at Rochester, a third war had been fought against the Dutch, this time with the French as allies of England instead, as in 1666, of Holland. It had been the personal friendship of Charles and Louis, assisted powerfully by a gift of 600,000 pistoles in gold from the French treasury to help Charles in his financial difficulties, which more than anything else had brought the two countries into uneasy partnership. The war had produced three battles at sea, none of them a conclusive victory for either side, and had at last come to its end as much by the mutual respect of the English and Dutch peoples as by the mutual distrust of the English for their Allies. The peace had been signed at Westminster on February 4th, 1674, and had been further cemented three years later by the marriage of Mary, daughter of the Duke of York, to William, Prince of Orange. It was a match that, though it might bring present benefits to the House of Stuart through better relations with the Dutch, yet had potent in it the threat of that House's final overthrow. For William of Orange was the European champion of Protestantism and the Test Act of 1673 had shown the future James II as a convinced and confirmed papist.

In the summer of 1678 the *Vanguard* was launched. And on September 28th of that same year, Titus Oates sprung upon a credulous and suspicious England the fantastic revelations of the famous Popish Plot, which swept so many innocent Catholics to their doom. At the same time it swept quite a number of innocent Protestants into prison, and one of them Pepys, who on May 22nd, 1679, was committed to the Tower on a trumped-up charge of popery. Six weeks later he was released on bail, but it took him a whole year of anxious collection of evidence before he was finally able to refute the charges brought against him by his Republican enemies—Buckingham, Shaftesbury, Harbord, Bennet, Sachaverell, and Meres being the chief of them. Even then Charles, frightened for once out of his complacency by the effect on the country of the revelations of Oates, false though he knew them to be, was unwilling to provoke public opinion against himself by re-instating Pepys in the Admiralty Secretaryship. It was not until five years later that the King felt it safe to bring him back into his service.

Those five years proved almost fatal for the new *Vanguard*. The "Thirty New Ships", which had caused so much commotion in Parliament and for which Pepys had fought so hard, were allowed to rot in harbour by the new Admiralty Commission with which the King had replaced the old at the height of the Popish Plot. "No king," wrote Pepys later, "ever did so unaccountable a thing to oblige his people by, as to dissolve a Commission of the Admiralty then in his own hand, who best understands the business of the sea of any prince the world ever had, and things never better done, and put it into hands which he knew were wholly ignorant thereof, sporting himself with their ignorance."

It was a stern rebuke, especially from so ardent a royalist as Pepys, but the condition of the ships warranted it.

"The greatest part of these *Thirty Ships*," stated a contemporary report in 1685, "(without having ever yet lookt out of *Harbour*) were let to sink into such distress, through *Decays* contracted in their *Buttocks*, *Quarters*, *Bows*, *Thickstuff* without *Board*, and *Spirkettings* upon their Gun-decks within; their *Buttock-planks* some of them *started* from their *Transums*, *Tree-nails* burnt and rotted, and *Planks* thereby become ready to drop into the *Water*, as being (without their neighbouring *Timbers*) in many places perish'd to *powder*, to the rendring them unable with safety to admit of being *Breem'd*,* for fear of taking fire; and their whole *sides* more disguised by *Shot-boards* nail'd, and *Plaisters* of *Canvas* pitch'd thereon (for hiding their *Defects* and keeping them above *Water*) than has been usually seen upon the coming in of a Fleet after a Battle; what several of them had been newly reported by the Navy-Board itself, to lye in danger of *sinking* at their very *Moorings*."

It was a disgraceful state of affairs and, when brought to the notice of Parliament, evoked from the Commission a suggestion that the cause was faulty construction and materials. This was another attempt to discredit Pepys, who had been responsible for their initial building. The great Secretary would have none of it. It amounted, he suggested, "to nothing less than a plain detection of the vanity of those suggestions touching the root of this calamity", and showed that the damage had been caused only by, "the plain omission of the necessary and ordinary cautions used for the preserving of new-built ships". He had himself been down to inspect them and had, with his own hands, gathered toadstools, "growing in the most considerable of them as big as my fists". After listing the damage found and showing its causes, he wrote:

"From which, and other like omissions, it could not but fall out (as indeed it did) that some of these unfortunate ships were already become rotten, while others built of the very same stuff, at the same place, by the same hand, and within the very same time for merchant service, succeeded well and continued so."

The death of Charles in 1685 and the accession of James to the throne saw a great change in the fortunes of the Navy. Almost his first act on ascending the throne was to strengthen the Commissioners

---

* Breaming; bringing a ship aground and careening her to burn off weeds growing on her bottom. At that period usually done with reeds or broom, sometimes with old ropes.

of the Navy by the appointment of four new men—Sir Anthony Deane, Sir John Berry, William Hewer, and Balthasar St. Michel. The hand of Pepys could be discerned very plainly in these new appointments, for Deane, the shipbuilder, was an old friend of many years' standing, Hewer was his chief clerk and life-long companion, and "Balty" St. Michel was his brother-in-law. But they were, nevertheless, the very type of men the Navy needed, for their lives had been spent in its service.

They set about unravelling the tangled skein of naval affairs which Charles had left as a legacy to his brother, and so well did they do their work that, a little over two years later, they had had all the old ships made serviceable, the new ones repaired and altered where necessary, the dockyards manned by experienced workmen, and the store-houses filled with every possible requirement for the fleet, all of the best and, moreover, economically purchased. The Navy Estimates were overhauled and brought into order and a system evolved whereby a close check could be maintained on all financial dealings, under which all the old avenues of wholesale fraud were effectively closed. And finally they liquidated the whole of the Navy debt, that running sore of Charles's days. Every officer and man in the Navy was paid up to the last farthing owing to him and the Victuallers' accounts were squared.

The Commission was dissolved on October 12th, 1688, on the completion of its work, having saved the country a sum of no less than £307,570 9s. 4d. on the money voted by Parliament. It was a formidable achievement.

History has had little to place on the credit side of James's account during his short reign, having largely ignored his work for the Navy. But certain it is that, on the administrative side, he laboured long and successfully to improve the fleet. That he threw it away in 1688 by the folly of his political actions and because of his religious beliefs cannot disguise the fact that, both in ships and men, the Navy was in better heart when he was forced to quit the throne than ever before.

But if James was a successful administrator, he was a poor judge of a man. There was still throughout his reign the scandal of the gentleman captains, for James had his favourites no less than Charles. When Pepys was asked to use his influence to obtain a command for a gentleman named Clinton, who had been recommended by Captain Killigrew, "by reason he hath been with him a whole year at sea and in three engagements where he saith he behaved himself like a gentleman and an understanding man", the great Secretary commented that this was

"a character which I confess wants a good deal of that which must lead me to think a man fit to make a sea officer of: I mean downright diligence, sobriety, and seamanship, without which no man can serve his Majesty as he ought, or at least will ever be thought by me to do."

And James Houblon, a London merchant writing to Pepys, urged him to press on with the work of reforming the officers of the fleet so that

> "you will at last do the great work which all honest men would rejoice in, that is that the management of the King's fleet in all particulars may be executed by sober, discreet and diligent persons and men of business, and that all drinking, swearing and gaming and expensive and sumptuous eating may be banished the Fleet, and particularly that the King's ships may not be made bawdy-houses nor the captains publicly carry and entertain their whores on board as some of them have formerly done, and that from port to port in the Mediterranean, to the great scandal of our religion and government, both amongst Turks, Jews, and Christians."

Pepys, indeed, was a persistent traveller along this road which was designed to lead to an improvement in the type of the naval officer of the times. One of the many reforms he instituted at about this time was his "Establishement for Lieutenants", under which were laid down the conditions for promotion to that rank. They included at least three years service in the Navy, with one year as a midshipman, and though Prince Rupert and others protested against the midshipman's clause as, "a service beneath the quality of a gentleman", Pepys's draft received the King's approval and was adopted into the Navy.

Captains, too, were subject to Pepys's drive for reform. They now had to furnish exact copies of their journals to the Admiralty at stated periods, an attempt to stamp out the evil of "good voyages", which were putting so many illicit pennies into the captains' pockets. These "good voyages" had sprung from the custom of sending bullion in men of war when shipped abroad, a reasonable precaution against the prevalent piracy of the times. Bullion, however, had now grown into merchandise and some captains went so far as to advertise the freight rates at which they were prepared to carry general goods from port to port. Its growth had led to intolerable abuses, so that the King's ships were employed less and less on the King's business and more and more on the private ventures of their captains. Finally they undercut the merchants to such an extent that the whole trade of the country was in danger of becoming ruined.

But while Pepys was able to do much to improve the general efficiency of the Navy, he was powerless to prevent James from appointing his favourites to command ships and fleets. James's most foolish action and, as it turned out, most fatal one, was the appointment in 1688 of Sir Roger Strickland as Commander-in-Chief of the fleet in place of Admiral Herbert. Strickland, an avowed Roman Catholic, was heartily disliked by the seamen and, when he introduced priests on board the ships to say Mass, there was uproar and mutiny. Many of the priests barely escaped serious injury and it took all the persuasive powers of the officers to prevent the sailors, "from offering

the priests as human sacrifices to King Neptune". Herbert, a strong
Protestant, followed by Captain Edward Russell, equally strong in
the faith, made their way to Holland, there to hitch their fortunes to
the star of Protestantism in the form of William of Orange. Both were
excellent seamen and their loss, both to James and the Navy, was
considerable.

As the year drew towards its close, James grew daily in unpopu-
larity in the country, hag-ridden as it was by the fear of popery. The
fleet remained largely loyal, for it still remembered him as a successful
admiral and a great administrator, under whom the lot of both officer
and man had been considerably improved. But Strickland's appointment in command had strained that loyalty almost to breaking point.
When James at last realized the false step he had made and replaced
Strickland by Lord Dartmouth, the damage had been done. Discontent
and mistrust had already swept through the fleet and there were
political meetings almost daily in captains' cabins and in forecastles.
The leading Protestant lights in the fleet were Matthew Aylmer,
captain of the *Mary*, and George Byng, First Lieutenant of the
Defiance. Both were in communication with Herbert, now in Holland,
and both worked tirelessly to convert as many officers serving in
Dartmouth's fleet as possible to the Protestant cause of William of
Orange. Byng, "he had been in his youth a resolute, able, enterprising
fellow, mercenary and knowing in his business", was the more active
of the two, and the more successful.

Events came to a head in October. Dartmouth, the better to keep
a watch on the movements of the Dutch fleet, stationed his ships
in the Shipwash so as to be ready to fall upon the invading ships of
William should they make their way either north towards the Humber,
or west down the Channel. This decision shows so remarkably poor
an appreciation of the strategical situation that one wonders whether
Dartmouth were not already in secret sympathy with William's aims.
He had with him 40 men of war, 18 fireships, and three yachts, and
among his larger vessels was the *Vanguard*, commanded by Captain
Christopher Mason. William, with a fleet of 50 ships of the line, 25
frigates, 25 fireships, and 400 transports carrying 4,092 horse and
11,090 foot, was at the mouth of the Maas. He was all set for the
great adventure.

On the night of October 19th he made a start, setting his course
for the Humber, but was forced back by heavy weather on the 21st.
Dartmouth, lulled into a feeling of security by the news of William's
swift return, took the opportunity to send down yards and topmasts
in his ships for re-rigging and overhaul. Eleven days later, with the
English fleet still largely immobilized with their yards and topmasts
down, William set sail on his second attempt. He was again bound
for the Humber, but changed his mind while at sea and altered course
for the English Channel, intending to land in Torbay. A brisk wind
from the north-east helped him on his way. In command of his fleet

was yet another Evertsen, this time Cornelis, "the Youngest", son of "the Old", and Admiral Herbert was flying his flag in the *Leijden*. The ships were sighted by Dartmouth as he lay in the Shipwash, but the English admiral was in no case to follow and William and his fleet sailed down Channel unmolested and unchallenged.

Four days later William landed at Torbay and, on the same day, Dartmouth at last got clear of the Shipwash. The English fleet sailed in William's track and looked into Torbay, but was driven back up Channel by a contrary wind. The ships anchored off St. Helens and there Dartmouth called a Council of War, attended by all captains. It was decided not to fight the Dutch, provided that an action could be avoided, "with honour". But there was, indeed, no chance now of any action, honour or no honour, for William was already ashore with his army and everywhere was being greeted with enthusiasm on his march towards London. Dartmouth, too, was left in no doubt as to the temper of his captains who, thanks to the work of Aylmer and Byng, were on William's side almost to a man. There was no more he could do now but to await the outcome of events ashore.

He gave leave of absence to Byng, "to visit a relative in Huntingdon-shire", and apparently expressed no surprise when Byng set off from the fleet disguised as a farmer. The indefatigable lieutenant reached William at Sherborne and, after reporting the general mood of the fleet, was

"sent back with an answer to the officers of the fleet, and with a letter to Lord Dartmouth to acquaint him with the necessity of his coming over, and of his intentions to continue him at the head of the fleet; with promises that Admiral Herbert should not be advanced over him. This letter the prince advised Mr. Byng to put into the stuffing of his saddle; lest, in case he was seized, it should not be found upon him; but he thought it best to quilt it in the rollers of his breeches. So Mr. Byng, taking his leave, returned safely to the fleet again."

9

The letter was left on Dartmouth's dressing-table.

It had the desired effect. Dartmouth made submission to William, and the fleet was firmly in the hands of the new king. Those few captains whose loyalty was suspect were sent ashore and on the 30th the ships dispersed, the *Vanguard* and most of the other large ships sailing to the Nore. There she went into dock at Chatham for the renewal of much of her planking, which was showing ominous signs of dry rot. It was a legacy of those years of neglect directly after her building.

It was for this reason that she missed the operations off the coast of Ireland and the Battle of Kinsale. James, with the active help of Louis, was eager to regain the kingdom he had lost and, in an attempt to do so, landed with a French army on the Catholic shores of Ireland. William, as eager to retain the kingdom he had gained, himself led the English army in defence of his crown and, by a series of brilliant victories, brought James's hopes to naught. Once again it was war, but this time the allies were changed. France was now the enemy and William had no difficulty in bringing in his countrymen, the Dutch, on the side of England.

The *Vanguard* was still in dockyard hands when Herbert, now Earl of Torrington, fought his ill-starred battle off Beachy Head on June 30th, 1690, against the French under the command of the Comte de Tourville. But she was in commission again early in 1692, still with Mason as her captain, and joined Admiral Russell's fleet in the Channel, reaching St. Helens on May 13th. There the English fleet, reinforced by a Dutch squadron of 36 sail under Admiral Allemande, lay for two days, a brave total of 99 sail of the line, mounting 6,676 cannon and manned by 41,621 seamen and marines. Against it Tourville could only muster 63 ships, though he was expecting a squadron from Toulon under the Comte d'Estrées.

The proceedings opened with the inevitable Council of War. There Russell explained to the assembled captains, Dutch and English, that Louis had collected a great army for the invasion of England, that it was drawn up at La Hogue with transports in readiness and that only the defeat of Tourville at sea could deny the waters of the Channel to the passage of the army. He read, too, a letter from Queen Mary— William at the time was in Flanders—to the effect that she was resolved to put her whole trust in her naval captains. There had been a wide-spread belief that the Navy was untrustworthy and that it might connive at a second restoration, this time of James. The Queen's message of confidence was enough to bring over any doubtful captain, had there been one, and they sent back to her an enthusiastic address.

> "God," they wrote, "direct your councils and prosper your arms by sea and land against your Majesty's enemies, let all people say 'Amen' with your Majesty's most dutiful and loyal subjects."

The *Vanguard* was in the Blue Squadron, under the command of Sir John Ashby, with George Rooke as Vice-Admiral. When Tourville was sighted early in the morning of May 19th, the fleet was formed up into line of battle, the Dutch leading in the van, Russell with the Red Squadron in the centre, and Ashby in the rear. Tourville, who had the advantage of the windward position, could accept or decline battle at will, but he crowded on all sail to bring his ships into action.

Two factors inclined him thus to bear down on the long English line, heavily outnumbered though he was. The first was the receipt of explicit orders from Louis to force the action, the second a belief that the English officers were largely Jacobite in their sympathies and would not fight. That there were some grounds for this belief would seem to be apparent from Russell's actions that morning. He had had himself rowed from ship to ship in the English squadrons and, addressing the men in each, had said to them, "If any of your officers play false, overboard with him, and with myself among the first."

By eleven o'clock the two fleets were in range and Tourville had discovered his mistake, for the English ships fought every bit as hard as they had done against the Dutch 20 years previously.

Tourville, for all his lack of numbers, fought most gallantly. He laid his ship, the *Soleil Royal*, alongside Russell in the *Britannia* and for two hours they exchanged broadsides until the French flagship was forced to tow out of the line because of the damage she had received to masts, rigging, and hull, and, "having so many men in her slain that the blood running out of the scuppers discoloured the ocean". At the head of the allied line the Dutch, stretching well out beyond the French van, were able to tack and come down to windward of the leading French ships, bringing them under two fires. Russell ordered a similar move on the part of the Blue Squadron, but it was so far astern and the wind so light that it was late in the afternoon before it could get up into action.

The *Vanguard* was next in the line to Ashby in the *Victory*, and it was nearly three o'clock before she was able to work herself up into range of the French rear. For an hour she was hotly engaged. And then, just when the case of the French looked completely hopeless, the battle was brought to a sudden stop by a thick fog, which came down at four o'clock. It cleared partially an hour later, and the French were seen to be in flight towards the westward. Russell ordered a general chase, but once again the fog prevented a general action. Before darkness fell the Blue Squadron, groping for the enemy in the general murk, bumped into one of their squadrons and for half an hour the *Vanguard* was again in the thick of the fighting. And once again the fog came down to shelter the French, this time thicker than ever. Russell was forced to signal to his fleet to anchor, hoping to find the French on the morrow. During the last half-hour of action, in which only Ashby's Blue Squadron had been engaged, four of the French ships had been sunk and the enemy thrown into even greater confusion.

It was still foggy when the morning of the 20th dawned, but a light breeze at about nine o'clock lifted it sufficiently for the Dutch squadron to discover the French. They made the signal for the sighting of a fleet and once again Russell ordered a general chase. The French, crowding on as much sail as they could carry, steered towards the west, anchoring as soon as the tide turned against them and they could make no more way over the ground. Russell did the same. At 10 p.m. that night the wind at last freshened and both fleets weighed. Russell's ship, the *Britannia*, lost her topmast in the breeze—it had been damaged in her duel the previous day with the *Soleil Royal*—and his squadron hove to while the damage was being repaired, the chase of the French meanwhile being carried on by the Blue Squadron and the Dutch.

It was the same on the 21st, though during the morning the *Soleil Royal*, pride of the French Navy and mounting 104 guns, ran ashore near Cherbourg. She had been so much damaged by the *Britannia* that she could not work to windward and so was unable to weather the dangers of the French coast. With her were the *Admirable*, of 90 guns, and the *Triomphant*, of 80, both fine ships. Russell promptly ordered Sir Ralph Delavell, Vice-Admiral of the Red, to take such ships as he required under his command and to destroy the three French vessels. Two of them, the *Soleil Royal* and the *Triomphant*, were successfully set on fire by two English fireships, the *Blaze* and the *Wolf.* The *Admirable* was stormed by the boats of the English ships, boarded and captured, and similarly set ablaze.

On the 22nd the French reached comparative safety. Twenty of the smaller vessels managed to round Cape La Hogue and, risking the dangerous passage of the Alderney Race, reached St. Malo, where they sheltered in the harbour. Twelve of the larger, unable to make so much distance to windward, worked into the Bay of La Hogue where, getting into as shoal water as they could, they placed themselves under the guns of Forts Lisset and St. Vaast. Ashore was the army destined by Louis for the invasion of England, and with it was James. As he stood with the Marquis de Bellefonds, Marshal of France and Commander-in-Chief of the army, he watched the French ships come to an anchor. Lifting his eyes he could see Russell's fleet standing in towards the bay. He could even hear the shouts of the English sailors as their anchors plunged into the sea. It was Sunday, and as he said his evening Mass no doubt he prayed for a happy issue of the inevitable fight on the morrow.

On the morning of the 23rd the 12 French ships worked their way yet closer inshore, six of them under Fort Lisset and six under Fort St. Vaast. The English were strangely quiet, though the army on shore could see much coming and going of boats between the ships. There was no sign of action in the afternoon, either, but as the tide rose in the evening the English showed their hand. Two hundred longboats, the *Vanguard's* among them, manned by officers and men of the fleet and under the command of Rooke, swept in towards the shore. The guns of Fort Lisset opened fire, but their noise was drowned by the cheers of the sailors. They pulled straight for the six three-deckers and so great was their eagerness to be first alongside that there was heavy wagering among the crews on the result of the race.

As they reached the ships the French crews fled. Lashing the ships together in pairs, the English sailors put them to the torch and, with little or no loss, rowed back to their own ships as the tide turned and began to ebb.

"They dropped out of the bay," wrote Grant, "with the ebb tide, leaving La Hogue one sheet of fire. During all the night the great ships blazed, and the explosion was heard from time to time of their loaded cannon as the fire reached them, till six culminating crashes announced that the flames had reached their magazines, and then sea and sky became sheeted with burning brands,"

There still remained the six ships anchored under St. Vaast. Rooke was back again with his boats on the morning tide of the 24th. Once again the ships were stormed and the crews routed. So close were they inshore that the French cavalry were ordered to assist in repelling the English boats. They waded into the water and were pulled from their horses by the sailors with boathooks. But nothing now could stop the English. The French ships were boarded and their guns turned against the fort ashore, silencing it while the seamen set about their work of further destruction. Again the ships were fired and burnt to the waterline. A number of transports and storeships, which had taken refuge up a creek in the bay, were added to the conflagration. The men then returned to their ships, cheering lustily and singing, "God Save the King".

It was the end of James's hopes, yet he could not resist a quick surge of pride in the achievements of the English sailors. "Ah," he said to the Duke of Berwick who was standing alongside him, another witness to the scene, "none but my brave English tars could have performed so gallant an action." But there is a touch of sadness in the letter he wrote to Louis after the burning of the French fleet and the disbanding of the army which was to have set him again on his throne.

> "Monsieur my Brother," he wrote, "I have hitherto borne with something of constancy and resolution those misfortunes which it hath blessed Heaven to lay upon me, so long as myself was the only sufferer; but I must acknowledge that this last disaster utterly overwhelms me. I am altogether comfortless in reference to what concerns your Majesty, through the loss that has befallen your fleets. I know too well that it is my unlucky star which has drawn this misfortune upon your forces, always victorious, save when they fought for my interests. And it is this which plainly tells me I no longer merit the support of so great a monarch—one who is always sure to vanquish when he fights for himself. For which reason it is that I request your Majesty no longer to concern yourself for a prince so unfortunate as I; but permit me to retire to some corner of the world, where I may cease to obstruct the course of your prosperity and conquest."

Louis promptly gave him a tolerably comfortable corner of the world at the Palace of St. Germain.

The Battle of Barfleur, with its attendant sequel at La Hogue, came as a severe shock to the French. Louis, for so many years the arbiter of European destiny, had received a devastating blow to his prestige. Though it did not mean the end of the war, which dragged on, with an interval of truce between 1697 and 1702, well into Queen Anne's reign, it did mean the end of the French Navy at sea. Louis was beginning to find the expense of his land war in Europe so great that he was financially unable to keep his big ships in commission. After the end of 1693 he laid up his fleet and resorted to a policy of sending out privateers to harry the English and Dutch trade. They were a nuisance, it is true, but they could not influence the war at sea. Russell had thus won a victory of great importance at Barfleur, though with his great superiority in numbers he could hardly have done less.

Burchett, who had followed Pepys as Secretary of the Admiralty, was of the opinion that he could have done a great deal more and blames him, the Dutch Admiral, and Ashby, for not accounting for the ships which escaped through the Alderney Race.

> "I cannot proceed," he wrote, "without lamenting the escape of those which the Dutch, and our Admiral of the Blue, were left to look after. I shall not lay the want of judgment, diligence, or ought else, to any one's charge; but since so fair an opportunity was offered for destroying the most considerably part of the French King's Navy, such ill success in that affair was the greatest misfortune to us; for had a happy push been made, the naval force of France could not in this age, whatever it might in the next, have given England any uneasiness."

But Burchett was less than fair. Both Ashby and Allemande had done all they could, being unable to catch the smaller French ships because of the lightness of the wind. It was impossible for them to follow through the treacherous waters of the Alderney Race, firstly because they had not the local knowledge as to the positions of the many rocks, and secondly because the pilots on board would not countenance so rash a course and refused to attempt the passage.

In England, news of the battle was received with mixed feelings. There was a tendency to feel that more should have been done and, in an attempt to find a suitable scapegoat, the unfortunate Rooke was picked upon for some unfavourable comment. The choice of him was entirely political. The Whigs were in power again after a long period of Tory rule, and Rooke was a Tory. But such comment as there was carried no weight with William, and Rooke did not suffer in his employment. His anonymous biographer is swift to dispute any reflection on the conduct of his hero.

Telling the story of La Hogue he recounts how Rooke went in with the boats,

> "wherein not only Mr. Rook and all the officers signalized themselves, but the men behaved themselves with greatest resolution and gallantry. Surely malice it self can never suggest any thing against an action so signal and gloriously executed. I have heard it often said that His Majesty was so extreamly well pleased with Mr. Rook's conduct, bravery, and intrepidity throughout the whole of it, that he settled a pension of 1000L a year upon him. If it was not so, every impartial man will allow he deserved it, and it was none of his fault that his merit did not meet with a suitable recompense. However it be, there is this satisfaction in it, that his fame will never dye as long as there are any annals of time to record it."

Rooke never got his £1,000 a year, which was no more than imagination on the part of his biographer, but the annals of time have certainly preserved his name.

For a few days after La Hogue the *Vanguard* remained on the French coast. She was in a small squadron of twelve ships under Ashby sent by Russell to look into Havre de Grace in the hopes of finding five or six French ships from Tourville's fleet which had escaped to the eastward. They were disappointed in their quest and a fortnight later the weather, which was beginning to turn stormy, drove them back to Russell's anchorage at St. Helens.

During the next week or two there was much deliberation between the flag officers of the fleet and the generals of the army as to the next move. A suggestion to attack St. Malo and destroy the French ships which had taken shelter there was turned down because

> "it was the opinion of the flag officers that it was not practicable to attempt any thing against the enemy's ships at St. Maloe's with any part of the fleet until the town itself could be reduced by the land forces, as that ships might not receive any great annoyance from the enemy's guns in the attempt; and the general and field officers of the army were of opinion that the troops could not do any service at that place without the fleet."

A similar state of deadlock was reached over projected attacks on Brest and Rochefort and finally it was decided to keep the majority of the fleet safely at anchor in Spithead, and to send Ashby with a force of 25 ships to lie off the coast of Normandy in the hope of intercepting French vessels.

Ashby sailed two days after the Council of War had decided on this course and the *Vanguard*, now under the command of Captain John Bridges, was among his squadron. They cruised between the Ile de Basse and the French shore until the severity of the weather sent them back to St. Helens again on September 10th. During their time on the Normandy coast the ships sighted nothing, returning empty-handed. It had been hoped that they might catch the 20 ships at St. Malo should they venture out and attempt to make Brest. But the French were not to be caught with so obvious a piece of strategy. They slipped out of St. Malo on the very day the English ships returned to St. Helens, and two days later were safe again in Brest.

The *Vanguard*, on her return, was paid off for the winter at Portsmouth, being recommissioned again the following spring. She was one of the fleet under the joint command of Henry Killigrew, Sir Cloudesly Shovell, and Delavell, which escorted the huge "Smyrna" convoy of 1693, just over 400 merchantmen, as far as the south-west of Ushant, from whence they were to proceed into the Mediterranean under the guardianship of Rooke and his squadron. The main fleet returned to Torbay on June 21st, while Rooke, sailing to the southward, fell into a neatly-laid trap set for him by the French admirals, Tourville and d'Estrées, in Lagos Bay. Ninety-two of the convoy were lost and the value of their merchandise was put at over £1,000,000 sterling.   18

No sooner was the news received in England than the fleet was again ordered to sea. But it was much too late to do anything to rectify the damage. The ships cruised aimlessly off Ushant till July 13th, when a severe storm sent them home after having done considerable damage to masts and rigging. The *Vanguard* was docked at Portsmouth during September for repairs, but was found to be in such very poor condition that it was decided to send her round to Chatham, where better facilities for docking existed. She was sailed round under a jury rig, anchoring in the Medway on her arrival. There she lay for the next eight years, paid off and out of commission. With the disappearance of Louis's fleet from the seas after the end of 1693, there was no further call for her services, especially as her repairs were estimated to cost a considerable sum.

She was still there on November 26th, 1703, when for two days was fought the greatest naval battle of the war. It was not against the French, nor against any mortal enemy, but against the most disastrous storm ever known in the history of the country. For two days it raged over southern England, the wind from west-south-west and "resembling thunder at a distance and being attended with terrible flashes of lightning". The English fleet, lying in the Downs and off the Gunfleet, put to sea as best they could, there to try and ride out the enormous waves and to fight the fury of the wind. With them went thousands of merchantmen and, "for a week to come the North Sea was covered with English shipping in every sort of peril".   1

The destruction on land was as great as that on sea. The underground warehouses at Bristol were flooded by the high tide swept up by the wind and the harbour was littered with wrecked vessels. At Wells Palace Kidder, Bishop of Bath and Wells, was killed by the roof falling in as he lay in bed with his wife. In London the leads on the roofs of the churches were rolled up like great scrolls, and once again London Bridge was in danger of capsizing by the mass of barges and smaller boats, torn from their moorings and forced down against it by the ferocity of the wind. In the Palace at St. James's, Queen Anne defied her gout and, rising painfully from her bed, stood at the window with her husband and watched great avenues of ancient trees in the park being bowled over like ninepins.

The storm lasted two days and blew itself out on the 27th. But it was many days before the full loss at sea was known. Gradually, one by one, the ships came home, their sails in ribbons, their masts gone by the board. Thanks to the quality of English seamanship, the loss was not as great as was at first feared. Yet it was grievous enough, for when the full count was known, it was found that 13 men of war had gone to the bottom, carrying with them 1,519 seamen.

Among the 13 was the *Vanguard*, driven on to a mudbank in the Medway and overset. She remained there throughout the winter months, but in the early spring was refloated, pumped out, and towed up to the yard at Chatham. There she lay for seven more years, idle and neglected, until in 1711 she was reconditioned and recommissioned for service. But her only service was as guardship at the Nore, and at the end of 1712 she was paid off again.

Finally, in 1723, she ceased to be the *Vanguard*, for by a sudden whim of the Lords of the Admiralty she was re-named the *Duke*. So she passed out of the line of *Vanguards*, having added the victory of Barfleur to the ship's list of battle honours.

CHAPTER X

THE EIGHTEENTH-CENTURY PATTERN

THE fourth ship in the line of *Vanguards* was classed as a Third-rate, although she was, in fact, larger than any of the other three vessels which had previously borne her name. Unlike her immediate predecessor, she was a two-decker, with a burthen of 1,414 tons, and a total complement of 520 men. She mounted 70 guns, carrying 26 on either deck, 24-pounders on the lower and 12-pounders on the main. Fourteen 6-pounders were carried as stern-chasers on the quarter-deck and four of the same size as bow-chasers on the fore-castle. Her gun-decks were 160 feet in length, her keel 131 feet 4 inches, her extreme beam 45 feet, and depth in her hold 19 feet 4 inches. Her final cost, when ready for sea, was £25,175.

She was built at Cowes, Isle of Wight, as the result of experience gained at sea during the "War of Jenkins's Ear" against the Spaniards, 1739–1742, and the longer war to which it gave birth, that of the Austrian succession, from 1743 to 1748. It had been found then that the three-decked ships, though useful for certain special purposes, had great limitations in their employment, since they needed to be paid off and laid up through each winter. They were too unwieldy to survive successfully the stress of winter storms, and as late as 1745 Admiral Vernon was writing to the Admiralty pointing out the dangers of keeping the three-deckers at sea during the winter and enumerating the great losses in these ships from wreck and loss of masts and sails. But the Third-rates, two-decked ships carrying from 64 to 80 guns each, had proved to be an ideal size for all-round work. They were big enough to lie in the line of battle and stout enough to remain at sea in all weathers. A large number of these excellent ships were built, no fewer than 27 of them between the years 1752 and 1760. One of them was the fourth *Vanguard*.

Her time came during the Seven Years' War, that great conflict against France which set the future pattern of the British Empire and which finally wrested power at sea from France. She was with Admiral Boscawen's fleet which took Louisbourg, the key to the St. Lawrence River, in 1758. She was with Admiral Saunders's fleet which penetrated the St. Lawrence and made possible the capture of Quebec, the key to the whole of Canada, in 1759. She was with Admiral Rodney's fleet which took Martinique and Grenada from the French in 1762 and, but for Rodney's disregard of orders from London, would have been with Admiral Pocock's fleet which captured Havana from the Spanish in the same year. During those seven years of war from 1756 to 1762 she was able to play a notable part in the territorial

By courtesy of the National Maritime Museum

Sir Edward Berry, captain of the *Vanguard*, 1798
From an oil painting by Copley

By courtesy of the National Maritime Museum

The Battle of the Nile, 1798

From an oil painting by Pocock

expansion of Great Britain which was to form the greatest empire which the world has ever known.

But before looking a little more closely at her battles at sea, it is interesting to glance at the conditions under which life was lived in this fourth *Vanguard*. In some ways they were an improvement on those of the Commonwealth and Restoration periods, in some ways worse.

Her captain during these years, Robert Swanton, wore a uniform. It had been introduced into the Navy in 1748 to add some sort of regularity in a great Service in which, till then, captains and other officers had worn whatever they fancied. The colours of the uniform were blue and white, inspired it is said by the pleasing sight, in the eyes of George II, of the Duchess of Bedford's riding habit, which was blue with white facings. He had happened to admire her while riding in the park just at the time when the new uniforms were under discussion.

Swanton wore a blue coat, heavily embroidered, without a collar and with a bunch of lace at his throat. Its sleeves were on the short side with white turned-up cuffs to reveal more lace at his wrists. Under his coat he wore a white kerseymore waistcoat with long sleeves. His breeches were white and he wore white silk stockings, and on his feet were black shoes with silver buckles. On his head he carried a three-cornered hat trimmed with tarnished silver, or gold, lace. He was allowed a certain amount of discretion as to the extent of the embroidery he had on his coat and also to the amount of gold or silver lace with which he decorated his person. The buttons on his coat were of brass and engraved with a rose.

Swanton was entitled to carry 20 servants on board the *Vanguard*, four for each hundred of her complement. Not all were necessarily personal servants; many "captain's servants" were young friends or relatives obtaining their first taste of service at sea. It was a recognized method of recruitment for officers and there was always keen competition to get a boy, who wished to make the Navy his career, accepted by a captain as his servant. But most captains went to sea with at least 10 or 12 retainers on board—footmen, waiters, a tailor, a barber, musicians—even sometimes a painter if the particular captain had leanings towards art or wished to keep an elaborate record of his travels. Swanton took his own food and wine to sea with him and only on long periods of service out of sight of land did he have to rely on the ordinary provisions supplied to the ships by the Victualling agents. He lived in a spacious cabin under the quarter-deck. His lieutenants, in not quite so grand a uniform and not quite so spacious a mess, yet lived well and had cabins, made with canvas screens, on the main deck in which to sleep.

Junior officers were not so fortunate. They lived down below decks in the cockpit, a part of the ship to which daylight and fresh air never penetrated. Frequently it was alongside the store-rooms and the smell

H

of rancid butter and rotting cheese was never absent for long. Captain Edward Thompson, writing in 1756, gave some pregnant advice to young gentlemen about to go to sea, which reveals the conditions prevailing at the time.

"Here," he wrote, "are no back doors through which you can make your escape, nor any humane bosoms to alleviate your feelings; at once you resign a good table for no table, and a good bed for your length and breadth; nay, it will be thought an indulgence, too, to let you sleep where day ne'er enters, and where fresh air only comes when forced. Your light for day and night is a small candle, which is often stuck at the side of your platter at meals, for want of a better convenience; your victuals are salt, and often bad; and if you vary the mode of dressing them, you must cook yourself. I would recommend you always to have tea and sugar; the rest you must trust to, for you'll scarce find room for any more than your chest and hammock, and the latter at times you must carry on deck to defend you from small shot, unless you keep one of the sailors in fee with a little brandy (which is a good friend at sea, but always drink it mixed with water).

"Low company is the bane of all young men; but in a man of war you have the collected filth of jails. Condemned criminals have the alternative of hanging, or entering on board. There's not a vice committed on shore but is practised here. The scenes of horror and infamy on board a man of war are so many and so great that I think they must rather disgust a mind rather than allure it. I do not mean, by this advice, to have you appear a dull, inactive being, that shudders amidst these horrors. No; I would wish you to see them in their proper shapes, for, to be hated, they need to be seen. You will find some little outward appearance of religion—and Sunday prayers!—but the congregation is generally drove together (like sheep by the shepherd) by the boatswain, who neither spares oaths nor blows."

He had more to say in criticism of this lot of the young gentleman and in suggestions for better conditions, under which he might reasonable grow into the type of naval officer which the Service needed.

"The disagreeable circumstances and situations attending a subaltern officer in the Navy are so many, and so hard, that, had not the first men in the service passed the dirty road to preferment to encourage the rest, they would renounce it to a man. It is a most mistaken notion that a youth will not be a good officer unless he stoops to the most menial officer; to be bedded worse than hogs, and eat less delicacies. In short, from having experienced such scenes of filth and infamy, such fatigues and hardships, they are sufficient to disgust the stoutest and the bravest, for, alas! there is only a little hope of promotion sprinkled in the cup to make a man swallow more than he digests the rest of his life. The state of inferior officers in his Majesty's service is a state of vassalage, and a lieutenant's preferment the greatest in it; the change is at once from a filthy maggot to a shining butterfly. Many methods might be introduced to make the lower officers of more consequence on their duty, and their lives more agreeable to themselves; for that power of reducing them to sweep the decks, being lodged in the breast of a captain, is often abused through passion or caprice; besides it is too despotic an authority to exercise on a man who has the feelings of an Englishman.

"We are likewise to recollect that all commanders of men of war are not gentlemen, nor men of education. I know a great part are brave men, but a much greater, seamen. I allow the maxim of learning to obey, before we command ourselves; but still there is no reason to be vulgar, for we are to consider these young people are the active machines of duty, the wheels which give motion to the main body; and it is absolutely necessary to give them authority in their office to carry on the duties of the ship: but rendering them low in the eyes of the people creates a contempt for midshipmen in general, and turns that necessary respect due to them into contempt.

"I propose to warrant this body of officers and make them answer to the Board of Admiralty for their conduct. They should possess a third table in the ship and have the countenance of their superiors. This would enliven their servitude, and make them of consequence on their duty."

It is pleasant to record that Thompson's recommendations bore fruit after the Napoleonic wars and that the dignity of midshipmen, as junior officers, was upheld by giving them a separate mess in the gun-room.

The ordinary sailors, though their lot was immeasurably harder even than that of the junior officers, were not quite so bestial in their behaviour as Thompson suggests. Not all of them were the sweepings of the gaols, not all of them were pressed men. Quite a number used to volunteer for the naval service, attracted either by the bounty payable on joining up, sometimes as much as five pounds when men were desperately needed, or by the very real chance of earning prize money, which occasionally amounted to a considerable sum if the prize were a rich one. The men who were pressed frequently settled down well to life in a warship at sea, and a letter written by a pressed man a few years before this fourth *Vanguard* was launched brings eloquent testimony of how some of them managed to forget the brutalities of the press-gang and adapt themselves to the vagaries of sea life. It was written by a sailor in Admiral Vernon's squadron at the taking of Portobello in 1739 and addressed to his wife. Its charm is as fresh today as it was when written over 200 years ago.

"My dear Life," he wrote,
"When I left you hevens noes it was with an akin hart to be hauld from you by a gang of rufins but hover i soon overcome that when I found that we were about to go in ernest to rite my natif contry, and against a parcel of impodent Spaniards, by whom I have often been ill treted and god nows my hearrt I have longed this fore Years past to cut of some of their Ears, and was in hopes I should haf sent you one for a sample now, but our good Admiral God bless him was to merciful we have taken Port

Belo with such coridge and bravery that I never saw before, for my own
Part my heart was rased to the clouds and woud ha scaled the Moon had
a Spaniard been there to come at him, as We did the Batry. Jack cox
is my messmate you know he was always a hevy ased dog and sleepy
headed, but had you seen him clime the Walls of the Batry, you would
never forget him for a cat coud not xceed him in nimbleness, and so in
short it was with all of us I belief I myselfe coud now overcum ten
Spaniards for I remember when I was in Spain that the Spaniards calld
the Englis Galen den mare, but we shall now make them kno that we are
the Cox of the Seas for our Admiral is of true Game breed had you se us
english Salor, now what altration what countnances what bravery can
xceed us tha tell us we shall meet a French Squadron by am by but i wish it
may be so And by God well jurch um Our dear cok of an Admiral has
true english blood in his vains; and thank god all our captins and officers
haue to a Man now we are in ernes but lying in harbours and letting our
timber rot and our provision to be devoured with Rats; was bad as I haf
sene. When our canons had left of firing by order our men could hardly
forbear going on. My Dere I have got some token of Suces to show you I
wish I could have sent some of them to you. Our dear Admiral ordered
every man some Spanish Dollers to be immediately given which is like a
Man of Honour, for i had rather have 10 dollers in hand, than to have
100 for sefen Years together, and perhaps compond it at last for—owed
by me—i am and so is every Man of us resolved either to lose our lifes or
conker our enemys. true british spirit revives and by God we will support
our King and contry so long as a drap of blood remains. Jo Wilks is as
good a Sailor as the best of um, and can now bear a hand with an Able
Sailor and has vowed never to take the Shittle in hand till we have
reduced the pride of Spain help them who will the more the better true
blews will never flinch. I cant help mentoning the Soldiers we took with
us from Jamaca who were as harty cox as ever took Musket in hand and
behaved with glorious coridge but all for the honour of England, I wish
we coud se one of those Plundrers the garda costaes especially him by
whom I once met was with when i lost 16 months wages if i did not cut of
the captain's ears may I be damed my dear i am well getting money
Wages secure, and all Revenge on my Enemies, fiteing for my King and
Country.

i am Your for ever."

Naturally there were some hard cases in every ship; the method
of recruitment made certain of that. But a good captain who treated
his men justly and with humanity could very easily make a ship a
happy one. Much has been written, and quoted, of the savagery of
the sailor's life during the second half of the 18th century, but these
cases on the whole were the exception rather than the rule. Some
captains, it is true, made their ships into living hells for the seamen,
having recourse to the "cat" on the slightest provocation, and inventing
in addition a number of other punishments, "all more or less beastly
and hurting", as their ingenuity could devise. Nor is it difficult, among
the records of the courts-martial of the times, to find instances of men
being ordered 300, 400, or even 500 lashes with the cat-o'-nine-tails.

But it should be remembered that it was these few cases which attracted the public eye and that for each brutal captain there were a score or more who were humane and kindly men.

Discipline on board a man of war was strict, necessarily so when a proportion of her crew inevitably came from the gaols. On the whole the better elements of a ship's company approved the strictness, for it kept in check the troubles which an unruly minority could cause in a ship. It was an age, too, of general inhumanity, when men ashore flocked in their thousands to see mains at cock-fighting, the baiting of bulls and bears, or to enjoy fights between specially-trained savage dogs. Human life was held cheaply in those days and the savagery of a sentence of 500 lashes with the cat did not make the heart run cold then as the thought of it does now.

Victuals in the fleet were still a source of trouble. Fresh provisions were difficult to procure and the methods of preserving food for a long voyage were still crude. Complaints from sea were still numerous and would-be reformers flooded the country with pamphlets calling for an enquiry in Parliament into the scandals. A typical one, dated 1761, produces the following evidence about the food supplied to the Navy:

"As a few more circumstances to prove how indispensably necessary it is that a Parliamentary enquiry should be made into that part of the public money which is appropriated for the victualling of the Navy, I shall therefore introduce the following, viz:

"That mariners in the King's ships have frequently put their 24 hours' allowance of salt provisions into their tobacco-boxes.

"That seamen in the King's ships have made buttons for their jackets and trowses with the cheese they were served with, having preferred it, by reason of its tough and durable quality, to buttons made of common metal; and that carpenters in the Navy-Service have made trucks to their ships' flagstaffs with whole cheeses, which have stood the weather equally with any timber.

"That the flour in the King's ships has been devoured by weevils, and become so intolerably musty, and cemented into such hard rocks, that the men have been obliged to use instruments, with all their feeble power, to break and pulverise it before they could make use of it, as though, in a comparative degree, they had been stubbing to pieces the ruins of an old fortification.

"That their bread has been so full of large black-headed maggots and that they have so nauseated the thoughts of it, as to be obliged to shut their eyes to confine that sense from being offended before they could bring their minds into a resolution of consuming it.

"That their beer has stunk as abominably as the foul stagnant water which is pumped out of many cellars in London at midnight hour; and that they were under a necessity of shutting their eyes, and stopping their breath by holding of their noses before they could conquer their aversion, so as to prevail upon themselves in their extreme necessities to drink it.

"That the same provisions have been issued from His Majesty's

Victualling Office which have been rejected by the officers of the ships they were sent to, and afterwards returned to the said Office and issued again three times to different ships belonging to His Majesty before they could be passed off, because they were so extremely bad.

"That the pork, which the Fleet under the command of the late Admiral Boscawen was served with, was so rotten, that when boiled it wasted away to mere rags and crumbs, so that it could be eaten with a spoon, and that when the liquor it had been boiled in was drawn off, it flowed out of the cock of the ship's boiler like curds and whey: it was also so nauseous that it made the men sick who did eat of it; and therefore resolving to fast rather than eat any more of it, they have thrown it privately out of their ship's port-holes to prevent being discovered by the officers of their ship."

Even worse than the food, if possible, was the water. It was stored in large casks in the hold and soon went slimy and putrid. There was no known way of distilling fresh water from salt and a ship had to wait till she made the land before she could renew her supply from rivers and streams.

Contemporary documents also talk of the evil smells on board. They arose partly from the bilges, partly from the smell of food in the store-rooms. Since ventilation was almost unknown the foul odours would hang about the ship more or less permanently. Men were even known to have died of asphyxiation from the dreadful stench below decks, Boscawen, for instance, reporting three men suffocated in his ship, the *Namur*, when they passed close to the well of the ship while the bilges were being pumped out.

The food, the water, and the foul air on board were all conducive to an excessive rate of sickness in the fleet. Scurvy was the greatest scourge of the period, the men dying by hundreds during a long cruise. It was caused by the salt provisions and by the almost total lack of fresh vegetables and fruit. After a single voyage across the Atlantic in 1756, the *Stirling Castle*, for instance, "had now one hundred and fifty-nine people ill in fluxes, scurvies, and fevers", out of a total complement of 480 men. And that was not an unduly high proportion for the times.

Drunkenness was an evil that was to endure for another 30 or 40 years, and the moral behaviour, both of officers and men, left a lot to be desired by modern standards. Women were still allowed on board in harbour and, indeed, frequently accompanied the ships to sea. Thompson, mentioning in his letters how he had found that the West Indian negroes were highly malodorous, wrote: "But bad smells don't hurt the sailor's appetite, each man possessing a temporary lady, whose pride is in her constancy to the man she chooses; and in this particular they are strictly so. I have known 350 women sup and sleep on board on a Sunday evening, and return at daybreak to their different plantations."

Such was the pattern of life on board the fourth *Vanguard* during those strenuous years between 1756 and 1762. It was rough and hard, but it had its compensations, even though they were not the compensations which might appear desirable today. Drink was plentiful, women were easy, and during a war it was an extremely unfortunate ship that did not earn for its men a reasonable amount of prize money in addition to their wages.

CHAPTER XI

THE SEVEN YEARS' WAR

By October, in the year 1754, the leisurely peace which had been ushered in on a war-torn Europe by the signing of the Treaty of Aix-la-Chapelle in 1748 was once again in danger. Aix-la-Chapelle had brought the War of the Austrian Succession to an end, but had left in abeyance those issues which divided the British and the French in the North American continent. They were to be settled by peaceful negotiation, but as is so often the way in negotiation, they had become bogged down in an indiscriminate mass of paper. The original point at issue had been reasonably clear—a settled line of demarcation between the French settlements in Canada and the English colonies further south between Pennsylvania and Virginia. Eighteenth-century diplomacy, however, was unequal to the task.

For six years learned lawyers had been adding to the confusion by writing long treatises on trading rights, on the law of prior discovery, on the effects of obscure treaties signed with the Indians in past years, on anything which could conceivably be thought to bring some point of vantage to one side or the other. Interminable letters had passed between the negotiators, and under the mass of paper thus accumulated the original dispute lay obscured and unresolved.

It was all brought to a head by the dream of the French Governor, Galissoniere, assisted after 1753 by the Marquis Duquesne, who had been sent from France to succeed him and carry out his plans. Galissoniere had had visions of a new French empire in the west, based upon the occupation of Canada and a claim to the mouth of the Mississippi, where the little town of New Orleans had been established. If this claim could be extended to embrace the whole of that great river, the British colonies could be restricted in their growth westward and all the rest of the continent brought under the French flag. It was a vision that found immediate acceptance at Versailles, for it would not only add considerably to French possessions overseas, but would also curb British expansion and, if successful, give the old enemy a nasty blow to her pride.

In Galissoniere's eyes, the problem offered few difficulties. The French could probably substantiate their claim to the Mississippi and to its tributary rivers, which would bring them as far north as the head waters of the Ohio. From Canada, they could claim as their boundary the St. Lawrence and the Great Lakes. There remained but the narrow strip between the southern shore of Lake Erie and the head waters of the Ohio. What could be simpler than to build there a chain of forts in what, at the best, was little more than no man's land?

Duquesne was just the man to carry out Galissoniere's dream. He set about the task with energy and by mid-April of 1754 needed but one more fort to complete the chain. And here, just in the nick of time, he was forestalled. The Government of Virginia, awake at last to the French danger, decided to build their own fort on the Alleghany River and so keep open a doorway to the west. In the course of the building they were surprised by the French and driven out by Duquesne's men. On the foundations which the Virginians had made for their own fort, Duquesne built the last of his chain and named it after himself, Fort Duquesne. But in doing so he had committed the first act of the Seven Years' War and, though no declaration was to follow for another two years, there was unofficial war between France and England.

A second unofficial act of war came during the following year. The British agent in Brest furnished the Government at home with a list of the French squadron at Brest and Rochefort, reporting that they were well advanced and that they would be sailing with reinforcements to Canada in April. A fleet was hurriedly got together and placed under the command of Admiral Boscawen, whose explicit orders were, should he fall in with any French ships of war or other vessels having on board troops or warlike stores, to "do your best to take possession of them. In case resistance should be made, you will employ the means at your disposal to capture and destroy them." But the fog was to defeat Boscawen and only two French ships were taken. The rest got safely into Louisbourg and Quebec. A second act of war had been committed and relations between the two countries became more and more strained. Yet even now the declaration of war was delayed and it was not until the French landed in the Island of Minorca in April of the following year that a formal declaration was made.

The *Vanguard's* first taste of action came in 1757, when she was one of a fleet of 15 sail of the line, under the command of Hawke and Boscawen, which was sent out in an attempt to intercept a home-coming French squadron from Canada. The British ships sailed from Spithead on October 22nd, bound for a rendezvous off Ushant, but shortly after their arrival there they were scattered by a storm. For three days the wind was at gale force, blowing from the west, and that same gale which swept the English ships off their station carried the French squadron, under the command of M. Dubois de la Motte, through Hawke's rendezvous. They were unobserved, except by one English ship, which caught a fleeting glimpse of the enemy on November 23rd. She was the *Vanguard*, with Robert Swanton as her captain, and she squared away before the wind in chase of the flying French.

For some hours she was in action with three or four of the French ships, but it was at long range and little damage was done on either side. De la Motte was more intent on bringing his squadron safe home to Brest than in exchanging broadsides with a British ship, even though she were alone, for he knew that Hawke and Boscawen were somewhere in the neighbourhood and he had no desire to force a general engagement. Though Hawke had not yet fought the Battle of Quiberon Bay, nor Boscawen that of Lagos, their reputations were sufficiently well-known to daunt even the most courageous of French admirals. The French fleet, by reason of their superior sailing qualities, had little difficulty in shaking off the *Vanguard* and making Brest in safety. Swanton rejoined the rest of the fleet off Ushant and, after reporting the escape of the French, sailed back with it to England, reaching Spithead on December 15th.

She was, however, not to remain at home for long. Pitt, the great Prime Minister to whom England owed so much of her empire, was even now fired by the same dreams which had caused Galissoniere to recommend the erection of forts in North America. He could appreciate the immense value of a victory in Canada to the cause for which the country was fighting and his mind was already engaged on the possibilities of something far beyond the defeat of the French and the driving of them back to their own boundaries in Canada. This was the conquest of the whole country, his "Glorious Enterprise" as he called it.

It called for a great deal of planning and a patience that could wait for two years before the result could be brought to final completion. As Pitt saw it, the key to the St. Lawrence was Louisbourg, on the Island of Cape Breton, and its capture must be the first step in the great plan. If that could be followed by the taking of Quebec from the sea and by the taking of Montreal from the land, then the whole of Canada must fall.

So Pitt made his plans. Early in 1758 he selected his favourite admiral, Boscawen, for the command of a fleet which was to take Louisbourg. General Abercrombie was sent out to take over command of the army from Lord Loudoun, with instructions to invade Canada by way of Lake George and Lake Champlain. The "Glorious Enterprise" was afoot.

The *Vanguard* was one of Boscawen's fleet, though she sailed for the New World in advance of the main squadron. She was with Rear-Admiral Sir Charles Hardy, who flew his flag in the *Captain*, and left in company with her for Halifax in January. Hardy's orders were to take under his command those ships which were wintering at Halifax and to institute a close blockade of Louisbourg as soon as the weather would permit. Boscawen followed with the main fleet and the troop transports on February 19th. In command of the land forces for the attack on Louisbourg was Major-General Amherst, with Brigadier James Wolfe as his second in command.

Hardy, with the *Captain* and the *Vanguard* and the other ships he found at Halifax, established a close blockade off Louisbourg during March. It was maintained with considerable difficulty in face of the fog and gales which are so distinct a feature of the Canadian spring.

At one period during April a westerly gale drove the British ships back to Halifax, and it was at this exact period that a French squadron under M. de Chaffault arrived off the coast after slipping out of Brest unobserved. Finding the way into Louisbourg unexpectedly clear Chaffault left there six sail of the line to assist in the defence and with the rest of his squadron entered the St. Lawrence and continued up to Quebec. Hardy managed to capture one small ship, the *Foudroyant* of 22 guns, but the remainder reached their destination in safety.

So, when Boscawen arrived at Halifax on May 9th, he found Louisbourg reinforced and the garrison heartened by the receipt of stores from France. He set about his task with characteristic energy. By the 28th he had collected his unwieldy flotilla, numbering no fewer than 167 ships and anchored them in Gabarus Bay, about six miles west of Louisbourg. No sooner were the anchors on the bottom than he had the ships' boats away taking soundings and reconnoitring for a possible landing-place. His speed at first rather disconcerted the easy-going Amherst, who was brought up in the leisurely siege technique of contemporary military thought, but it found an enthusiastic supporter in Wolfe.

"Wasted no time," wrote Boscawen in his journal. "Sent the generals ashore to reconnoitre, ordered all launches and pinnaces to be manned and armed. Sent the boats away to make an alarm in order to thereby discover where the strength of the enemy's force was posted. Between 10 and 11 saw some rockets thrown from the boats."

It was decided to attempt a landing at Cormorant Cove, in the Bay, and to risk the fury of the French fire. Three days later Boscawen gave the order and the boats went in, "but the swell running so very high and breaking so strong upon the shore", the whole operation had to be postponed.

A second attempt was made early in the morning of June 8th and once again the soldiers were crowded into the boats of the fleet.

"At 4 o'clock," wrote Boscawen, "I saw the boats rowing towards the shore with the troops, and the sun's rising, the *Kennington* and *Halifax*, frigates, began to fire upon the enemy to cover the landing, which was instantly followed by the *Sutherland* and the rest of the frigates placed ashore. At about 5 o'clock the enemy began a very smart fire at the boats with both cannon and small arms, which continued about 15 minutes, when it ceased, part of the troops having landed and driven the enemy out of their entrenchments."

The landing, in fact, did not go as smoothly as Boscawen's journal suggests. Wolfe was in the first flight of boats and, as they approached the shore, they were met with a furious reception from the French. So hot was the fire that Wolfe was convinced that the landing there was impossible and ordered the boats to return. Just at that moment, two subalterns noticed a strip of beach which was masked from the French fire and, making a dash for it, got successfully ashore. They attracted Wolfe's attention and he, quick to see the possibilities, directed the boats to follow the first two. It was rough off the little beach, with rocks strewn in the entrance. Several of the boats were broken to pieces on the rocks and many men drowned, but sufficient were got ashore to withstand the first charge of the French grenadiers when they discovered the landing. Soon more were ashore and the French driven back into their trenches. And as further troops were landed, threatening to cut the French retreat, the defenders broke from their positions and made the best of their way back to the town.

With the army safely ashore, the fleet was busy landing guns and stores, keeping a close blockade on the harbour and bombarding the fortifications of the town and the French ships lying in the port. Amherst, ever a cautious soldier, made a slow, plodding advance against the fortifications, throwing up breastworks, mining and tunnelling, establishing his batteries stage by stage and drawing a slow, yet ever-closing cord round the throat of the French defence. Such operations had been hallowed by time and were in the approved Continental fashion. Wolfe, more dashing, marched his brigade round the bay under cover of a fog and managed to occupy the eastern arm of the harbour. There, taking the high ground with a spirited assault, he set up a battery of naval guns landed by the sailors of the fleet and began a harassing fire on the French defences.

The *Vanguard*, having assisted in covering the initial landing in Gabarus Bay, was sent by Boscawen to rejoin Hardy off the town. The French governor of Louisbourg, the Chevalier de Drucour, alarmed by this show of force and knowing something of the methods of British naval attacks, promptly closed the entrance of the harbour by sinking the *Apollon*, *Fidèle*, *Biche*, and *Chevre* in the channel. Inside the now blocked port were five more ships, the *Entreprenant*, of 74 guns, *Celèbre*, 64, *Capricieux*, 64, *Prudent*, 74, and *Bienfaisant*, 64. On Saturday, July 22nd, Boscawen

"observed a large explosion in the harbour which proved to be the *Entreprenant*, of 74 guns, blown up by a shot from our Marines battery. She fell athwart the *Celebre* and *Capricieux* of 64 guns and burnt them, and at half past 8 observed a large smoak to arise which proved to be the barracks on fire."

Louisbourg was now nearing the end of its resistance, though it had stood the siege much longer than had at first been hoped. Pitt's original plan had called for the quick capture of Louisbourg, to be followed the same year by the assault on Quebec. The time-table was sadly upset, partly by Boscawen's slow voyage across the Atlantic, partly by the dilatory tactics of Amherst. Of the first Wolfe wrote that :

"From Christopher Columbus's time to our own days there perhaps has never been a more extraordinary voyage. The continual opposition of contrary winds, calms, or currents, baffled all our skill and wore out all our patience."

and of the second:

"Our next operations were exceeding slow and injudicious, owing partly to the difficulty of landing our stores and artillery, and partly to the ignorance and inexperience of our engineers."

Nor was Boscawen entirely blameless for the delay. As early as June 25th he could have entered the harbour with the fleet and destroyed the French ships, Wolfe having by then silenced the batteries on the eastern arm of the harbour. It seems as though Boscawen, perhaps with memories of his commission as a Major-General in the Army during his abortive campaign in the East Indies the previous year, fancied the military side more than the naval. Certainly he spent more time ashore with the army than afloat with the navy, and denuded the fleet of men, guns, stores, and boats to help on Amherst and Wolfe.

"Mr. Boscawen," wrote Wolfe, "has given all and even more than we could ask of him. He has furnished arms and ammunition, pioneers, sappers, miners, gunners, carpenters, and boats, and is, I must confess, no bad *fantassin* himself, and an excellent back-hand at a siege."

As a model of harmonious co-operation between Navy and Army, Louisbourg stands out in vivid contrast against the bickering and confusion of former amphibious attempts, but it was woefully slow.

Finally, on the night of July 25th, Boscawen again turned his thoughts to the naval side of the operations. He planned a brilliant and daring little operation which, if successful, could hardly fail to bring the complete surrender of the town. And successful it was. The boats of the fleet, manned by sailors from Hardy's squadron, rowed into the harbour to cut out the two remaining French ships. The *Prudent*, being aground, was set on fire and burned to the waterline, the *Bienfaisant* was towed out after her capture and made a prize.

It was the end of the French resistance. At ten o'clock on the 26th, all firing ceased and articles of capitulation were signed by Drucour. The English flag was hoisted in the garrison on the following day and the key to the St. Lawrence was safe in British hands. But it was too late for any thoughts of Quebec that year, for the season was now far advanced and ice would close the river before the fleet could be got up. That it would close it to the French, too, was a cheering thought and provided at least one grain of comfort over the unduly prolonged operations off Louisbourg. Pitt's plans were not necessarily endangered by the delays, merely postponed. With Louisbourg in

British hands, he could look forward to 1759 with something of confidence, for the first important step in the "Glorious Enterprise" had been successfully taken.

With Louisbourg was surrendered the whole island of Cape Breton and also that of St. John, renamed Prince Edward Island. The capture of the town had provided 3,600 French prisoners and 216 French guns. At St. John's Island another 5,000 prisoners were gathered in. Eleven French warships, mounting in all 498 guns, were sunk, taken, or burnt, and the total British losses were 525 officers and men.

On August 31st Boscawen detached Hardy to cruise in the mouth of the St. Lawrence. With him were the *Royal William, Bedford, Vanguard, Devonshire, Lancaster*, four frigates, and 10 transports filled with soldiers under Wolfe. Hardy's orders were to do as much damage to the French settlements in the river as possible before it froze up for the winter. The squadron was responsible for the burning of 125 houses, and 176 fishing boats and the destruction of all the fish and gear in the French fishing stations round the St. Lawrence estuary. Many prisoners were taken as well and on the completion of this raiding expedition the ships returned to Halifax. During October the *Vanguard* was out cruising off Newfoundland, Cape Race and St. Paul Island, the Belle Isle Straits, and the Bay of Fundy, in search of French warships. But the seas were empty of the enemy and, with the icing up of the St. Lawrence in November and in the sure knowledge that no ship, French or British, could now reach Quebec, she returned to Halifax, to spend the winter there with a few other men of war under the command of Rear-Admiral Philip Durell.

As the new year came round Pitt returned to his darling project with all the old force and skill. With Boscawen now appointed as Commander-in-Chief in the Mediterranean, the man he chose to direct the naval side of the operations against Quebec was Vice-Admiral Charles Saunders, an appointment which was heartily approved by Lord Anson, the First Sea Lord. Saunders had been with Anson in his great voyage of circumnavigation 20 years before and he held the old man's confidence to a remarkable degree. For the operations ashore there was one man who stood out head and shoulders above all others, Wolfe. His brilliance at the capture of Louisbourg was enough to secure that, and Pitt made no mistake in his choice.

At the very start of the year orders were sent to Durell in Halifax to take his ships into the St. Lawrence at the earliest possible moment and to prevent at all costs any French ship from reaching Quebec. So important was this point that Pitt himself wrote to Saunders asking him

"to take the earliest opportunity to renew the said orders in the strongest manner, as nothing can be so essential to the success of the important expedition against Quebec as effectually blocking up the river St. Lawrence as early in the year as shall be practicable."

The land attack was, at the same time, to be pressed to its utmost to bring the French under attack from two sides.

Saunders's fleet, carrying Wolfe and 9,200 soldiers, sailed from Spithead on February 17th, confident that, on the arrival of the ships, they would find Durell and his squadron in the St. Lawrence, denying it to the French. Intelligence of a French convoy bound for Quebec had been received before Saunders sailed, but it had caused little concern in view of the stringent orders sent to Durell. Indeed, it was hoped and expected that the convoy had fallen into Durell's hands.

As Saunders approached Halifax on April 30th, he saw the masts and yards of ships lying in the harbour. They were Durell's. Saunders and Wolfe were furious, for the delay in blocking the St. Lawrence might well have let the French reinforcements through. Durell had been waiting for definite news of the break-up of the ice in the St. Lawrence before taking his squadron there. It was a faulty piece of reasoning, for the news would certainly take some days to reach him at Halifax and still more days would elapse before he could arrive with his squadron on his station. He must have realized that they were vital days in the execution of the plan, if only from the repeated stringency of his orders.

Saunders immediately ordered Durell to sea and he sailed the same day with the *Princess Amelia, Vanguard, Captain, Devonshire, Pembroke, Prince of Orange, Centurion, Sutherland,* and six frigates. But he was too late. The damage had been done and the convoy from France had entered the river and reached Quebec before the British ships arrived to stop them. It was a bitter blow to Saunders and Wolfe and hardly an auspicious start to the great adventure.

But if Durell had failed in his main task, he made noble amends. Instead of leaving his big ships at the Isle of Bic, the rendezvous fixed with Saunders, he had pushed on with his whole squadron to the Isle of Coudres, 100 miles farther up the river and only 65 miles below Quebec itself. He had lain here for 10 days, sending ashore a battalion of soldiers to occupy and fortify the island. Not content with that, he had pushed on yet farther. This was a formidable task, for 20 miles above the island lay the infamous "traverses" of the river through which, in the opinion of Canadians, no large ship could pass without a local pilot. Yet Durell did it, sending up the *Vanguard, Pembroke,* and *Sutherland,* with the *Mercury* frigate, and buoying the difficult channels for the fleet which was following him under Saunders. The three ships of the line had been led up by the *Mercury,* whose master was James Cook. It was this same Cook who, 20 years later, was to write his name even more boldly in the pages of history by his three great voyages into the Pacific, his discovery of Australia and New Zealand, and his pioneer work in stamping out the scourge of scurvy from the Navy.

When Saunders arrived at the Isle of Bic and found that Durell had gone on up-river, he made the decision which was to stamp him as one of the greatest, if not the best known, of English admirals. The plan originally had been for the battle fleet to remain off the St. Lawrence and Louisbourg, sending only the smaller ships up to Quebec with Wolfe. But as a result of unavoidable delays because of fogs and the late breaking of the ice, Wolfe's timetable was falling sadly behind schedule. There was also the set-back of the French convoy which had slipped through. Saunders therefore decided to take his whole fleet up-river as far as the Isle of Coudres, and leaving only the largest of his ships there, carry on with the remainder in the path which Durell had set. It was a feat which was considered impossible by the Canadians.

On June 5th the *Vanguard* and her three companions had reached the Isle d'Orleans, at the entrance to the Quebec basin. Their arrival through the treacherous rapids of the river had given the French their first premonitions of coming disaster. And where Durell had led, Saunders could follow. As the great fleet worked up-river, mile by mile, its steady advance brought an added chill to the defenders of Quebec. The "traverses" were successfully negotiated and on June 27th Saunders, with most of his fleet and all the transports, had joined the *Vanguard*, *Pembroke*, and *Sutherland* at the Isle d'Orleans. It was a superb feat of seamanship.

Saunders's next move was even more remarkable. On the night of July 18th he sent the *Sutherland*, the *Diana*, and the *Squirrel*, under cover of Wolfe's batteries, up-river past Quebec. The narrow channel past the town itself was dominated by French guns, but so completely unprepared was the defence for this move that the ships were past before the enemy gunners had time to find the range. Only the *Diana* failed, running aground opposite the town. She was got off in the morning and brought down-river to safety, though badly damaged by the French fire.

Wolfe now decided to launch his attack above the town. On the night of the 20th orders were given for nine companies of grenadiers, all the artillery, and 1,400 seamen and marines to be ready for embarkation in two hours time. There was immense preparation in the fleet, boats being got ready and landing parties arranged. An hour later the whole operation was cancelled, only to be revived again after another hour had passed. Once again it was countermanded, and the indecision began to breed despondency in the fleet.

"Within the space of five hours," wrote one of the *Vanguard's* officers, "we received at the General's request three different orders of consequence which were contradicted immediately after their reception to the no small amazement of everyone who has taken the liberty of thinking. . . . I am told that he (Wolfe) asks no one's opinion."

Wolfe, indeed, was playing a lone hand. He was moody, ill, worried, and even dispirited. He was impatient of advice from his

By courtesy of the National Maritime Museum

The French flagship *L'Orient* blowing up, 1798
From a line engraving after P. J. de Loutherbourg

By courtesy of the Parker Gallery, 2 Albemarle Street, London

The sixth *Vanguard* firing a salute in the Channel

From a lithograph by H. J. Vernon-Day and Haghe

juniors and turned down with abrupt discourtesy a suggested plan of attack submitted by the three Brigadiers under him. Certainly, the task facing him was immense. Montcalm, the French commander, was firmly established with his troops on the Heights of Abraham, above Quebec, and there seemed no possible way to come at him. The town itself was under a heavy bombardment, both from batteries erected ashore and from the ships of the fleet, but Quebec looked as far from capture as ever it had done. A more effective enemy than Montcalm, even, was the approaching autumn. Time was running short and it could not be long now before the Canadian climate brought a complete stop to all operations. It was a desperate Wolfe who turned over and over in his restless brain the ways and means of attack.

He could not know that, just as he was worrying about the means of bringing the French to action, so Montcalm was also worrying as to the best way of parrying the expected attack. On August 31st Saunders managed to get some more of his ships above Quebec, the *Seahorse*, *Lowestoft*, and *Hunter*, and their progress up-river caused Montcalm to doubt the strength of his original dispositions and to wonder whether the main attack were not to be directed some miles above Quebec. He, too, was becoming rattled. Against all the teachings of military strategy he divided his forces and sent a large number of men up-river to keep a watch on the English ships there. It was the chance for which Wolfe had been waiting.

During one of his many personal reconnaissances to study the ground, Wolfe had noticed a cleft in the cliffs on the northern bank of the river, known as the Anse du Foulon. He now set out to study it again, wearing a private's greatcoat over his uniform to disguise his interest from the French. He was seen and reported both to Montcalm and Bougainville, who was in command of the party detached to watch the ships up the river. There were, wrote the French officer who noticed the reconnaissance, "*beaucoup d'officiers vêtus de plusieurs couleurs. Il y en avait un qui dessous un surtout bleu était fort galonné*". The officer *fort galonné*, heavily decorated, of course was Wolfe. He had seen all he had wanted, and fortunately neither Montcalm nor Bougainville heeded the warning of the reported reconnaissance. The date was September 11th, and Wolfe's study of the Anse du Foulon had shown him that the path looked practicable though at one point it was broken. It would mean a tough scramble for his soldiers, but it was not for nothing that he had asked for a regiment of Highlanders to be included in his command.

Wolfe, his mind made up at last, wasted no time. On the following day, after a brief conference with Saunders, he gave orders for the attempt to be made that night. Boats were concentrated and manned, soldiers, guns, and necessary equipment embarked, detailed orders sent to the ships above Quebec, and Captain Chads told off to command the boats. The arrangements for the naval side of the operation were

I

in the hands of Rear-Admiral Holmes, who was in the *Sutherland* above Quebec.

Of the Navy's part in the battle which won Quebec, and indirectly all Canada, for Great Britain, little has been written. Most of its work was dull and undramatic, and largely eclipsed by the drama that was subsequently played out on the Heights of Abraham. Yet without it, Wolfe could not have mounted his attack. It was in the boats of the fleet, under Chads, that the soldiers were put ashore on the north bank. His task had been to bring the boats down, silently and without giving any sign to the French, through 15 miles of racing river in the darkest part of the night, and to land the soldiers at the exact spot a little before daybreak. It called for an exactness and a precision that only the Navy knew how to provide. Chads accomplished his difficult task to perfection. He had one stroke of good fortune on the way down, learning from the *Hunter*, which he passed, the French challenge and reply for the night. It worked admirably as the boats swept past the enemy sentries, and they were able to reach the Anse du Foulon undetected.

There the sailors formed a living chain up the narrow and precipitous path, helping the soldiers to reach the top. Then, their work still not done, they manhandled the heavy guns up the steep slope, first the military pieces and then, in case there should not be sufficient, a number of naval 24-pounders to assist in the assault. In the meanwhile, Saunders had brought up the ships of the fleet as close to the walls of the citadel as he could, ready in the morning to bombard the lower town with every gun that could be brought to bear.

At ten o'clock Wolfe's action against Montcalm on the Heights of Abraham was begun. Exactly one hour later his corpse was carried up the gangway of the *Lowestoft*. But by then the battle had been won. Montcalm, like Wolfe, was lying dead and the beaten French were streaming back from the field towards the gates of Quebec.

The town itself held out for another 16 days, hoping against hope for relief by one of the many French forces in the neighbourhood. But Brigadier Townshend, who succeeded Wolfe in the military command, turned a stern front towards the French hurrying towards Quebec and effectively prevented any communication with the city. In Quebec itself the end had come. The garrison, half starved and desperate, could fight no more and on the 29th the Union Jack was flying from the battlements.

It had been as successful an operation as that of Boscawen and Amherst at the taking of Louisbourg the previous year. Both had been achieved by a perfect understanding between the naval and military commanders and by the unflagging efforts of every sailor and soldier, working together in complete harmony.

"I should be wanting," wrote Townshend in his final despatch to Pitt, "in paying my due respects to the admirals and naval service if I neglected this occasion of acknowledging how much we are indebted for our success to the constant assistance and support received, and the perfect harmony and correspondence which has prevailed throughout all our operation in the uncommon difficulties which the nature of this country presents to military operations of a great extent, and which no army can in itself solely supply. The immense labour on the transportation of artillery stores and provisions, the long watchings in boats, the drawing of our artillery even in the heat of the action, it is my duty, short as my command has been, to acknowledge for that time how great a share the navy has had in this successful campaign."

As soon as Quebec had fallen, Saunders's task was over. He sent Durell home with the larger ships and himself followed a week later on October 11th, leaving the *Northumberland* and four more ships of the line at Halifax for the winter, and the *Oxford* at Quebec. She was to remain there and prevent any movement of the French frigates higher up the river—those which had got up ahead of Durell in the spring—until the winter season and its attendant ice made all movement on the river impossible. Colonels Murray and Burton were left in command of the garrison at Quebec, with as many provisions as could be spared from the fleet. They would have to hold the town until relief could come the following spring and the third and final stage of Pitt's "Glorious Enterprise" put into operation.

Saunders's share of the capture of Quebec is often forgotten and he himself is denied in history the real place to which his brilliance entitles him. Sir Julian Corbett, in his excellent book, *England in the Seven Years' War*, pays him a worthy tribute.

"The feat," he wrote, "which the French privateers accomplished in forcing their way through the ice ahead of our advanced division was a brilliant one, but what Saunders had accomplished quite overshadowed it. To carry such a fleet as his up such a river, to maintain it there for three months in spite of gales and batteries and two attacks by fireships, to preserve it in perfect harmony with the sister service, to judge and take every risk soberly, and yet to the extremity of daring; and finally, to bring it forth again at the last moment with the loss of but one ship, was a stroke of conduct without parallel. It is enough to have placed him in the first rank of sea commanders. But by the frailty of human judgment such a place can only be won by a successful action—a test which often has not called forth a tithe of the admiralship which Saunders's more sober triumph entailed. Though he lacked the genius of Wolfe, his hand throughout was the surer of the two; and, dazzling as was the final stroke by which Wolfe snatched victory from failure, the steadier flame of Saunders's exploit is worthy to burn beside it without loss of radiance for all time."

While Saunders and Wolfe were bringing to a successful close the attack on Quebec, England's cause was prospering in other seas. Hawke, watching the French in Brest, was in a few days to fight his great battle at Quiberon Bay. Boscawen, in the Mediterranean, had chased the Toulon fleet under M. de la Clue and caught it at Lagos, destroying over half of it and sending the remainder to be blocked up at Cadiz. In Indian waters Admiral Pocock was fighting his long-drawn-out duel with M. d'Aché, consolidating the advantages which Clive had won at Plassey and Admiral Watson at Calcutta. It was indeed the *annus mirabilis* and well might Englishmen sing, "Come cheer up my lads, 'tis to glory we steer". The Hearts of Oak had carried all before them.

On his way home a gale struck Saunders's ships and scattered them. Only three were in company on November 19th, when he was within 50 miles of the Lizard, the *Somerset,* in which he was flying his flag, the *Vanguard,* and the *Devonshire.* On that day he fell in with the frigate *Juno* and from her learnt that Admiral Conflans was out with his fleet and that Hawke was hot in pursuit of him. At once he turned back to the south-westward.

> "I have only time," he wrote to Pitt, "to acquaint you that I am making the best of my way in quest of Sir Edward Hawke, which I hope His Majesty will approve of."

It was a move typical of the man, wearied as he was with the North American campaign and with his three ships torn by storm.

> "The part," wrote Lord Hardwicke, "which Admiral Saunders has taken voluntarily is, I think, the greatest I ever heard of."

And even the vitriolic Horace Walpole, whose cutting wit was so often directed against the reigning admirals and generals, was moved to praise.

> "That admiral," he wrote of Saunders, "was a pattern of most steady bravery, united with the most unaffected modesty. No man said less or deserved more."

Saunders and his ships were just too late to join in that exciting action at Quiberon Bay. He heard news of the victory as he reached Morbihan. He turned again and made for home, and the *Vanguard* dropped anchor at Spithead early in December. The "wonderful year" of 1759 had closed with the victory of Quiberon Bay, and all round the world, from India to Canada, the French had been defeated. "It will soon be as shameful," wrote Walpole, "to beat a Frenchman as to beat a woman."

The war, which had gone so well in 1759, went even better in 1760, though for a moment in Canada it was touch and go. The garrison left in Quebec had been unmolested throughout the winter, but with the arrival of spring and a return of campaigning weather, its situation

was causing anxiety. Supplies were running short and the attacks
on the last French stronghold of Montreal from the land side, under
Amherst and Haviland, were making such slow progress that no help
for Quebec could be counted on from them. And there were still
those French frigates which had given Durell the slip in 1759. Once
the river was free of ice they could operate above the town on the
French flank and so bring Quebec under two fires. Nor was this all,
for the lack of fresh vegetables and fruit throughout the winter had
brought on a severe attack of scurvy in the garrison. Murray's 9,000
men were reduced by the sickness to no more than 3,000 fit for action.

Quebec's situation now was desperate, and the French knew it.
De Levis, Montcalm's successor in command of the army, concentrated his troops on the Heights of Abraham, there to wait for the
inevitable fall of the town should help be late in coming. Murray, in
desperation, wrote to Amherst to say that he would hold out as long
as possible, but that if he could not do so he would retire to the Isle
d'Orleans and there await reinforcements. His letter, which was sent
on to Pitt, caused consternation in England.

While the situation in Quebec was giving rise to such anxiety,
two squadrons were crossing the Atlantic, each unknown to the other.
One was French, bringing reinforcements and supplies to the forces
in Canada. The other was English and under the command of Swanton,
now promoted to Commodore, in the *Vanguard*. He was also bringing
reinforcements and supplies to Canada. The fate of Quebec hung on
the first to arrive.

Murray held on gallantly in Quebec. De Levis, using the path
discovered by Wolfe, brought his frigates down to the Anse du Foulon
and began to haul up siege guns and stores, preparatory to his attack
on the town. Progress was slow, for Murray made a number of sorties
with his little garrison to upset and hinder the French concentration.
Both sides were waiting for their convoy, for the French, no less than
the English, were desperately short of stores.

On May 9th the watchers on the battlements of Quebec saw the
topsails of a frigate standing up-river. She flew no flag and her nationality could not be determined. Slowly she forced her way through the
swift current. The guns of Quebec were loaded and manned, ready
to greet her with a storm of shot should it prove to be the Tricolour
of France that she hoisted. She reached the basin, and as the watchers
in the city saw her anchor plunge into the water, they saw also a
flag creep up to the masthead. As at last it broke clear they could see
that it was the Union Jack, and a tumult of cheering rose from the
garrison on the city battlements. Quebec was saved.

No less, indeed, than the whole fate of Canada hung on that timely
arrival. The ship was the frigate *Lowestoft*, returning to the scene of
her activities of the previous year. She was the forerunner of Swanton's
squadron and a few days later the *Vanguard's* topsails were sighted
as she made her way up the difficult river. With her came the storeships

and transports, sail after sail, to crowd the basin below Quebec and to bring relief to Murray's sorely-tried men.

On the day after his arrival Swanton attacked the French squadron in the river above Quebec. The battlements were lined with excited and cheering soldiers as the *Vanguard* and her consorts drove the French off with considerable loss. While Swanton anchored the *Vanguard* in a position where she could pour a flanking fire into the siege works which de Levis had so painfully constructed, he ordered his frigates to chase the French flotilla and destroy it. De Levis found his situation impossible to hold and was forced to retire, leaving his big siege guns behind him. As he drew his men back towards Montreal he, too, knew that it could only be a matter of weeks at the most before the whole of Canada was lost.

And so it was. Amherst and Haviland were advancing with their columns by the land route into the heart of Canada and approaching Montreal, the last centre of French resistance. Their encircling movements were steady, methodical, sure, and the French were unable to stop them. Gradually they drew tighter the relentless net they had cast round Montreal, and by September 6th both columns had met on the island on which Montreal stands. It was the end. No further resistance was possible and a final battle could only mean useless sacrifice. Two days later, on September 8th, all was over and the whole of Canada was transferred to the British crown under the terms of the capitulation.

In London, when the news of Swanton's relief of Quebec was received, Pitt was in the highest spirits. Here was his "Glorious Enterprise" at last fully and irrevocably achieved, a brilliant jewel in King George's crown.

> "Join, my love," he wrote to his wife, "with me in the most humble and grateful thanks to the Almighty. The siege of Quebec was decided on May 17th, with every happy circumstance. The enemy left their camp standing, abandoned forty pieces of cannon, etc. Swanton, with the *Vanguard*, destroyed all the French shipping, six or seven in number. Happy, happy day! My joy and hurry are inexpressible."

The war, which in 1759 and 1760 had added so many new territories to the British Empire, languished in 1761. There were tentative moves by both sides to reach an agreement for peace. They were shattered on August 15th by the "Family Compact", signed by the kings of France and Spain. It amounted to no less than an offensive-defensive alliance between the two countries and meant that Spain was now to be brought into the war on the side of a faltering France. The actual declaration of war was not made until the January of 1762, but in the meantime the Spaniards were busily employed in bringing their armed forces into fighting trim.

While the threat of Spanish intervention was still hanging over the country, Pitt turned his eyes towards the West Indies. There were plums ripe for the picking there. Martinique and the other small French islands in the neighbourhood might well be added to the territories already won from France, while if Spain were eventually dragged in, there was the rich island of Cuba with its capital at Havana ready for plucking from his Most Catholic Majesty. With France totally driven out of North America there were no lack of troops nearly on the spot for these adventures. It would be a simple matter to gather them at Barbados and Jamaica.

Pitt, however, was not destined to direct the course of the war in these waters, for he fell from power on October 4th. But within a few days of his relinquishing the post of Prime Minister he saw one of his cherished plans set into operation. It was the expedition against Martinique. Rear-Admiral Rodney was given command of a fleet of 17 sail of the line, flying his flag in the *Marlborough*. Among his ships was the *Vanguard*, still under Swanton's command.

The fleet reached Barbados on November 22nd. There they waited for a month till the army they were to accompany was collected, men from England, from North America, from Canada. The ships and transports weighed anchor on December 27th and arrived off St. Pierre, the capital of Martinique, on January 8th. A small squadron under Commodore Sir James Douglas had been lying off the harbour since November to prevent any reinforcement of the island and Douglas had spent his time in silencing the St. Pierre batteries. As the result, Rodney had a safe enough anchorage for his ships.

The main objective, if the island was to be captured, was not St. Pierre, but the French strong-point of Fort Royal, a few miles further to the south. Rodney detached Swanton with a small squadron and two brigades of troops to the Bay of Petite Anse d'Arlet, below Fort Royal, directing him at the same time to fly an admiral's flag in the *Vanguard* to confuse the enemy and to induce them to believe that the main landing was to be there. He himself took the remainder of the ships and transports to St. Anne's Bay, on the southern tip of the island. After a preliminary bombardment of the French batteries on the shore, the soldiers were landed, only to find the ground impossible. It was a desolate expanse of rocky ravines, across which no guns could be transported without superhuman efforts. The attempt was made, but progress was so slow that it would have taken weeks of ceaseless toil to come within striking distance of Fort Royal. The project was abandoned and two days after going ashore the troops were back in their transports again.

Swanton, too, had been busy. The *Vanguard's* guns had soon destroyed the French defences at the Petite Anse, and also at the Grande Anse, just above it. Here the troops were put ashore but, as at St. Anne's, the rugged nature of the ground made any advance impossible.

There was nothing for it now but to make a direct attack on Fort

Royal itself, well defended and heavily gunned as it was. A suitable landing-place in the Bay was selected at Cas Navires, just to the northward of Fort Royal itself, and on January 16th the whole fleet stood in to attack the numerous batteries with which it was defended. The ships did their work thoroughly and during the night that followed, with Swanton in charge of the boats, the soldiers and marines were successfully landed. A thousand seamen from the fleet were sent ashore to assist in getting the guns in position for a bombardment of the citadel.

"As soon," wrote one of the army officers, "as we were all safely disembarked at Cas Navire, our engineers were immediately set to work in raising batteries, as well to establish our footing on the island as to cover us in our approaches to dislodge the enemy from their posts. For this purpose, all the cannon, and other warlike stores were landed as soon as possible and dragged by the jacks to any point thought proper. You may fancy you know the spirit of those fellows, but to see them in action exceeds any idea that can be formed of them. A hundred or two of them, with ropes and pullies, will do more than all your dray-horses in London; let but their tackle hold and they will draw you a cannon or mortar on its proper carriages up to any height, though the weight be ever so great. It is droll enough to see them tugging along with a good heavy twenty-four pounder at their heels. On they go, huzzaing and hollowing, sometimes up hill, sometimes down hill, now sticking fast in the brakes, presently floundering in the mire, swearing, blasting, damning, sinking, and as careless of every thing but the matter committed to their charge, as if death and danger had nothing to do with them. We had a thousand of these brave fellows sent to our assistance by the admiral; and the service they did us, both on shore and on the water, is incredible." [2]

Although the difficulties were still immense, the soldiers pushed the attack with great dash and by February 3rd Fort Royal was in British hands. The Governor of the island, M. la Touche, retired with the remainder of his forces to St. Pierre, "determined either to die sword in hand like Montcalm before Quebec or preserve the place". [2] His defiance of the English was not to last long, however, for by the 15th his ardour had cooled and he signed the final terms of capitulation which surrendered Martinique to the British crown.

Rodney decided at once to implement the capture of Martinique to its fullest extent. He sent the *Vanguard*, with one brigade of troops under Hunt Walsh, to Grenada, and another to St. Lucia and St. Vincent. On his arrival off the island, which was defended by a small fort, Swanton summoned the governor to surrender. It was refused. The *Vanguard* stood in towards the shore, her guns ready to attack the fort and silence opposition to a landing. The threat was sufficient and the island was surrendered without a shot being fired. With it were yielded the group of smaller islands nearby, known as the Grenadines. The terms of surrender were signed on board the *Vanguard*.

For the next few months the *Vanguard*, acting as Commodore's ship of a squadron of 10 sail, cruised in the Spanish Main in search of prizes. She had, in fact, been specifically detailed by orders from London to join Admiral Pocock's fleet for an attack on Havana. Rodney, in a fit of pique at having a senior officer sent out to take command in his station, had thought fit to ignore the order. What had happened, and what Rodney did not yet know, was that war had been declared on Spain and that the proposed expedition against Havana was the result of a decision in London to prosecute the war vigorously against Spanish possessions in the West Indies. By the time Pocock arrived, the damage was done. The *Vanguard*, together with nine other ships of Rodney's fleet, was out of reach and carrying out a purposeless cruise in the Caribbean. Her presence at Havana, together with those of the other nine vessels, would have made Pocock's task immeasurably easier.

The capture of Havana was the last act of the Seven Years' War,

"a war which the perfidiousness of Britain's enemies made her undertake, wherein she acquired at least ten millions of plunder, had destroyed or taken above one hundred ships of war, had reduced a considerable number of cities, towns, forts and castles; conquered twenty-five islands, and a track of continent of immense extent. The news of her victories have sounded in most parts of the globe, and her conquests have added greatly to her territories in America, Asia, etc., and may one day become as famed and more powerful than any empire under the canopy of heaven; and wherever her streamers fly and her cannons roar, may Britannia always be triumphant!"

Preliminaries of peace were signed at Fontainebleau on November 3rd, and under the treaty Martinique was to be returned to the French. The *Vanguard* rejoined Rodney there at the end of her cruise in the Spanish Main, lying for a few days in the harbour at Fort Royal which she had helped to capture. They were days of rest and peace in that sun-drenched island of laughing Creole women who carried themselves like caryatids of the Parthenon. As the *Vanguard* lay there, one of them gave birth to a daughter, who was to cast a shadow over Europe in the years to come, when a fifth *Vanguard* sailed the seas. She was christened Josephine, "la belle Créole", and she came to France as the wife of M. de Beauharnais, the gentle scholar. After his death, when revolution stalked through the land, she became the mistress of Director Barras and, later still, the mistress of a black-haired captain of artillery, who made amends by marrying her. His name was Napoleon Bonaparte.

In the same year an English child was born, who was to cast an equally great shadow. Amy Lyon was her name, and when she reached womanhood she changed it to Emma Hart. For some years she was a prostitute and finally was sold by her paramour, Charles Greville, to the British Ambassador at Naples for £7,000. He, too, made amends by marrying her and giving her his name of Hamilton,

It is, perhaps, idle to speculate on the effect, if any, that these two women had on the fortunes of the fifth *Vanguard*. But perhaps Josephine inspired Napoleon in his dream of Eastern conquest that took him to Egypt in 1798. And perhaps Emma Hamilton inspired Nelson to the glorious achievements of his three great victories. In the first of them the destinies of these two men mingled with the guns of the fifth *Vanguard* in Aboukir Bay.

CHAPTER XII

THE REVOLUTION IN FRANCE

THE fourth *Vanguard* was sold out of the service in 1774, two years before the American Declaration of Independence and the long and painful war which that act entailed. Eleven years later when, in 1787, the fifth *Vanguard* was built at Deptford, the map of North America had been greatly changed as the result.

This fifth *Vanguard* was, like her predecessor, a Third-rate, of 1662 tons, and one of the famous "seventy-fours", of which nearly 60 had been built by the end of the 18th century. Although pierced to carry 74 32-pounders on her two decks, main and lower, she in fact carried 82 guns, as an Admiralty order of November 19th, 1794, directed all ships of her class to mount two additional 32-pounder carronades on the forecastle and six 18-pounder carronades on the poop. These carronades, so called because they were cast by the Carron Company of Scotland, were known as "smashers" in the Navy because of their destructive effect against the timber of ships. The new *Vanguard* was manned by a ship's company of 604 men and 32 boys.

Although this *Vanguard*, completed in 1787, is generally recognized as the fifth in the line, the name had, in fact, been given to a small vessel in 1780. There are few details of her existence and even fewer of her achievements. She was a prize captured from the Spaniards by Captain Sir Roger Curtis and brought into Gibraltar. There her possibilities as a small defensive craft were recognized and she was purchased from Curtis by the naval authorities and fitted out as a "gunboat", a class of ship which at that time had no official status in the Navy. She was stationed at Gibraltar in 1781 and on August 7th of that year is mentioned as having come to the assistance of the sloop *Helena*, which was being attacked by 14 Spanish gunboats off the harbour. Curtis took this *Vanguard*, and another small gunboat, the *Repulse*, into action against the Spanish ships and drove them off. He then towed the *Helena* into Gibraltar "amid the cheers of a vast body of spectators who had collected to witness his gallant efforts".

After that episode, this little *Vanguard* disappears from history. There is a note on the official record of her existence, "not to be entered", an indication that she was never considered to be a purely naval vessel and never listed on the official strength of the Royal Navy.

During the first few years of the fifth *Vanguard's* service events in Europe were taking a new and sinister turn. The revolution in France was having repercussions all over the continent as the down-trodden classes saw for themselves a gleam of hope in the excesses in Paris.

Liberté, Egalité, Fraternité, had a golden and exciting ring about them and there was a potent charm in the pictures they conjured up. Even in England the call was heard. On November 28th, 1792, deputations from various revolutionary societies in Britain were received at the bar of the Convention in Paris, and the Government in London was denounced by "those incredible mountebanks in France", as St. Vincent called them, in no uncertain terms.

To the young Mr. Pitt, Prime Minister son of a Prime Minister father, the call from Paris sounded ominous. Behind it he could hear the rumbling undertones of the coming war. On December 1st he called out the militia and on the 15th he advised the King to summon Parliament from its Christmas recess. The members met on the appointed day, to be greeted with another decree from the Convention across the Channel, this time pledging itself to overthrow the government in every country to which its armies could penetrate. That was a serious threat in a world grown inflammatory, as was the world of 1792, and made even more serious less than a month later when Louis XVI and Marie Antoinette were hustled off to the guillotine. Cromwell could behead a Stuart in 1649 and keep the matter a domestic one because the rest of Europe was not ready for revolution. But when Robespierre and his companions took the life of a Capet 150 years later, its repercussions were felt all over Europe, for most governments were seated precariously on national volcanoes of discontent. The only answer was war, as much a channel to divert subversive thoughts into the paths of patriotism as to retain the old and tried ways of life.

But Pitt was cautious. For its maximum effect on the country the actual declaration of war would be better if coming from the other side. So he held his hand and for the moment did no more than order the commissioning of all available ships of war, of which the new *Vanguard* was one. It was a gesture designed to prove to France that Great Britain was ready to accept the challenge so loosely thrown down by the Paris Convention and at the same time a warning that the French decree could have no other ending but war if it were to be persisted in. Persisted in it was, and the new Republic of France declared war on Great Britain and Holland on February 1st, 1793.

The *Vanguard* was commissioned under the command of Captain John Stanhope and joined the Channel Fleet, under Lord Howe, who flew his flag in the *Queen Charlotte*. The *Vanguard* sailed with the fleet on October 27th for a cruise in the Bay of Biscay in search of a French squadron under Commodore Vanstabel in the *Tigre*, which was known, from intelligence reports received, to be ready for sea.

There followed a weary three weeks of boisterous weather and hard gales from the south-east in which the Channel Fleet tossed and laboured in the waters off Ushant. They were ended on November 18th when the *Latona*, one of Howe's advanced frigates, flew the signal for the sighting of a strange fleet. It proved to be the French and Howe at once hoisted the signal for a general chase. Vanstabel, setting whole topsails and even top-gallant sails, had the heels of the English ships and soon began to draw away to the westward. Howe's ships were under reefed topsails because of the weight of the gale, and an attempt to carry more sail only ended in disaster. When the topsail reefs were shaken out the *Defence* lost her fore and maintopmasts, the *Russell* her foretopmast, and the *Vanguard* and *Montagu* their maintopmasts. As a result they were all compelled to bear up for the Channel, to be followed a few days later by Howe and the rest of the fleet. Vanstabel, whose squadron consisted of new ships and the fastest sailors in France, returned to Brest unscathed. He had the good fortune, after giving Howe the slip, of falling in with a British convoy from Newfoundland, from which he captured 17 rich merchantmen.

Early in 1794 the *Vanguard* was ordered to the West Indies to join the fleet of Admiral Sir John Jervis, who was later to become Earl of St. Vincent and, as First Sea Lord, the man on whom the brunt of the naval war effort was later to fall. The *Vanguard* was commanded by Captain Charles Sawyer and on her arrival on the new station flew the broad pendant of Commodore Thompson. She arrived at Martinique shortly after its capture from the French in the beginning of April. Early in June, Thompson joined the Commander-in-Chief at Guadeloupe, which had fallen to a combined assault from land and sea during May, but was now being re-attacked by the French.

While the fleet had been absent from Guadeloupe at the end of May, a French squadron, which had slipped out of Rochefort un-noticed by the British blockade, had arrived at the island and succeeded in landing a considerable force. They had recaptured almost the whole of it before Jervis could get back. In an attempt to hold on to the gains of a month or so previously, Jervis ordered the seamen of the *Vanguard* and the *Veteran* to be landed under Sawyer's command as a reinforce-ment to the military. The sailors recaptured the village of Gosier, near Grand-terre, but it proved to be no more than a temporary success. A number of small skirmishes followed, but the French were in too great a force to be dislodged and the seamen were re-embarked on July 3rd. The remaining British forces held out for a few months longer, but by December 10th the French were again in undisputed possession of the whole island.

The *Vanguard* remained in the West Indies for the next two years, but after the initial engagements at Martinique and Guadeloupe, there was little activity at sea. The war was being fought mainly in Europe and almost entirely on land, where Napoleon's armies were biting deep into Italy and Austria. Because of his vast and never-ending calls for men and supplies for the land war, the French fleet was kept largely starved of seamen and French ships rarely took the seas in force. There were a few small actions, both in the Mediterranean and the Atlantic, but none on a large scale. The only events of interest on the *Vanguard's* station in the West Indies were the capture in 1796 of Demerara and

Essequibo from the Dutch and of St. Lucia, St. Vincent, and Grenada from the French.

During these first four years of the Revolutionary War, matters had gone almost entirely in favour of the French. Their troops had quickly overrun Holland, making of that country an enemy of England instead of, as at the start, an ally. Similarly, Spain had become an enemy in 1796 when a treaty of alliance between the French and Spanish governments had been signed on August 19th of that year. French successes in Italy and Austria had forced an uneasy peace in those areas of Europe, so that in 1797 only England was still standing out against the French tyrant. She, too, was becoming hard pressed.

The defeat of the Dutch and that country's consequent adherence to the French cause called for an English fleet in those waters to prevent any junction of Dutch warships with those of the French squadrons at Brest and Rochefort. Adam Duncan was placed in command of it. Napoleon's successes in northern Italy had made the Mediterranean almost untenable by British ships for lack of bases, and Corsica, taken from the French in 1794, had to be evacuated two years later. There was nothing for it but to retire from the Mediterranean and on December 1st, 1796, Jervis withdrew his fleet to Gibraltar. On that date, for the first time for over one hundred years, no British ship sailed in Mediterranean waters. Napoleon was in high spirits. "The expulsion of the English," he wrote, "has a great effect upon the successes of our military operations in Italy. We must exact more severe conditions of Naples. It has the greatest moral influence upon the minds of the Italians; assures our communications; and we will make Naples tremble even in Sicily."

It was at this stage of the war that the *Vanguard* returned home, after nearly three years in the West Indies. She arrived at a time when the unsatisfactory state of the war was causing uneasiness throughout the country and when the continued successes of Napoleon almost daily brought news of fresh disasters. With fleets off the Dutch coast, in the Channel, and at Gibraltar, with squadrons in the East Indies, off South Africa, and in the western Atlantic, British naval force was stretched to the limit. Even the capture from the Dutch, in 1796, of Amboyna, in the East Indies, following that of the Cape of Good Hope, in 1795, had failed to raise English spirits.

Into this atmosphere of gloom, early in 1797, had come news of the Battle of St. Vincent when, on February 14th, Jervis met the Spanish fleet under Admiral Don José de Cordova and soundly defeated it. It was a gleam of light in an overcast sky and the first step towards the second stage of the war with France, in which the *Vanguard* was to play an important part.

On her arrival in England, the *Vanguard* was paid off at Chatham. Having no crew on board she was not concerned with the great mutinies of 1797 at Spithead and the Nore. Those unhappy affairs, ending in dignity at Spithead, in tragedy at the Nore, were perhaps the lowest ebb to which the British Navy sank during the Revolutionary Wars, but from them it emerged in better heart than before. A number of legitimate grievances had been aired and rectified and a new spirit was abroad in the sailors as the result.

The position in which England found herself at the end of 1797 was hardly hopeful. Overtures for peace made in the summer had been met by terms too humiliating to contemplate. She was now the only country at war with France; all the former allies, Holland, Spain, Prussia, Austria, having dropped out of the fight. By the treaty of Campo Formio, signed with Austria in October of that year, Belgium had been added to metropolitan France, bringing her eastern boundary to the Rhine. Venice, as a sovereign state, had disappeared, the town itself being given to Austria, her lands and islands to France. The Italian republics, Switzerland, and Holland were occupied by French armies. Prussia remained neutral and death, in 1796, had removed, in the person of the Empress Catherine of Russia, another potential enemy of France. Apart from the unrelenting hostility of England, Napoleon saw his way clear to newer and wider victories.

As 1797 faded into 1798, Bonaparte made his new plans for extending the empire of France. He had cast his eyes as far afield as India, where Tippoo Sahib was proving something of a thorn in the side of the English administration there. A previous plan to send a French expeditionary force to India in 1797 under the command of Villaret-Joyeuse had been abandoned for the more attractive, though ill-prepared, attempt to land in Ireland. That had been beaten back before achieving anything, and now Napoleon himself was proposing to take his army out east. It was spectacular and grandiose, and thus wholly attractive to the all-conquering genius of military operations.

Yet, even while contemplating action so many thousands of miles away, Napoleon still had not lost sight of the main requirement of ultimate success. England, still the greatest sea power in the world, for all the navies of France, Spain, and Holland, would have to be beaten at home before Napoleon would bask in the full glory of ambition achieved. Writing on April 13th, 1798, he said:

"In our situation we ought to wage a sure war against England, and we can do so. Whether in peace or war, we should expend from forty to fifty millions (francs) in reorganizing our navy. Our army need not be of greater or less strength, so long as the war obliges England to make immense preparations that will ruin her finances, and destroy the commercial spirit, and absolutely change the habits and manners of her people. We should employ the whole summer in getting the Brest fleet ready for sea, in exercising the sailors in the road, and in completing the ships that are building at Rochefort, Lorient, and Brest. With a little activity in these operations, we may hope to have, by the month of September, 35 sail of the line in Brest, including the four or five which may then be ready at Lorient and Rochefort.

"We shall have by the end of the month, in the different ports of the

Channel, nearly 200 gunboats. These must be stationed at Cherbourg, Havre, Boulogne, Dunkerque, and Ostende, and the whole summer employed in inuring the soldiers to the sea. In continuing to allow to the commission for the coasts of the Channel 300,000 francs per decade (a period of ten days) we shall be enabled to build 200 gunboats of larger dimensions, capable of carrying cavalry. We shall then have, in the month of September, 400 gunboats at Boulogne and 35 sail of the line at Brest. The Dutch can also have ready, in this interval, 12 sail of the line in the Texel.

"We have in the Mediterranean two descriptions of line-of-battle ships: 12 of French construction which, between this and the month of September, may be augmented by two new ships; and nine of Venetian construction. We may perhaps be able, when the expedition which the government projects in the Mediterranean is over, to send the 14 ships to Brest, and to retain in the Mediterranean only the nine Venetian ships; which will give us, in the month of October or November, 50 ships of the line at Brest, and almost an equal number of frigates.

"We may perhaps then be able to transport 40,000 men to any spot of England we wish, by avoiding, however, a naval action, if the enemy should be too strong: in the meanwhile, 40,000 men threaten to put off in the 400 gunboats, and about as many fishing vessels of Boulogne, and the Dutch fleet and 10,000 men threaten a descent upon Scotland. The invasion of England, put in practice in this manner in the months of November and December, would be almost certain. England would waste herself by immense efforts, but these would not secure her from our invasion.

"In fact, the expedition to the East will oblige England to send six additional ships of the line to India, and perhaps twice as many frigates to the entrance of the Red Sea: she would be obliged to have from 22 to 25 ships of the line at the entrance of the Mediterranean, 60 before Brest, and 12 before the Texel, forming a total of 100 line-of-battle ships, without reckoning those she now has in America and the Indies, and the ten or twelve 50-gun ships, with 20 frigates, which she would be obliged to have ready to oppose the invasion from Boulogne. We should always remain masters of the Mediterranean, since we should have there the nine Venetian ships of the line."

It sounded so easy to Napoleon. One hundred and fifty years later it was to sound almost equally easy to Hitler. But what Napoleon forgot, and what Hitler forgot, was that English ships of war are not so easily beaten from the seas. It is comparatively simple on paper, to reckon out the possible force which can be massed at one particular point by joining up the squadrons from the different bases round to coast. It is another matter to make the concentration in practice. To do that, ships must go to sea, must evade the blockade or fight their way out. And the English had an uncomfortable habit of winning their battles at sea.

It was against this background that the *Vanguard* was re-commissioned in the last days of 1797. Already St. Vincent, blockading the Spanish fleet in Cadiz, was worrying about reports of a fleet fitting-out at Toulon, and worrying even more about an order from Lord Spencer, First Lord of the Admiralty, to send a squadron into the Mediterranean.

"I am much at a loss," he wrote, "to reconcile the plans in contemplation to augment this fleet and extend its operations, with the peace which Portugal seems determined to make with France, upon any terms the latter may be pleased to impose; because Gibraltar is an unsafe depot for either stores of provisions, which the Spaniards have always in their power to destroy, and the French keep such an army in Italy, that Tuscany and Naples would fall a sacrifice to any the smallest assistance rendered to our fleet."

St. Vincent was now 64 years old, in poor health from his long stay at sea in front of Cadiz, and careworn by the weight of responsibility he was carrying as Commander-in-Chief.

In that mood of depression he asked for Nelson to be sent out to him. He suggested to Spencer that the *Foudroyant*, of 80 guns, would make a suitable flagship for the new admiral—Nelson's promotion to Rear-Admiral of the Blue was dated February 20th, 1797—but she could not be made ready in time. Nelson's wound, received during the attack on Teneriffe when he lost his right arm, had responded to the doctors' treatment and healed more rapidly than had been expected. The ligature on the artery had sloughed away on December 4th. Until then he had been in constant pain, only getting sleep by the use of opium, but the healing of the artery brought immediate relief.

At once he was impatient to get to sea. Four days after the ligature came away, on December 8th, he was writing to Captain Edward Berry, who was to be his flag-captain, to say that he was fit again and asking him to hurry the commissioning of his new ship. It was the *Vanguard*, selected by Spencer in place of the *Foudroyant*.

She was floated out of dock at Chatham on December 19th, and by March was round at Portsmouth, where she took on board ammunition and provisions. On the 29th, at eight o'clock in the evening, Nelson hoisted his flag, Blue at the mizen, on board the *Vanguard*, and on April 10th, after being delayed at St. Helens for a week by head winds, she sailed for Lisbon, escorting the Portugal, Gibraltar, and Mediterranean convoy. Nelson arrived at the Portuguese capital on the 23rd and handed over his charge. Four days later the *Vanguard* sailed for Cadiz, where she joined the fleet under St. Vincent.

K

CHAPTER XIII

NELSON'S FLAGSHIP

"I DO assure your Lordship," wrote St. Vincent to Spencer on May 1st, "that the arrival of Admiral Nelson has given me new life. You could not have gratified me more than in sending him. His presence in the Mediterranean is so very essential that I mean to put the *Orion* and *Alexander* under his command, with the addition of three or four frigates, and to send him away (the moment the *Vanguard* has delivered her water to the in-shore squadron) to endeavour to ascertain the real object of the preparations making by the French."

The Commander-in-Chief was referring to the French activities at Toulon. A considerable army amounting to 40,000 troops, including cavalry, had been collected there and it was known that Napoleon himself had arrived. There were 15 sail of the line reported to be ready for sea, and numberless transports. It all pointed to a considerable expedition. Admiral de Brueys, who was flying his flag in the great 120-gun ship *l'Orient*, was in command of the fleet.

The possible destination of this expeditionary force was a cause of much speculation in London. Spencer, in making his guess, favoured Naples, and followed that with further guesses of Portugal and Ireland, "for the former, most probably, by landing somewhere in Spain; for the latter, by pushing through the Straits and escaping our vigilance". Sicily and the West Indies were also mentioned as possible objectives of Napoleon, and even the island of Corfu had some adherents. Dundas, Minister of War, also joined in the guessing game.

"My dear Lord," he wrote to Spencer on June 9th, "Did the instructions to Lord St. Vincent mention that Egypt might be in the contemplation of Bonaparte's expedition? It may be whimsical, but I cannot help having a fancy of my own on that subject."

St. Vincent lost no time in detaching the *Vanguard* to look into the Mediterranean and to attempt to unravel the tangled skein of Napoleon's movements. On May 2nd she parted company with the fleet off Cadiz and spread her sails to a north-westerly wind which would carry her to Gibraltar on the first stage of her new mission. As her topsails disappeared over the horizon a new phase in the war was beginning, though few could discern it yet. Her presence in the Mediterranean, the swift building up of Nelson's fleet, the great victory but three months ahead, all these were to combine in bringing a new confidence to Europe and to making possible Pitt's "Second Coalition" in the great fight against France.

The *Vanguard* reached Gibraltar on May 4th, and there Nelson found the two ships he had been promised by St. Vincent, the *Alexander*, commanded by Captain Alexander Ball, and the *Orion*, under Captain Sir James Saumarez. Also there were the frigates *Alcmène, Emerald, Terpsichore,* and *Bonne Citoyenne.* Taking all these under his command, he left Gibraltar late in the evening of May 8th, trusting to the darkness to prevent his easterly course being seen by agents of the French. It was a moment of considerable historical importance. For the first time for over two years British ships were again in the Mediterranean, and the sea power of Britain was beginning to draw tight the cords which were to restrict, and finally to bind, the continental adventures of Napoleon.

The small squadron of three 74's and four frigates made its way into the Gulf of Lyons and on the 17th the *Terpsichore* captured a small French corvette, *Le Pierre*, of eight guns and 65 men. Nothing definite could be learned from her except that the soldiers at Toulon were already being embarked in the transports. The information did little but add a note of urgency to Nelson's immediate task, though the men of the squadron were in high spirits at the chance of so early an encounter.

Three days later the *Vanguard*, from being one of the finest sailing vessels in the Royal Navy, was lying dismasted and useless in the troughs of enormous waves. They were south of Hyères at the time and had been caught by a gale which sprang up without warning. One of the most vivid descriptions of the catastrophe was given by Berry, the *Vanguard's* captain, in a letter to his father-in-law.

"After arriving at the height of our wishes at sea," he wrote, "and elated beyond description at being so fortunate as to be the detached Squadron in the Mediterranean, and surrounded by enemies, and but little chance of seeing anything else on these seas—our Squadron though small being very choice—the passage from Gibraltar to the Gulf of Lyons being favourable in all respects, fine weather, and not discovered by the enemy, though close to their ports, we thought ourselves in the height of our glory: what more could we wish for?

"But alas! how liable to a reverse, and how it was verified! Sunday, the 20th of May, being exactly in the situation for intercepting the enemy's ships bound into Marseilles, Toulon, etc., and that afternoon having captured a tolerably rich prize, we stood in towards Cape Sicie, off Toulon, with a moderate breeze: towards sunset the weather did not appear so promising; we consequently got down our top-gallant yard, etc.; before 12 at night the gale came on and increased with rapid violence, which obliged us to furl all the sails, and try under a main storm staysail.

"At about two the main topmast went over the side, with the topsail yard full of men. I dreaded the inquiry of who were killed and drowned; fortunately only one man fell overboard and one fell on the booms and was killed on the spot. At half-past-two the mizen-topmast went over the side; the foremast gave an alarming crack, and at a quarter-past-three went by the board with a most tremendous crash and, what was very extraordinary, it fell in two pieces across the forecastle.

"Our situation was really alarming: the wreck of the fore topmast and foremast hanging over the side and beating against the ship's bottom; the best bower anchor was flung out of its place and was also thumping the bottom; the wreck of the main topmast swinging violently against the main rigging; every roll endangering the loss of the mainmast which we expected to fall every moment—thus circumstanced we endeavoured, though with little hopes of success, to wear, having no headsail and knowing we were driving on an enemy's shore. Fortunately there was a small rag of the spritsail left, and by watching a favourable moment we got her on the other tack. The bowsprit did not go, though it was sprung in three different places.

"The ship rolled and laboured dreadfully but did not make any water, more than we shipped over all. We cut the anchor from the bows and got clear of the wreck, with the loss of a boat and topsail yard, etc., and were not apprehensive of our bottom being damaged. The gale did not abate in the smallest degree and the main rigging, from being new, stretched to that degree that it was no support to the mast; we struck the mainyard, which eased it greatly, and secured the rigging as well as laid in our power. We shipped so much water that it was necessary to scuttle the lower deck, still we were consoled that she did not leak.

"Here I have to lament the loss of a most active young man, a Midshipman of the name of Meek, recommended by Mr. Coke, of Norfolk. He showed himself so particularly active at the time everybody admired him: by accident he was suddenly killed.

"For want of masts we rolled dreadfully. The storm did not abate till Tuesday afternoon, which enabled the *Alexander* to take us in tow. Our situation on Tuesday night was the most alarming I ever experienced: we stood in for the Island of Sardinia and approached the S.W. side of the island, intending to go into Oristan Bay, which we were not acquainted with, but it was absolutely necessary to go somewhere. Finding we could not fetch Oristan, the Admiral determined to try for St. Pierre's, which we could have fetched had the breeze continued, but unfortunately it fell light airs, and at times almost calm; so much so, that we determined to order the *Alexander* to cast off the hawser, and desire her to shift for herself—trust to our own fate, but not involve any other ship in our difficulties.

"All this time there was a heavy western swell driving in towards the shore, so that at midnight we were completely embayed. You may easily figure to yourself our situation, and the feeling of those who *knew the danger*, when I tell you I could easily distinguish the surf breaking on the rocky shore; still there was hope anchorage might be found, though we knew of none. We therefore bent our cables and prepared for the worst, anxiously wishing for daybreak, which at length arrived, and we found ourselves about five miles from the shore, the western swell still continuing to drive us in and no wind to enable us to get off.

"Indeed, the *Vanguard* was a perfect wreck, but the *Alexander* still had us in tow. Fortunately, at about six o'clock on Wednesday, the 23rd of May, a breeze sprang up, the *Alexander's* sails filled, we weathered the rocks to windward of the island of St. Pierre's, and before 12 we anchored in six fathoms and fine smooth water—a luxury to us scarcely to be equalled, and if ever there was a satisfaction at being in distress, we felt it.

"The ready assistance of our friends Sir James Saumarez, captain of the *Orion*, and Captain Alexander John Ball, of the *Alexander*, 74, by their united efforts, and the greatest exertion we all used, the *Vanguard* was equipped in four days and actually at sea, not bound (I would have you observe) to Gibraltar or any English port to be refitted, but again cruizing after the enemy on their own coast! with a main topmast for a foremast, and a topgallantmast for a topmast, consequently everything else reduced in proportion. By our superiority of sailing with other ships, we find the loss trifling to what it would have been to the generality of ships. With such perseverance you will say we deserve success."

Nelson himself looked upon the dismasting of his ship as a judgment on his pride.

"My dearest Fanny," he wrote to his wife, "I ought not to call what has happened to the *Vanguard* by the cold name of accident. I firmly believe that it was the Almighty's goodness to check my consummate vanity. I hope it has made me a better officer, as I feel confident it has made me a better man. I kiss with all humility the rod.

"Figure to your self a vain man, on Sunday evening at sunset, walking in his cabin with a Squadron about him, who looked up to their chief to lead them to glory, and in whom this chief placed the firmest reliance, that the proudest ships, in equal numbers, belonging to France, would have bowed their flags; and with a very rich prize lying by him. Figure to yourself this proud, conceited man when the sun rose on Monday morning, his ship dismasted, his fleet dispersed, and himself in such distress that the meanest frigate out of France would have been a very unwelcome guest. But it has pleased Almighty God to bring us into a safe port where, although we are refused the rights of humanity, yet the *Vanguard* will in two days get to sea again as an English man of war. . . . If the ship had been in England, months would have been taken to send her to sea: here, my operations will not be delayed four days and I shall join the rest of my fleet on the rendezvous."

While the *Vanguard* lay dismasted at San Pietro, in Sardinia, important decisions were being taken in London and Toulon. From the former came urgent orders from Spencer to St. Vincent to detach a powerful squadron from his fleet off Cadiz and send it into the Mediterranean to reinforce Nelson. At the same time the First Lord promised to hurry out a squadron from England under Sir Roger Curtis to bring St. Vincent's fleet up to full strength. In Toulon, and all along the Riviera coast, soldiers were being hurriedly embarked and ships of war prepared for sea. On the 19th, the day on which the *Vanguard* and her squadron had been driven off their station by the storm, Napoleon gave the order to proceed.

Fifteen sail of the line, two of which were armed *en flûte*, 14 frigates, and a host of transports made their way out of Toulon and set a course towards the east. As the unwieldy mass of ships sailed slowly along the

French coast, each little harbour and port contributed yet more transports to swell the great convoy, the last of them from Genoa. By then the fleet numbered 72 ships of war and over 300 transports, the whole armada being under the command of Vice-Admiral de Brueys, with Rear-Admirals Villeneuve, Blanquet de Chayla, and Decrès in the junior posts. In the transports were 36,000 men under Napoleon, with Generals Kléber, Desaix, Bon, Regnier, Vaubois, Menou, Duqua, Dumas, and Dumuy as commanders of divisions.

From the Gulf of Genoa Napoleon turned south and lay off Corsica for 10 days, awaiting a further convoy of transports from Civita Vecchia. When, 10 days later, they had still failed to arrive, he grew tired of inactivity and sailed from Corsican waters on June 3rd, passing Mazzaro del Vallo, on the south-west coast of Sicily, on the 7th. The Civita Vecchia convoy joined on the 9th, in sight of Malta, and on the 10th French troops were landed at seven points on the island. Resistance was of the slightest, and five days later, Malta, Gozo, and Comino, were firmly held in Napoleon's grasp. With the islands he captured two ships of the line, one frigate, and three galleys. Waiting in the island only long enough to load on board *l'Orient* the priceless treasures of the Knights of St. John, he ordered the fleet to sea on the 19th and disappeared into the blue of the Mediterranean waters.

In the meantime, Nelson had been busy. With the *Vanguard* refitted in record time he returned to his station off Toulon only to find that the French had flown. He was back there on May 27th, expecting to see the four frigates of his squadron and to learn from them the course on which the French expedition had sailed. But the seas off Toulon were empty. On June 5th, with his three 74's widely spread in search of the frigates, he was joined by the *Mutine* sloop, whose captain, Thomas Hardy, brought him news of the reinforcements which St. Vincent was sending him—ten more 74's under Captain Troubridge in the *Culloden*. Hardy also solved the puzzle of the missing frigates. He had met them on his way up to Toulon from Gibraltar. They had witnessed the dismasting of the *Vanguard* and, confident that such considerable repairs could only be made good in a dockyard, had set a course for Gibraltar in the conviction that the *Vanguard* would of necessity join them there. But the frigate captains did not know Nelson's ways and their action was to prove an almost calamitous error. Instead of four frigates to scout for him, Nelson was now reduced to a single brig-rigged sloop, the *Mutine*.

In the *Culloden* came new orders for Nelson from St. Vincent. He was

"to proceed in quest of the armament preparing by the enemy at Toulon and Genoa, the object whereof appears to be either an attack upon Naples or Sicily, the conveyance of an army to some part of the coast of Spain for the purpose of marching towards Portugal, or to pass through the Straits, with a view to proceeding to Ireland."

Nelson himself had a different opinion. Napoleon had left Toulon with a north-west wind, which had remained steady ever since. It was a reasonable assumption that his course must be eastward, and to Nelson had come an anxiety for the safety of India.

"If they pass Sicily," he wrote to Spencer on June 15th, "I shall believe they are going on their scheme of possessing Alexandria, and getting troops to India—a plan concerted with Tippoo Saib, by no means so difficult as might at first view be imagined . . . but be they bound to the Antipodes, your Lordship may rely that I will not lose a moment in bringing them to action."

So Nelson sailed eastward with his fleet, bound for Naples and Sicily, hoping and expecting to get news of the French movements there. He drew a blank at both places, but surmised from the apparent calm of the two courts that neither felt themselves in any danger from the French. On June 22nd he called a council of his most trusted captains, Saumarez of the *Orion*, Troubridge of the *Culloden*, Ball of the *Alexander*, and Darby of the *Bellerophon*, and in the cabin of the *Vanguard* put to them his beliefs, that Napoleon was gone to Alexandria. On that day, and with the complete concurrence of his four captains, he made up his mind. It was a bold decision and Saumarez, his second-in-command, could write:

"I am just returned from on board the Admiral and we are crowding sail for Alexandria; but the contrast to what we experienced yesterday is great indeed, having made sure of attacking them this morning. At present it is very doubtful whether we shall fall in with them at all, as we are proceeding upon the merest conjecture only, and not on any positive information. Some days must now elapse before we can be relieved from our cruel suspense; and if, at the end of our journey, we find we are upon a wrong scent, our embarrassment will be great indeed. Fortunately, I only act here *en second*; but did the chief responsibility rest with me, I fear it would be more than my too irritable nerves would bear."

Six days later, on June 28th, the fleet was off the Pharos Tower of Alexandria. Nelson hailed the *Mutine* to close the harbour and report on the shipping there. Hardy returned an hour or two later with the news that the port contained no more than one Turkish ship of the line, four Turkish frigates, and about 60 sail of merchantmen of various nationalities. It was a terrible disappointment.

Had Nelson had with him those four frigates which even then were still lying inactive at Gibraltar, he would by that date have won his victory. As his fleet sailed to the eastward after leaving Sicily on the 22nd, it passed through the same waters, and within an hour or two, at the same time, as the much slower French convoy, which had left Malta on the 19th. With frigates spread ahead on a line of search he could hardly have missed Brueys and the great straggling armada of transports. There would inevitably have been a fleet action at sea, and Nelson's genius in command would have been a sufficient guarantee of a victory. "It would have been my delight," he wrote to Fanny, "to have tried Buonaparte on a wind, for he commands the fleet as well as the army." There might well have been the spectacle of Napoleon, a prisoner, walking the decks of the *Vanguard* as, 17 years later, he was to walk the decks of the *Bellerophon*.

Nelson sat down to write to St. Vincent. It was a curious letter, half justification for his actions, half defence against a charge not yet made. After detailing every movement he had made after Troubridge had joined him with the ten 74's, he went on:

"I recalled all the circumstances of this armament before me, 40,000 troops in 280 transports, many hundred pieces of artillery, waggons, draught-horses, cavalry, artificers, naturalists, astronomers, mathematicians, etc. The first rendezvous in case of separation was Bastia, the second Malta—this armament could not be necessary for taking possession of Malta. The Neapolitan ministers considered Naples and Sicily as safe; Spain, after Malta, or indeed any place to the westward, I could not think their destination, for at this season the westerly winds so strongly prevail between Sicily and the Coast of Barbary that I conceive it almost impossible to get a fleet of transports to the westward. It then became the serious question, where are they gone? (Here I had deeply to regret my want of frigates, and I desire it may be understood that if one-half the frigates your Lordship had ordered under my command had been with me, that I could not have wanted information of the French fleet.) If to Corfu, in consequence of my approach (which they knew from Naples on the 12th or 13th) they were arrived by this time, the 22nd.

"Upon their whole proceedings, together with such information as I have been able to collect, it appeared clear to me that either they were destined to assist the rebel Pacha and to overthrow the present Government of Turkey, or to settle a colony in Egypt and to open a trade to India by way of the Red Sea; for, strange as it may appear at first sight, an enterprising enemy, if they have the force or consent of the Pacha of Egypt, may with great ease get an army to the Red Sea, and if they have concerted a plan with Tippoo Saib to have vessels at Suez, three weeks at this season is a common passage to the Malabar coast, when our India possessions would be in great danger.

"I therefore determined, with the opinion of those captains in whom I place great confidence [Saumarez, Troubridge, Ball, and Darby were summoned to a Council on board the *Vanguard* on June 22nd], to go to Alexandria; and if that place, or any other part of Egypt, was their destination, I hoped to arrive in time enough to frustrate their plans. The only objection I can fancy to be started is, 'you should not have gone such a long voyage without more certain information of the enemy's destination': my answer is ready—who was I to get it from? The Governments of Naples and Sicily either knew not or chose to keep me in ignorance. Was I to wait patiently till I heard certain accounts? If Egypt was their object, before I could hear of them they would have been in India. To do nothing, I felt, was disgraceful: therefore I made use of my understand-

ing, and by it I ought to stand or fall. I am before your Lordship's judgment, (which in the present case I feel is the Tribunal of my Country)
and if, under all circumstances, it is decided that I am wrong, I ought,
for the sake of our Country, to be superseded; for, at this moment, when
I know the French are not in Alexandria, I hold the same opinion as off
Cape Passaro—viz., that under all circumstances I was right in steering
for Alexandria, and by that opinion I must stand or fall."

It was sound reasoning, brilliantly sound as the event turned out.
Nelson's last information had been that the French fleet had left
Malta on the 15th, in point of fact it had left four days later, and
those four days made all the difference.

But if Nelson's lack of frigates had saved the French for the time
being, it still left Nelson in the dark and he was no nearer a solution
of the mystery. He stood north-westward towards the Palestine coast,
and then back towards Crete. Still there was no news. All he could do
now was to double back on his tracks and begin again his search for
intelligence of the French movements. He reached Syracuse on
July 18th, and entered the harbour to take on board water, wine,
lemons, and bullocks.

> "This," states the *Vanguard's* log, "was the first opportunity that the
> *Vanguard* had enjoyed of receiving water on board from the 6th of May;
> so that not only the stock of that ship, but of several others of the squadron
> was very nearly exhausted."

There was an outcry in England when the news reached home.
Nelson's appointment in the first instance had caused a certain amount
of ill-feeling, for he was junior in rank to Sir John Orde, already with
St. Vincent off Cadiz at the time of Nelson's arrival in the *Vanguard*
and his appointment to command in the Mediterranean. There were
others, too, with whom the appointment rankled. "How often have I
been questioned," wrote Admiral Goodall, a close friend, to Nelson,
"What is your favourite hero about? The French fleet has passed
under his nose, etc., etc." There were other criticisms in the same vein
and questions had been asked in the House of Commons. Fortunately
for Nelson's peace of mind, news travelled slowly in those days and
he did not hear till much later of the murmurings against him.

At Syracuse, where the fleet remained five days, there was still
no news of the French, and Nelson's letters at that time speak eloquently
of the anxiety of his mind. He had failed in his cast to the eastward,
yet all his powers of reasoning told him that he would find the French
there and nowhere else. The prevalent westerly wind spelled an easterly
destination. The great prize of India was surely a magnet powerful
enough to tempt Napoleon in that direction. And if not India, then
the tottering Ottoman Empire was yet another reason for Napoleonic
adventures in near Eastern lands. So Nelson decided to trust again to
his own beliefs and his own reasoning. On July 25th the *Vanguard*

led the fleet out of Syracuse and, squaring away to a wind still blowing from the west, once more set a course for Egypt.

On the 28th the *Culloden* was detached to look into the Gulf of Koton, in Crete, for information. Three hours later Troubridge rejoined the fleet with the news that, four weeks previously, the whole French armada had been sighted from the coast steering south-east. That could only mean Alexandria, and Nelson ran before the wind for Egypt. On the morning of August 1st the British fleet again lay off the Pharos of Alexandria. And again the harbour was empty. But this time Nelson had no qualms. The French fleet must be somewhere in the neighbourhood and the ships were signalled to stretch up the coast in search of them. Shortly after noon the mast-head look-out in the *Zealous* reported masts in Aboukir Bay. At 12.50 p.m. the *Alexander* flew the signal for "Enemy in Sight", and at 2.30 p.m. the *Zealous* signalled "16 ships of the line". It was the French fleet and the long chase was over.

CHAPTER XIV

THE BATTLE OF THE NILE

At half past two, secure in the knowledge that at last the French fleet had been found and that an action was inevitable, Nelson ordered dinner to be served in the cabin of the *Vanguard*. His mind was at rest now and he talked gaily with his officers as they sat round the table. There was no need for him to discuss a plan of action, no need to harass the fleet with a number of signals to indicate his intentions. In this, his first action in command of a fleet, the absence of unnecessary signalling was as marked as it was later at Copenhagen and Trafalgar. It was a tribute at once to his thoroughness and to the confidence he felt in his captains.

Nelson had long contemplated the possibility of finding the French at anchor and had communicated his plan of attack in such a situation at frequent conferences with his captains.

"The Admiral had," wrote Berry, "and it appeared most justly, the highest opinion of, and placed the firmest reliance on, the valour and conduct of every captain in his Squadron. It had been his practice during the whole of the cruize, whenever the weather and circumstances would permit, to have his captains on board the *Vanguard*, where he would fully develop to them his own ideas of the different and best modes of attack, and such plans as he proposed to execute upon falling in with the enemy, whatever their position or situation might be, by day or by night. There was no possible position in which they could be found that he did not take into his calculation, and for the most advantageous attack of which he had not digested and arranged the best possible disposition of the force which he commanded.

"With the masterly ideas of their Admiral, therefore, on the subject of naval tactics, every one of the captains of his Squadron was most thoroughly acquainted; and upon surveying the situation of the enemy, they could ascertain with precision what were the ideas and intentions of their Commander without the aid of any further instructions; by which means signals became almost unnecessary, much time was saved, and the attention of every captain could almost undistractedly be paid to the conduct of his own particular ship, a circumstance from which, upon this occasion, the advantages to the general service were almost incalculable."

And when the final plans had been thoroughly explained there had been a chorus of amazed delight from the assembled captains.

"If we succeed," had exclaimed Berry, "what will the world say?" "There is no 'if' in the case," Nelson had answered. "That we shall succeed is certain. Who may live to tell the story is a different question."

In the present situation, with the French fleet at anchor under the batteries ashore, every captain knew that the admiral intended to concentrate the whole of his force on a portion of the enemy fleet—van or rear. A single signal would indicate the part selected. The few details remaining to be settled could be decided as soon as he got a closer view of the French dispositions, and for this particular purpose Nelson had inserted additional signals in the book so that his tactical requirements might be quickly and easily understood. In the meantime he ate his dinner in high good humour and, as he rose from the table, announced to his officers, "Before this time to-morrow I shall have gained a peerage or Westminster Abbey."

The afternoon wore on and the British fleet, in a single line ahead, sailed steadily towards the French on a moderate northerly wind. Nelson paced the quarter-deck of the *Vanguard* and "viewed the obstacles with the eye of a seaman determined on attack, and it instantly struck his eager and penetrating mind that where there was room for an enemy's ship to swing, there was room for one of ours to anchor". At 4.22 p.m. the *Vanguard* flew the signal to "prepare for battle and for anchoring with springs, and sheet cable taken in at stern port". Half an hour later Nelson flew another signal to "attack the enemy's van and centre". No more was necessary. The wind, now slightly fresher at north-north-west, was blowing straight down the French line from van to rear. It dictated automatically the position of attack, for with the van to windward the rear ships were prevented from coming up to the assistance of those first engaged.

Brueys, for all the final result of the battle, had drawn up his ships with skill and selected the best possible position for defence, though the lie of the land could offer him little help. Aboukir Bay curves southwards and eastwards from Aboukir Point, and is further guarded by a shoal bank stretching north-east from the point. Near the end of the bank lay the Island of Béquieres, now known as Nelson's Island, where the French admiral had erected batteries. It was close under the shelter of the bank that Brueys had anchored his leading ship, the *Guerrier*, with the remainder in a single line stretching towards the south-east. Where Brueys had made his mistake was in permitting his ships to lie to a single anchor. To do so meant giving each ship room to swing to the full extent of her cable, so that his ships were some 160 yards apart. The distance between the *Guerrier* and the edge of the shoal was rather more, about 1,100 yards. Not only was there plenty of room for an English ship to pass ahead of the *Guerrier*, but also room to pass between the intermediate ships of the French line. Nelson's "eye of a seaman determined to attack" had at once picked out the one weak point of the French admiral's defence.

The main difficulty which the English ships had to negotiate was the shallow water round Aboukir Point. The only chart in the British fleet was a rough map drawn in pencil which had been found on board a small French prize, and it gave no soundings. As the ships came abreast the shoal Nelson hailed Hood in the *Zealous* and asked him if he thought the fleet was far enough to the eastward before rounding the point. Hood replied that he was in eleven fathoms and that he had no chart, "but if you will allow me the honour of leading you into battle, I will keep the lead going". Nelson gave him permission and, as Hood lifted his cocked hat in acknowledgement, the wind swept it out of his hand and sent it dancing down the waves to leeward towards the French. "Never mind, Webley," he said to his First Lieutenant. "There it goes for luck. Put the helm up and make sail." But in the end it was not the *Zealous* which led the fleet into action. Foley in the *Goliath* raced her in.

Following the *Goliath* and *Zealous* in the original line of approach came the *Vanguard*. Nelson, desiring to take up the usual admiral's position in the centre of the line of battle, backed his topsails to allow the *Orion* and *Audacious* to pass. Astern of them came the *Theseus* and as she drew abreast the *Vanguard* she was hailed by Berry to take up position next ahead of the flagship. As she passed, the *Vanguard* set her topsails again and took her place in the line. Astern of her were now the *Minotaur*, *Defence*, *Bellerophon*, *Majestic*, and *Leander*, with the *Culloden* some distance away to the northward towing a prize captured off the Gulf of Koton. Still farther astern, some miles away, were the *Alexander* and *Swiftsure*, which had been sent on ahead the previous day to close the land. The *Culloden* was signalled to cast off her prize and close the fleet, and the other two ships ordered to make all sail and rejoin.

Brueys, after an indeterminate attempt to make sail and weigh, decided to fight at anchor. He sent out two small brigs, the *Alerte* and *Railleur*, with orders to steer across the shoal in an attempt to decoy the leading English ships on to the ledge. It was a fruitless gesture. "The bait," wrote Guérin, the French historian, "was a clumsy one to put before a man like Nelson." The British van paid no attention and, with the lead going continuously, sounded their way in past the danger. They came under a distant and ineffectual fire from the French batteries on the Island of Béquieres and from the starboard guns of the anchored French fleet. But there was no answering fire from the English ships. "The silent progression of the English was observed by their enemies with astonishment," and it was not until the *Goliath* rounded the bows of the *Guerrier* that the first British gun was fired.

This was at a quarter past six, a few minutes after the French had opened fire. The *Goliath*, according to the original plan of action, was to have anchored opposite the leading ship, with the remainder of the van passing outside her and taking the next French ship astern in the order of their approach. But the *Goliath's* anchor hung up and by the time she had cleared it and let go, she had run down opposite the *Conquérant*, the second ship in the line. Hood, in the *Zealous*, seeing what had happened to Foley, anchored on the port bow of the *Guerrier*, bringing his broadside to bear from a position where he could only receive a return fire from the bow-chasers of the French ship.

Astern of the *Guerrier* and the *Conquérant*, the French line in order of their anchoring was the *Spartiate, Aquilon, Peuple Souverain, Franklin, Orient, Tonnant, Heureux, Mercure, Guillaume Tell, Généreux,* and *Timoléon.* The *Orion,* third British ship to reach the French line, passed outside the *Goliath* and *Zealous* as intended and brought up in a position where she could engage both the *Peuple Souverain* and the *Franklin,* while the *Theseus,* in her anxiety to get speedily into action, sailed inside the English ships and anchored ahead of the *Goliath* to divide her fire between the *Conquérant* and the *Aquilon.*

The third ship in the French line, the *Spartiate,* was attacked by the *Vanguard.* In order to bring the French under two fires she remained outside the line and let go her anchor to bring up within 80 yards of the enemy. For a time she was hard pressed, coming under the combined fire of the *Spartiate* and her next astern, the *Aquilon.* The *Audacious,* breaking through the line between the *Guerrier* and the *Conquérant,* anchored close on the port bow of the latter, to relieve the weight of fire directed on the *Vanguard* by engaging the whole attention of the *Aquilon.* The remainder of the squadron, following Nelson's lead down the outside of the French line, placed themselves alongside such ships as they could reach, the *Minotaur* engaging the *Aquilon,* the *Defence* alongside the *Peuple Souverain,* the *Bellerophon* alongside the *Orient,* Bruey's 120-gun flagship, and the *Majestic* alongside the *Tonnant.* The little *Leander,* carrying only 50 guns, most gallantly steered between the *Peuple Souverain* and the *Franklin,* anchoring almost in the French line in a position where she could rake both ships with her broadsides and be free of all but the bow and stern guns of her two enemies.

Nelson had thus concentrated eight of his ships on the leading five in the enemy line, a crushing advantage that was to have a swift result. Two more, the *Bellerophon* and the *Majestic,* were engaged in single ship actions farther down the line, while another three, the *Culloden, Alexander,* and *Swiftsure,* were fast coming up from astern under a press of sail. The unfortunate Troubridge in the *Culloden,* approaching the Bay in the darkness, ran aground on the point of the shoal and had to be content throughout the night with a distant and tantalizing view of the fury of the battle in which he was yearning to take a part. He had the presence of mind to hang a red light in his rigging as a danger signal to the *Alexander* and *Swiftsure,* still astern of him, to prevent them from sharing his unhappy fate.

All had gone almost exactly as Nelson had planned and by half past six the leading eight French vessels were all under a heavy fire, many of them from two or three English ships simultaneously. At this early stage the value of bringing cables through the stern port and anchoring from the stern could be fully appreciated. As the ships ran down on a following wind the stern anchors prevented their swinging round to the wind when they let go, so that their broadsides could

be engaged at once. Springs on the cables, led over the bows to the
capstan, enabled them to point their ships as required to bring the
fullest weight of fire in any desired direction.

Within a very short space of time the French van was almost
completely annihilated. The *Guerrier* had lost all three of her masts
overboard within 12 minutes of the first broadside and the other
four ships of the van were all more or less completely disabled shortly
afterwards. All of them had struck by half past eight, and Berry had
sent Galwey, First Lieutenant of the *Vanguard*, across to the *Spartiate*
with a party of marines to take possession of her. He returned with
Captain Emeriau's sword, which Berry presented to Nelson with the
news that six ships had struck and that though the *Tonnant*, *Orient*,
and *Heureux* had not yet been taken, "they were considered as completely in our power".

Berry's report was not quite accurate. The *Bellerophon*, which
had ranged up alongside the French flagship, had met the full force
of *l'Orient's* 60-gun broadside, to which her own of 37 guns was an
inadequate reply. Captain Miller had anchored alongside at seven
o'clock and for an hour had exchanged broadsides with his powerful
opponent.

> "At 8," wrote her master, Edward Kirby, in the ship's log, "the mizen
> mast was shot away and shortly after the main mast, which fell along the
> booms on the starboard side of the forecastle. At 9, observing our an-
> tagonist on fire in the middle gun deck, cut the stern cable and wore
> clear of her by loosing the sprit-sail. Shortly afterwards, the fore mast
> went over the larboard bow."

The *Bellerophon*, mastless now and out of control, drifted out of the
battle to anchor in a safe position where she could make jury repairs
to masts and rigging. But by this time the *Alexander* and *Swiftsure*
had arrived on the scene. They anchored one each side of the *Orient*
to finish off the good work so ably begun by the *Bellerophon*.

In the meantime, on board the *Vanguard*, Nelson had been struck
across the forehead by a piece of flying langridge, the chain shot used
by the French to damage sails and rigging. The forehead was cut to
the bone and a flap of flesh fell down to cover his remaining eye,
temporarily blinding him and bathing his face in blood. He fell back
into Berry's arms. "I am killed," he said, "remember me to my wife."
He was assisted down to the cockpit with the other wounded where,
fortunately, his hurt was found to be not so serious as had been thought.
Jefferson, the *Vanguard's* surgeon, left his work to come and dress the
admiral's eye, but Nelson, theatrical as ever, sent him back. "No,"
he exclaimed, "I will take my turn with my brave fellows."

Above, the battle raged as furiously as ever. It had become dark
at seven o'clock, "but the whole hemisphere was, with intervals,
illuminated by the fire of the hostile fleets". It was an illumination

made even more vivid shortly after nine o'clock by the fire on board the *Orient*, which had been started by the *Bellerophon*. Bruey's flagship had been repainting masts and yards during the day and her officers had failed to take the elementary precaution of sending below the paint buckets and oil jars before the start of the action. Instead they had been piled hurriedly on the port side of the upper deck. The fire reached them at about a quarter past nine and flames shot up mast high to catch the rigging alight.

Berry, coming down once again to the *Vanguard's* cockpit, brought news of the great fire to the little Admiral. He insisted on being assisted up to the quarter-deck, and stood there in the Egyptian night to witness the scene.

"The first consideration that struck his mind," wrote Berry, "was concern for the danger of so many lives, to save as many as possible of whom he ordered Captain Berry [the report was written in the third person] to make every practicable exertion. A boat, the only one that could swim, was instantly dispatched from the *Vanguard*, and other ships that were in a condition to do so immediately followed the example; by which means, from the best possible information, the lives of about seventy Frenchmen were saved. The light thrown by the fire of *l'Orient* upon the surrounding objects, enabled us to perceive with more certainty the situation of the two fleets, the colours of both being clearly distinguishable. The cannonading was partially kept up to leeward of the centre till about ten o'clock, when *l'Orient* blew up with a most tremendous explosion. An awful pause and death-like silence for about three minutes ensued, when the wreck of the masts, yards, etc., which had been carried to a vast height, fell down into the water and on board the surrounding ships. A port fire from *l'Orient* fell into the main royal of the *Alexander* the fire occasioned by which, however, was extinguished in about two minutes by the active exertions of Captain Ball."

In the disaster to the *Orient* perished her captain, Commodore Casabianca, who had with him on board his small son, aged ten years, "who stood upon the burning deck, whence all but he had fled". Brueys had already been killed. "*Un amiral français doit mourir sur son banc de quart*," he had said, refusing to be taken below after he had been nearly cut in two by a British ball.

The tragedy of the *Orient* took most of the spirit out of the French sailors, who till then had fought most gallantly against heavy odds. Those of the *Tonnant*, indeed, had fought in the very finest traditions of naval warfare. Her captain, Dupetit-Thouars, had had first his right arm taken off by a round shot, then his left arm by another, and finally his left leg by a third. He sent for a tub of bran and ordered his men to place him upright in it so that he could continue to direct the fight. His ship was being engaged by the *Majestic*, *Swiftsure*, and *Alexander*, and in spite of the odds she had succeeded in dismasting the former. His next order was to nail the French flag to the mast, a precaution that proved to be useless as shortly afterwards all three of the *Tonnant's* masts were shot away. Just before he became insensible from loss of blood he implored his sailors to fight to the end rather than strike. Among the many gallant deeds of that August night, the courage and resolution of Dupetit-Thouars stands out as a shining light of devoted service.

With the complete surrender of the French van, those English ships which were still able to sail weighed and passed down the French line to attack the rear. Spasmodic firing continued till five o'clock the following morning, and as the sun rose over the bay, it was possible to assess the magnitude of the victory.

It was an astonishing sight. Of the French fleet of 13 sail of the line, the *Tonnant, Franklin, Guerrier, Conquérant, Spartiate, Peuple Souverain, Heureux, Mercure,* and *Aquilon,* had been captured, the *Orient* and *Timoléon* burnt. Of the four frigates, the *Artemise* had been burnt and the *Sérieuse* sunk. Only two line of battleships, the *Guillaume Tell* and *Généreux,* and two frigates, *Justice* and *Diane,* escaped. They sailed at about noon, and only Hood in the *Zealous* was in any condition to chase.

"I immediately directed the *Zealous*," he wrote, "to keep close on a wind in the hope I should be able to bring them to action and disable them in such a manner as to allow our ships to come to my assistance (there being then none under sail), and that should I disable them at all they could not fetch out of the bay. I just weathered them within musket shot and obliged the *Guillaume Tell* to keep away to prevent my raking her; and though I did them a great deal of damage, they were so well prepared as to cut every bowline, boom, topmast and standing rigging, sails, etc., away. I intended to have boarded the rear frigate, but could not get the ship round for a short space of time; and when I was doing it Sir Horatio called me in by signal, seeing I should only get disabled and not stop them with such a superior force."

The victory, immense and devastating as it was, was won at a comparatively modest cost. The total English casualties were 218 killed and 677 wounded, the *Vanguard* losing three officers, 20 seamen, and seven marines killed, and seven officers, 60 seamen, and eight marines wounded. The French losses were far more serious, 5,225 being "taken, drowned, burnt and missing", with a further 3,105 sent ashore under cartel. Most of the English ships were more or less seriously damaged, the *Bellerophon* and *Vanguard* more heavily than the remainder.

On August 2nd and 3rd, Nelson was busy in his cabin in the *Vanguard* writing letters and despatches.

"Almighty God," he wrote to St. Vincent, "has blessed his Majesty's Arms in the late Battle, by a great Victory over the Fleet of the Enemy, who I attacked at sunset on the 1st of August, off the Mouth of the Nile.

L

The Enemy were moored in a strong Line of Battle for defending the entrance of the Bay . . . but nothing could withstand the Squadron your Lordship did me the honour to place under my command. Their high state of discipline is well known to you, and with the judgment of the Captains, together with their valour, and that of the Officers and Men of every description, it was absolutely irresistible. Could anything from my pen add to the character of the Captains, I would write it with pleasure, but that is impossible."

To his officers and men he sent his "most sincere and cordial thanks" and informed them that he "intends returning Public Thanksgiving for the victory at two o'clock this day; and he recommends every ship doing the same as soon as convenient".

He also received the congratulations of his captains—"I give you joy. This is a glorious victory," wrote Gould of the *Audacious*—and a joint letter from them requesting his acceptance of a sword and

"as a further proof of their esteem and regard, hope that he will permit his portrait to be taken and hung up in the room belonging to the Egyptian Club, now established in commemoration of that glorious day."

But perhaps the most striking souvenir of the victory came from Benjamin Hallowell of the *Swiftsure*.

"Herewith," he wrote to his admiral, "I send you a coffin made of part of *l'Orient's* mast, that when you are tired of this life you may be buried in one of your own trophies—but may that period be far distant is the sincere wish of your obedient and much obliged servant."

Berry was sent home in the *Leander* with the despatches, sailing on August 5th. Unfortunately, she fell in with the *Généreux*, one of the two French 74's which escaped from Aboukir Bay. Heavily out-gunned, she was forced to strike after a spirited defence in which a third of her crew was slain. Duplicate despatches had been sent in the little *Mutine*, which sailed on the 13th under the command of Capel, who had been signal lieutenant of the *Vanguard*, to Naples, and from there overland to London. They arrived on October 2nd, the first authentic news of the victory.

It was received with acclamation, made all the more delirious by the fever of uncertainty which had seized the country through lack of previous information. The last news received at the Admiralty had been a copy of Nelson's despatch to St. Vincent, written at Syracuse, stating that he had missed the French fleet in his first voyage to Egypt. The long silence from the Mediterranean since then had caused ministers and people alike to fear the worst, and again there were murmurs against the selection of so junior and so inexperienced an officer as Nelson to command the fleet. But now the gloom was riven by the bright light of Nelson's tactical genius and bonfires enlivened the London streets as the citizens danced in their glee.

Honours now were showered upon him. Nelson himself, in his bold, sloping handwriting, made a list of them.

"Presents," he wrote, "received for my services in the Mediterranean.

"From my own Most Gracious Sovereign, a peerage of Great Britain and a gold medal.

"From the Parliament of Great Britain, for my life and two next heirs, £2,000 per annum.

"From the Parliament of Ireland, not known, but supposed the same as given St. Vincent and Duncan, £1,000 per annum.*

"From the East India Company, £10,000.

"From the Turkish Company, a fine piece of plate.

"From the City of London a sword, and the Captains who served under my orders a sword.

"From the Grand Seignior, a diamond aigrette, or plume of triumph, valued at £2,000. Ditto a rich pelisse, valued at £1,000.

"From the Grand Seignior's Mother, a box set with diamonds, valued at £1,000.

"From the Emperor of Russia, a box set with diamonds, valued at £2,500 and a most elegant letter.

"From the King of the Two Sicilies, a sword richly ornamented with diamonds, valued at £5,000 and a most elegant and kind letter; and the Dukedom of Brontë, with an estate supposed worth £3,000 per annum.†

"From the King of Sardinia, a box set with diamonds, valued at £1,200 and a most elegant letter.

"From the Island of Zante, a gold-headed sword and cane, as an acknowledgement that had it not been for the battle of the Nile, they could not have been liberated from French cruelty.

"From the City of Palermo, a gold box and chain, brought on a silver waiter."

It was an impressive list, and as Nelson wrote it in his cabin in the *Vanguard* he must have been well satisfied with the tangible results of his first great battle. Only in one particular did he feel disappointment. He had expected more than a barony on his elevation to the peerage. Jervis had received an earldom for his battle of St. Vincent, Duncan a viscountcy for Camperdown. The Nile was a more decisive victory than either of those. It was pointed out in Parliament that Nelson, not being a Commander-in-Chief but only employed in a sub-command under St. Vincent, could hardly expect so lofty an honour as had been given to Jervis and Duncan, and that a barony was, in fact, "the highest honour that has ever been conferred on an officer of your standing in the Service".

* This was wishful thinking on Nelson's part, for Ireland gave him nothing. The grant was contemplated, but dropped on the question of Union being raised in Parliament.

† Nelson had been misled. The estate had once been worth this sum, but by now had fallen into ruin and was almost valueless.

The award of a barony—Baron Nelson of the Nile and of Burnham Thorpe—was strongly criticized in Parliament and throughout the country as too meagre a reward for so resounding a victory. That Nelson also thought it inadequate is confirmed in a letter he wrote to Berry, on the latter's receiving a knighthood when he finally returned to London with the delayed despatches. "As to both our honours," he wrote, "it is a proof how much a battle fought near England is prized to one fought at a great distance."

One further honour, if honour it can be called, was the addition of a fourth verse to "God Save the King". It delighted Nelson, who drew the attention of his correspondents to it in the numerous letters he wrote at this time. It was entirely unofficial, of course, and is said to have been written by Mr. Davenport, the editor of the *Poetical Miscellany*, though a rival claim to its authorship is put forward on behalf of Miss Knight, friend of the Hamiltons.

> Join we in Great Nelson's name, (it ran),
> First on the rolls of Fame,
> Him let us sing.
> Spread we his fame around,
> Honour of British ground,
> Who made Nile's shore resound,
> God save the King.

"I know you will sing it with pleasure," wrote Nelson to Fanny.

If there was criticism of the award of a barony to Nelson to be heard in England, it was even more pungent in Naples.

"If I was King of England," wrote Emma Hamilton, "I would make you the most noble present, Duke Nelson, Marquis Nile, Earl Aboukir, Viscount Pyramid, Baron Crocodile, and Prince Victory, that posterity might have you in all forms. Your statue ought to be made of pure gold and placed in the middle of London."

But by this date Emma was prejudiced. The heady flavour of Nelsonian admiration was proving too strong a temptation for her errant heart.

CHAPTER XV

NEAPOLITAN INTERLUDE

"The poor wretched *Vanguard*," wrote Nelson to Fanny on his arrival at Naples, "arrived here on the 22nd of September." She was in tow of the *Thalia*, frigate, her foremast having carried away during a squall on the 15th.

"I must endeavour," he continued, "to convey to you something of what passed; but if it were so affecting to those who were only united to me by bonds of friendship, what must it be to my dearest wife, my friend, my everything which is most dear to me in this world?

"Sir William and Lady Hamilton came out to sea, attended by numerous boats with emblems, etc. They, my most respectable friends, had really been laid up and seriously ill; first from anxiety and then from joy. It was imprudently told Lady Hamilton in a moment, and the effect was like a shot; she fell apparently dead and is not yet perfectly recovered from severe bruises. Alongside came my honoured friends: the scene in the boat was terribly affecting; up flew her Ladyship, and exclaiming, 'O God, is it possible?' she fell into my arms more dead than alive. . . . All Naples calls me 'Nostro Liberatore'; my greeting from the lower classes was truly affecting. I hope some day to have the pleasure of introducing you to Lady Hamilton, she is one of the very best women in this world; she is an honour to her sex."

The *Vanguard* had taken just over a month on her voyage to Naples. When Berry had been sent home in the *Leander* with the despatches, Nelson had promoted Captain Thomas Hardy out of the *Mutine* to be her new captain, and Hardy had had a difficult time of it in patching her up for the voyage to the west. She had suffered much in the battle, especially in her masts and rigging, and it was only by supreme seamanship on the part of her officers and men that she was kept in a fit state to take the sea.

The *Vanguard's* arrival at Naples marked the beginning of an unhappy chapter in Nelson's career. As one reads his letters, almost all dated from the *Vanguard*, it is difficult to escape the feeling that the adulation he received from every quarter of the globe had gone a little to his head. There was, too, the increasing attachment to Emma Hamilton which on occasions seems to have clouded his judgment. The temptation to stay at Naples and Palermo in the company of the Hamiltons was a probable cause.

Perhaps the first and most grievous of Nelson's errors of judgment at this time was his urging of Ferdinand of Naples to attack the French in the Roman Republic. It is true that the French lines of communication in central Italy were dangerously extended, and it is equally true that the British fleet, freed by the victory at Aboukir Bay, could make those communications extremely hazardous by operations along the Italian coast. A concerted attack by all countries together—those of Pitt's second coalition—might well succeed in driving the French out of Italy if properly handled and co-ordinated. But for Naples alone to precipitate action by an isolated attack on the French army was an act of folly. Yet it was just this that Nelson urged the King of Naples to do. He was aided and abetted by Lady Hamilton and by the impulsive Queen who, being a daughter of Maria Theresa of Austria, and sister to Marie Antoinette, had a burning hatred of republicanism in any, but especially in its French, form.

The strange mixture that was Nelson at this period yet retained enough strategic insight to grasp at the importance of the recapture of Malta, taken and garrisoned by Napoleon on his way to Alexandria. Ball was already lying off the islands in the *Alexander* and thither Nelson sailed in the *Vanguard* on October 15th, taking with him the *Minotaur, Audacious, Goliath,* and *Mutine.* He remained there for a week, during which time he witnessed the surrender of the island of Gozo. He left again for Naples on November 1st with the prisoners captured in the Castle of Gozo on board the *Vanguard,* leaving Ball to conduct the blockade of Malta with the *Alexander, Goliath, Audacious, Terpsichore,* and the fireship *Incendiary.* He hoped and expected a speedy capitulation, but it was to be nearly two years before the citadel of Valetta finally surrendered to the patient Ball. Before the end, rats were being sold in Valetta at 10*d.* each, and even they were so thin that there was little on them worth eating.

The *Vanguard* was back at Naples on November 5th.

> "I am, I fear," wrote Nelson to St. Vincent on the 7th, "drawn into a promise that Naples Bay shall never be left without an English man of war. . . . Who could withstand the request of such a Queen? . . . The King goes to the Army to-morrow, in three days he hopes to march. His Majesty is determined to conquer or die at the head of his army, which is composed of 30,000 healthy, good-looking troops."

Good-looking they may have been, but they were shockingly led. General Mack had been imported from Austria with a reputation as an experienced tactician and bold general, but his first efforts as a commander in the field filled all who witnessed them with terror and foreboding. Conducting manœuvres before an audience composed of the Royal Family and high-ranking British officers, and with the advantage of being able to command the movements of both sides in the mock battle, he got his forces so inextricably mixed that he finished the day with his own troops completely surrounded by those of the supposed enemy. "I have formed my opinion," wrote Nelson. "I heartily pray I may be mistaken."

For the naval side of the projected operations, Nelson embarked

5,000 Neapolitan troops in his squadron and sailed on November 22nd for Leghorn, arriving there on the 28th. A summons to the town to surrender received a hurried acquiescence in the face of such force, and the troops were landed that night. Nelson left Troubridge with a small squadron to act off the coast and to stop all traffic to the French armies, and by December 5th was back in Naples. As the *Vanguard* anchored in the bay he hurried ashore to learn the latest news of this private war against the French.

The situation was hardly encouraging. The King had set out, in full Neapolitan regimentals resplendent with gold lace and cocks' feathers, and had made a triumphal entry into Rome. As yet he had not had to fight. But as soon as he did, it was early discovered that 30,000 Neapolitans were no match for 15,000 disciplined Frenchmen. At the first shot the army of Naples disintegrated and the King, throwing away his gold lace and feathers, led the flight in civilian disguise back to his capital. "The Neapolitan officers did not lose much honour," commented Nelson, "for, God knows, they had not much to lose; but they lost all they had."

By mid-December it was obvious that the farce had run its tragic course. "Things are in such a critical state here," wrote Nelson to Troubridge on the 15th, "that I desire you will join me without one moment's loss of time. . . . The King is returned here and everything is as bad as possible." The only course left now was flight, but this was difficult to arrange without creating suspicion in the minds of the city's inhabitants. It was finally done through Lady Hamilton who, alone of the English colony in Naples, could move freely to and from the Palace.

"Lady Hamilton," wrote Southey, "arranged everything for the removal of the royal family. This was conducted, on her part, with the greatest address, and without suspicion, because she had been in habits of constant correspondence with the queen. It was known that the removal could not be effected without danger; for the mob, and especially the lazzaroni, were attached to the king; and as, at this time, they felt a natural presumption in their own numbers and strength, they insisted that he should not leave Naples. Several persons fell victims to their fury; among others was a messenger from Vienna, whose body was dragged under the windows of the palace in the king's sight. The king and queen spoke to the mob and pacified them, but it would not have been safe, while they were in this agitated state, to have embarked the effects of the royal family openly. Lady Hamilton, like a heroine of modern romance, explored, with no little danger, a subterraneous passage, leading from the palace to the seaside; through this passage the royal treasure, the choicest pieces of painting and sculpture, and other property to the value of two millions and a half, were conveyed to the shore and stowed safely on board the English ships.

"On the night of the 21st, at half-past eight, Nelson landed, brought out the whole royal family, embarked them in three barges, and carried them safely through a tremendous sea to the *Vanguard*. Notice was then

immediately given to the British merchants that they would be received
on board any ship in the squadron. Their property had previously been
embarked in transports. Two days were passed in the bay, for the
purpose of taking such persons on board as required an asylum; and on
the night of the 23rd, the fleet sailed."

On the following day the *Vanguard* ran into a storm.

"It blew harder," wrote Nelson to St. Vincent, "than I ever experienced since I have been at sea . . . but not a word of uneasiness
escaped the lips of any of the Royal Family. In the 25th, at 9 a.m.,
Prince Albert, their Majesties' youngest child, having eat a hearty
breakfast, was taken ill, and at 7 p.m. died in the arms of Lady Hamilton;
and here it is my duty to tell your Lordship the obligations which the
whole Royal Family as well as myself are under on this trying occasion
to her Ladyship. . . . Lady Hamilton provided her own beds, linen, etc.,
and became *their slave*, for except one man, no person belonging to
Royalty assisted the Royal Family, nor did her Ladyship enter a bed the
whole time they were on board. . . . I must not omit to state the kindness
of Captain Hardy and every officer in the *Vanguard*, all of whom readily
gave up their beds for the convenience of the numerous persons attending
the Royal Family."

Palermo was, if anything, even worse than Naples for Nelson
in his present mood. While the *Vanguard* lay at anchor in the harbour,
the Admiral lived ashore in a large house he rented and shared with
the Hamiltons. There they gambled nightly—it was no rare event
for Emma to lose as much as £500 in gold of Nelson's money in a
single sitting—and joined in the antics and absurdities of what was
probably the most dissolute Court in Europe. It was an unedifying
spectacle and gossip blazed round the persons of the Victor of the
Nile and the wife of the English Ambassador. While it was treated as
a great joke in Neapolitan society, its effect in the British fleet was
tragic.

While the *Vanguard* lay inactive at Palermo, the remainder of
Nelson's captains were fully employed afloat. Ball was blockading
Malta with the *Alexander*, *Audacious*, *Goliath*, and *Emerald*, Troubridge
was watching Alexandria with the *Culloden*, *Zealous*, *Swiftsure*, *Theseus*,
and four smaller ships, Louis had taken over at Leghorn with the
Minotaur and *Terpsichore*, and Darby, in the *Bellerophon*, was escorting
a convoy to Leghorn. Only the *Vanguard* remained at Palermo. For
a short space of time she, too, was employed when Nelson sent her
to reinforce Ball off Malta on January 31st, 1799. But she was back
again in a fortnight at her old anchorage. Two months later she was
at Tripoli, carrying a strong letter of protest from Nelson to the Bey,
who had been flirting with the French. The arrival of the *Vanguard*
had an immediate effect and the Bey renounced his former actions.

To the westward, where St. Vincent watched with a heavy heart
the behaviour of his favourite admiral, events were beginning to

The seventh *Vanguard*, 1869

The eighth *Vanguard*, 1909

H.M.S. *Vanguard*

move. The Commander-in-Chief, old and tired, was a very sick man, on the verge of returning to England and handing over his fleet to his Second-in-Command, Lord Keith. Further north, Lord Bridport was on the Brest station, watching Admiral Bruix and the French squadron in that port. On April 25th, apparently under a mistaken impression that the French were contemplating a descent on Ireland, Bridport withdrew his squadron to the northward. It was the chance for which Bruix had been waiting and he slipped out of Brest with a squadron of 25 sail of the line and five frigates.

As soon as Bridport discovered that the French were gone he sent a message to Keith, off Cadiz, and to St. Vincent, at Gibraltar, and himself took his squadron to Cork, leaving the way wide open for Bruix. The French admiral turned south and, although sighted by Keith on May 4th, slipped into the Mediterranean unscathed. The French ships passed Gibraltar on the 5th, and by May 13th were safe in Toulon.

The French objective was to concentrate sufficient naval forces in the Mediterranean and repeat the situation of 1796, when the English had been forced to leave those waters. When Keith, in pursuit of Bruix, left his station off Cadiz, it had opened the way for the escape of the Spanish fleet under Admiral Massaredo, consisting of 17 sail of the line. They followed Bruix into the Mediterranean and on May 20th reached Cartagena, though rather battered by a storm and in need of repair.

It was an interesting situation. Had Bruix been a "seaman determined on attack" he might have achieved the French plan, for the British ships were well scattered. But St. Vincent, old as he was, moved too fast for him. From Minorca, which he had reached, he sent orders to Keith to detach Commodore Duckworth with four ships of the line to reinforce Nelson and himself sent 12 of the line to Keith off Toulon. He also sent him instructions to concentrate his ships at Rosas Bay, where he would be in an ideal position for preventing a junction between the French and the Spaniards.

Nelson, still in the *Vanguard* at Palermo, received all this information with mixed feelings. He was deeply committed to his Neapolitan adventure and was planning a close blockade of Naples with the object of returning there with Ferdinand and his queen. He called in his outlying ships, with the exception of the *Alexander* off Malta, and cruised in the Sicilian channel in case, as he suspected, the French were to make a dash to Naples. With no sign of a French movement towards the east, he returned to Palermo, "to offer myself for the service of Naples where I knew the French fleet was going". His offer, naturally enough, was accepted and Nelson sailed with the whole of his fleet for the Bay of Naples, arriving there on June 24th. He found the city already retaken by the Neapolitans, with only the castle of St. Elmo holding out. When it fell on July 13th, all Naples was free again.

While Nelson and his squadron were thus occupied in the service of the King of Naples, the slowness of Keith in obeying St. Vincent's orders to concentrate in Rosas Bay had enabled Bruix to leave Toulon and link up with Massaredo. Had the Spanish ships been in better shape, Bruix would have had a fleet with which he could have dominated the Mediterranean. But he decided that he was not strong enough to tackle the English and instead set a course for Gibraltar and the Atlantic. He passed through the Straits on July 7th. As soon as Keith heard of his destination, he decided to chase with the whole of his fleet. Before he finally left the Mediterranean, and fearing that Minorca might be a French objective should it be left completely unguarded, he sent orders to Nelson to detach a small squadron to take over the defence there.

The orders arrived when Nelson was in the very midst of his Naples expedition. He decided to ignore them. And in the meanwhile Keith was away in chase of Bruix. It meant that for a period the western Mediterranean was left without an English ship in it. As matters turned out, no harm was done, for the French took no steps to profit from the lack of ships at Minorca. Keith was back again by the end of July to restore the balance, but annoyed to find that his orders had been disregarded by his junior.

On June 8th, Nelson had shifted his flag from the *Vanguard* to the *Foudroyant*, taking Hardy with him as his flag captain. As a result the captain of the *Foudroyant*, William Brown, exchanged into the *Vanguard*, and it was as a private ship that she finished her commission in the Mediterranean.

For a short time she joined Ball off Malta, assisting in the blockade, and later was with Duckworth at Port Mahon, in Minorca. But by the end of 1799 it had become apparent that the repairs carried out at Naples after the Battle of the Nile were not extensive enough to keep her fully seaworthy. She had received so much damage during the action that only a complete refit in a dockyard could bring her back to full efficiency. It was decided to send her home and in December she passed through the Straits of Gibraltar. Eighteen months before, she had made minor history by being the first British warship to enter the Mediterranean after nearly two years of French domination there. Now, when she left again, the inland sea was firmly in the hands of the British Navy and French ships sailing there did so only at the risk of being brought to a speedy action. The great battle in which she had fought as Nelson's flagship had ensured that once again the British flag flew unchallenged over the waters of the Mediterranean.

CHAPTER XVI

BALTIC OPERATIONS

THE years of 1800 and 1801 saw the *Vanguard* in home waters after her Mediterranean commission, for the most part in dockyard hands for repairs. 1801 was the year which saw Nelson's second great victory, that of Copenhagen, and also the end of the continental war between France, Austria, and Prussia. With the treaty of peace signed at Luneville on February 9th, England was again the only nation left in the struggle.

Once more Napoleon turned his thoughts towards invasion across the Channel.

"Tous les moyens propres à entretenir la haine de la nation contre la Grande-Bretagne furent employés avec activité et avec succès. Les autoritiés, les orateurs du gouvernement, les écrivains publicistes, rivalisèrent de zéle pour prêcher cette espèce de croisade contre l'éternelle ennemie de la France."

But no matter how furiously "the authorities, the government orators, the journalists, outrivalled each other in their zeal to preach this crusade against the eternal enemy", there still remained the English Channel to cross and the British Navy to defeat.

As soon as she came out of the dockyard, the *Vanguard* joined the Channel Fleet, under the command of St. Vincent, and spent her time in anti-invasion duties. Exactly how far, at this stage, Napoleon was seriously considering the invasion of England is difficult to estimate. Certainly he assembled a large fleet of barges at Boulogne and adjacent ports, and equally certainly a large army was camped ashore in the immediate neighbourhood. But at the same time as these rather obvious preparations were being made, negotiations for peace were in train between the Directory in Paris and Addington, Pitt's successor as Prime Minister. Indeed, they had been in train for some months. Whatever hopes Napoleon may have had of getting an army across the Channel must have been dashed in July when Nelson, home from Copenhagen, was appointed Second-in-Command of the Channel Fleet. He had already had one taste of this admiral's quality in the Mediterranean. But by October the Napoleonic bogey was laid, temporarily at any rate, when a treaty of peace between England and France was ratified on the 9th of the month.

The *Vanguard's* next commission was dictated mainly by French actions. In December 1801 a strong French squadron commanded by Vice-Admiral Villaret-Joyeuse, with an army of 21,000 men under General Leclerc, was sent to the West Indies where trouble at San Domingo was causing some embarrassment to the French.

Napoleon, in a fit of republican enthusiasm, had appointed the negro general Toussaint-Louverture as Commander-in-Chief of the colonial army there. He had celebrated his commission from the First Consul by writing a new constitution for the island under which he had appointed himself President and Governor for life. He followed this by expropriating all the French estates and diverting their revenues to himself. He was safe enough while the war lasted, for he knew he could count on the help of British warships should the French attempt to send an expedition against the island. But with the peace of 1801 his period of immunity was over and a swift retribution followed. The unfortunate Toussaint died a painful death in the prison of Fort de Joux in France.

It was this act of domestic politics on the part of France which decided the *Vanguard's* next scene of operations. The appearance of a powerful French squadron in the West Indies, even if it were only sent out to deal with the recalcitrant Toussaint, was a latent threat to British interests in those waters. Few, either in England or France, were deceived by the precarious peace and in both countries preparations for a renewal of the war were being actively pressed forward. So, during 1802, an impressive fleet of 28 sail of the line, under the command of Rear-Admiral Sir John Duckworth, was sent out to Caribbean waters. Among the ships was the *Vanguard*, now commanded by Captain Charles Inglis. The fleet arrived at Port Royal, in Jamaica, during the early part of April and lay there for some months.

They were tragic months for the English ships. An epidemic of yellow fever broke out in the fleet and claimed an ever-increasing number of victims. Men were dying by hundreds, and the great heat of the summer months accentuated the rapidity with which the disease spread. In the *Vanguard* one of the victims was her captain, Inglis, and he was replaced by Captain James Walker, under whom the operations of the next year or two were conducted.

With the renewal of the war in 1803, Duckworth instituted a close blockade of San Domingo. He sent the *Theseus*, Captain John Bligh, to lie off the port and there to take the *Vanguard* under her orders and maintain the blockade. Bligh left Port Royal on December 19th, but on arrival off San Domingo was unable to make contact with the *Vanguard*. On January 15th, 1804, these orders were followed by new ones, instructing Bligh to lift the San Domingo blockade and to sail to Curaçao with the *Hercule, Vanguard,* and two frigates, and there demand the surrender of the island from the Dutch. Again the *Vanguard* was missing. Bligh proceeded with his force but found the opposition too strong for him and on February 25th was forced to re-embark his men and return to Jamaica. The incident is remarkable only as an example of the poverty of Duckworth's staff work, for all the time the *Vanguard* was cruising off the island of San Domingo, Walker having received no orders to join Bligh and being in total ignorance of the design against Curaçao. His presence there might well have given Bligh sufficient margin of strength to reduce the island.

In the meantime, however, the *Vanguard* had figured in two small actions which had ended favourably. On June 30th, 1803, when in company with the *Cumberland*, off Cape St. Nicholas Mole, San Domingo, she had sighted a large French frigate trying to make the harbour. It was the *Créole*, of 40 guns, Captain Jean Marie Pierre Lebastard. The two 74's gave chase and soon were within range. The *Vanguard*, first up with the frigate, gave her a couple of broadsides and forced her to haul down her colours. On board were found General Morgan, second-in-command of the island, his staff, and 530 troops. The *Créole* was added to the British Navy, but was so inefficiently repaired at the dockyard at Jamaica that she foundered on her way home to England.

The *Vanguard's* next action was on July 25th. On the previous day the French squadron blockaded in the harbour at San Domingo, consisting of the *Duguay-Trouin*, *Duquêsne*, and *Guerrière*, had taken advantage of a heavy squall and slipped out of port in an attempt to clear the blockade and return to France. They were sighted and followed, but separated during the night. The *Duguay-Trouin* and *Guerrière* steered to the eastward and were chased by the *Elephant*. The *Duquêsne* made off westward, hotly followed by the *Vanguard*, *Bellerophon*, and *Theseus*, together with the *Aeolus* and *Tartar*, frigates.

By noon on the 25th the *Vanguard* and the *Tartar* had caught the French 74 and opened a heavy fire on her. The *Duquêsne*, luffing up to escape the *Vanguard's* broadsides, found herself being cut off by the *Bellerophon* and *Aeolus* and promptly surrendered to the *Vanguard*. She was a fine new 74 of 1901 tons and was added to the British Navy only, like the *Créole*, to be wrecked the following year. The *Vanguard's* casualties in this action were one man killed and one wounded.

The *Duguay-Trouin*, after a series of adventures with British ships, both in West Indian and European waters, reached Corunna in safety. She was with the combined fleet of France and Spain at Trafalgar and, escaping after that battle, was captured three weeks later by Sir Richard Strachan. She was added to the British Navy under the name of *Implacable* and after a distinquished career in the Baltic operations of 1808 and 1809, she finished her life as a training ship at Portsmouth. It was only in 1949, her timbers rotted beyond repair, that she was taken out into the Channel and sunk off the Sussex coast, sole survivor, apart from the *Victory*, of Nelson's third great victory at Trafalgar.

Two more small vessels fell to the *Vanguard* during this summer of 1803, the *Papillon*, of six guns, and the *Courier de Nantes*, a schooner, of two. Both were captured off St. Marc, San Domingo, the first on September 4th and the second on the following day.

The *Vanguard* was ordered home in 1805, the year of Trafalgar. She was, in fact, very nearly a participant in that great battle, for on her arrival home in English waters she was taken in hand and hurriedly refitted with a view to joining Collingwood's fleet off Cadiz.

Nelson, in the *Victory*, sailed on September 15th, but the *Vanguard* was not ready to accompany her. She put to sea a few weeks later, but before she was clear of the Channel news had come in of the great victory and her presence farther south was no longer required. She returned to Portsmouth and joined the Channel Fleet for the next two years.

While the *Vanguard* was in home waters during 1806 and 1807, the war in Europe was reaching a new pitch of intensity. At sea, the staggering victory of Trafalgar had shattered the French naval power and removed once and for all the threat of an invasion of England. But though defeated at sea, there was as yet no stopping Napoleon on land. A swift campaign in Prussia in 1807 had ended in the annihilating victory of Friedland, and once again the pendulum had swung back. Friedland had opened the way to the Treaty of Tilsit and the subjection of Russia, Prussia, and Austria to the military prowess of France. Again there was a pause in the continental war and for the third time only England was left to uphold the standard of freedom.

The Treaty of Tilsit gave Napoleon the opportunity of organizing his "Northern Confederacy", under which the Sound and the Belts, dividing Denmark and Sweden and forming the only entry into the Baltic, were to be closed to British shipping. At the same time a Napoleonic decree prohibited all trade between the northern group of countries and Great Britain. But this, however, was not the only danger. In those northern waters lay the fleets of Denmark, Russia, and Sweden, and together they amounted to some 60 sail of the line. Great Britain acted swiftly. Friedland was fought on June 14th, armistice negotiations with Russia and Prussia were concluded on the 25th, and the two peace treaties signed at Tilsit on July 7th and 9th respectively. Seventeen days later a British fleet under Admiral James Gambier sailed from Yarmouth Roads bound for the Baltic. Gambier's orders were to occupy the Sound and to demand the handing over of the Danish fleet under a promise to return it undamaged at the end of the war. In the event of the Danes refusing, the ships were to be seized by force.

With Gambier's fleet sailed the *Vanguard*, now under the command of Captain Alexander Fraser. By August 1st the British ships were off Göteborg, and Gambier detached the *Ganges*, flying the broad pendant of Commodore Keats, with the *Vanguard*, *Orion*, and *Nassau*, to block the Great Belt and prevent any assistance being sent up to Copenhagen.

By August 15th all was ready. Gambier's fleet closed in on the town and General Lord Cathcart, in command of the military side of the operation, landed his troops and began to erect batteries on the high ground above the city. A demand was sent to the Crown Prince of Denmark to surrender the Danish ships, to which he returned a polite rejection. There was no other course but to resort to force and at 7.30 p.m. on September 2nd the first British shells fell on Copenhagen. In a few minutes large fires had been started. The bombardment was continued on the 3rd, but less hotly. On the 4th, the Danes still being unwilling to surrender their ships, it was re-opened with great fury and, within a couple of hours, huge conflagrations were sweeping through the city.

So it continued through the whole of the 5th, till it seemed that all Copenhagen must be reduced to ashes. But at last the Danes asked for an armistice and by the evening of the 6th articles were drawn up under which the Danish fleet was surrendered. On October 21st Gambier returned to England with his fleet, escorting 18 Danish sail of the line, 11 frigates, and a number of smaller craft. Only the *Vanguard*, with a few frigates and smaller vessels, was left to show the British flag in northern waters. She made a few cruises in the Great Belt until the severity of the winter brought all activities to a stop. In February 1808 the Great Belt froze over and the *Vanguard* remained gripped in the ice until it broke up again at the end of March.

The Treaty of Tilsit, however, had repercussions in England more far-reaching than the seizure of the Danish warships. It had also brought Denmark and Russia into active partnership with France. Although, while Gambier's fleet lay in the Sound and off Copenhagen, the Czar had kept notably silent about his new alliance, he wasted no time in breathing defiance as soon as Gambier was safely home and the winter had closed the Baltic to British ships.

The new danger lay with Sweden. Alone of the northern countries she had refused to join Napoleon's "Confederacy". Her fleet numbered 12 sail of the line and six frigates. That of Russia consisted of 20 new line of battleships, mounting 1,588 guns, and 14 frigates, carrying 426 guns. The ships of Sweden were a temptation that the Czar was not strong enough to resist. Fortunately, the wintry weather of early 1808 had kept the Russians locked in their harbours and by the time they were ready to venture forth, another British squadron was already operating in the Baltic. It was commanded by Admiral Saumarez, who had fought so gallantly at the Nile, in Nelson's flagship at Trafalgar, the *Victory*. Second in command to him was Hood, another Nile veteran, in the *Centaur*. Of the ships that had fought in that battle, the *Vanguard*, now under the command of Captain Thomas Baker, the *Orion*, and *Goliath* were included in the fleet. Also among them was the *Implacable*, which as the French *Duguay-Trouin* had escaped from the *Vanguard* in 1803.

The operations of 1808 in the Baltic were strenuous, if unproductive of any outstanding result. During August a Russian fleet under Vice-Admiral Hanickoff, composed of 12 ships of the line, sailed from Cronstadt and anchored in Hangö Bay, in Swedish Finland. Nearby, in Oro Roads, lay the Swedish fleet, weakly manned because of an epidemic which had swept through the ships and decimated their crews. On August 20th Hanickoff arrived off the Roads with his squadron, and on the same night Hood reached the same place with the *Centaur* and *Implacable*. The two ships slipped safely past the

Russian blockade to bring a welcome reinforcement to the weakened Swedes.

Five days later the combined fleet of English and Swedish ships weighed anchor and stood out to sea. Led by the *Centaur*, they formed a line of battle and set a course for the Russians. The sight was too much for Hanickoff who, setting every sail his vessels could carry, made off to the eastward and home.

The *Centaur* and *Implacable*, under a press of sail, soon outdistanced the undermanned Swedish ships and were hot in pursuit of the flying Russians. Early in the morning of the 26th they were 10 miles ahead of the rest of the fleet, with the *Implacable* about a mile in advance of the *Centaur*. At 6.30 a.m. the Russian 74-gun *Sewolod* was within range of the *Implacable's* guns, and after half an hour's brisk action was forced to strike her colours. But she was not to be captured yet for Hanickoff, seeing that the *Implacable* was unsupported, ran down with his fleet to the *Sewolod's* assistance and forced the *Implacable* to fall back on the fast-approaching *Centaur*.

It was, however, not the end of the action, for as the Russian fleet was entering the harbour of Rogerswick, the *Centaur* and *Implacable* again managed to cut off the crippled *Sewolod*. Again she struck her colours, and again the prize was denied to the British ships. For this time she was hard aground and all the efforts of the *Centaur* and *Implacable* were insufficient to tow her off into deep water. Instead, she was put to the torch and burnt to the waterline.

The *Vanguard*, during this brush with the Russian fleet, was in the western Baltic, patrolling the Great Belt and preventing the movements of any French or allied ships. For three more years she remained in Baltic waters, engaged on minor operations in hampering the French campaign in the north. Finally, in 1811, she was ordered home after little short of five years in these inhospitable waters.

But if there had been little for her to do during her last three years in the Baltic, there was even less for her in English waters. The war at sea, to all intents and purposes, was over, ended by the crushing defeat of the French at Trafalgar which had crippled her sea-power. Now the blockade of Europe, carried out by the British Navy, was slowly strangling Napoleon's continental operations. The disaster of the 1812 campaign against Russia was a terrible blow to the French Emperor and the equally great disasters of the Peninsula campaign had brought his end yet nearer.

Slowly, surely, the net around Napoleon was now beginning to draw in. As 1814 gave way to 1815, the curtain rose on the last act of the great drama, now to be played out to its bitter finale. The banishment to Elba, the return to France, the "Hundred Days", the march on Brussels, this was the prelude to that fateful day when the French Emperor and the English Duke met for the first time on the field of Waterloo. It was the end of French tyranny in Europe, and the streets of Paris echoed to the tramp of victorious allied soldiers.

After nearly twenty years of fighting, peace had come again to Europe.

We can catch one more glimpse of the fifth *Vanguard* before she disappears from history. It shows her after her return from the Baltic, during those years when there was little for the Navy to do. Captains were beginning to pay more attention to the looks of their vessels, and a ship's efficiency was more often judged by the degree of "brightening of brass heads, of bitts and capstan hoops", than by the skill and seamanship of her officers and men. The sailors disliked the extra labour of this "spit and polish", and even more the discipline which accompanied it. It was a common sight to see a man lashed to a grating at the gangway and given the "cat" for trivial offences.

"A week rarely passed," wrote Sloane-Stanley, "at this period without some man receiving his three or four dozen lashes at the gangway. The first time I witnessed corporal punishment I was horror-struck and, after the first minute or so, averted my eyes to avoid the ghastly sight; but after a time I became so used to seeing what was called 'scratching a man's back', that I could contemplate the spectacle from beginning to end without shrinking. . . . I must have seen some hundreds in my day."

An anonymous sailor on board the *Vanguard* composed a song which in its way is a little epitome of life on the lower deck of those days. It achieved a certain popularity throughout the Navy.

Come, all you seamen, stout and bold, and listen to my song,
It's worth your whole attention, I'll not detain you long.

Chorus

*Then let us sing the Vanguard's praise, proclaim her valiant name,
Cruel usage I have met with since I sail'd in the same.*

Concerning of the *Vanguard*, a ship of noble fame,
With her r—— commander, Mickey Walker call'd by name.

At four o'clock you must turn out, the decks to holystone;
One and all you must go down upon your marrow bones.

Then Mr. Croycraft comes on deck, and he'll begin to curse
    and swear;
Both watches of gunners send up on deck to see your lashings
    are all square.

At eight o'clock it's up top-gallant yards, to the mast-head
    you must run,
And if you are not the first ship, your name is taken down.

Then down from the mast-head to the gangway you must repair,
And there is the gratings rigged ready to punish you there.

M

And when on shore by leave you go, if beyond your time you
    stay,
Then you are put on the stage party for the space of sixty days.

Then next you're put in chokey, boys, you get both thin and
    white;
And if you break your liberty, scrub copper from morning till
    night.

But if you are in the black list, as true as I'm a sinner,
Then you must polish brass-work while the crew are at their
    dinner.

But if a fighting you do go, you'll never get any rest;
They will drive you off the lower deck, in the galley for to mess.

And when you are in the galley mess, your heart is fill'd with
    woe;
Your monthly money it is stopt, on shore you must not go.

Now, you seamen of the *Vanguard*, you had better not get
    drunk;
You will be laid upon your back, and they'll use the stomach
    pump.

If your hammock it is dirty, and you know no reason why,
Then you must scrub it in the head, carry it on a boat-hook
    to dry.

There's a man on our lower deck, he is called Jondy Cross;*
If I had my will of him, I'd overboard him toss.

But when on shore the bully comes, if with him you should
    fall in,
The whore that gives to him a drubbing shall have a gown
    and a gallon of gin.

So now to conclude, and finish my song;
I am a saucy mizen-top man, to the *Vanguard* does belong

But if to sea I go again, I'd sooner swing in a halter,
Before I'd sail in any ship commanded by Mickey Walker."

This fifth *Vanguard*, the most famous of them all, had served in
stirring times.

"It was," wrote Clowes, "a period of extraordinary triumphs. It saw
the exhaustion by the steady force of sea power, of the greatest military
organization that the world has ever known; and it exhibited the

---

* Jondy, Master-at-Arms, the head of the ship's police.

influence of sea power under two distinct aspects. At Trafalgar, amid the roar of guns and with the terrible impressiveness that belongs to the critical moments of the world's story, the flower of the navies of France and Spain was destroyed. After Trafalgar, more quietly yet not less surely, what remained of the colonies, the commerce, the wealth and the resources of Great Britain's allied foes was slowly taken from them, until they were rendered so weak by the steady denial to them of any use of the sea, that even the small army of Great Britain was able to take a decisive share in the annihilation of the military horde which, for years, had terrorised Europe."

And in those years of decision, which settled the pattern of the world for the next century, the fifth *Vanguard* had played a decisive part.

CHAPTER XVII

FROM SAIL TO STEAM

THE story of the sixth *Vanguard*, though long in years, is almost completely devoid of action. The Revolutionary wars had come to an end with Napoleon's final defeat at Waterloo, and his death at Longwood, on the Island of St. Helena, in 1821, had brought to a final close the ambitions of France and had ushered in a long period of peace. The few occasions on which Her Majesty's ships were called upon to show their teeth were more in the nature of preventive actions to maintain the peace rather than of large-scale battles.

The new *Vanguard* was launched in 1835. She had been built to the designs of Captain Sir William Symonds, one of the most brilliant of the naval architects of the early 19th century. The ships designed by him, though broader, roomier, and with a greater height between decks, were yet faster and more stable than those which came from the drawing-boards of other architects. He realized the importance of finer lines in hull form and their influence on speed and stability. The "Symondite" ships, as they were called, represented the highest standard of perfection to which the sailing navy of England ever reached.

This sixth *Vanguard* was of 2,609 tons, with an overall length of 190 feet, a beam of 57 feet, and a draught of 23 feet 4 inches. She carried 80 guns, twenty 32-pounders and eight 8-inch on her lower deck, twenty-four 32-pounders and four 8-inch on her main deck. A further twenty-four 32-pounders were mounted on her upper deck. quarterdeck, and forecastle. An innovation was the 8-inch gun, which fired a 51-lb shell or a 56-lb plugged hollow shot. Like the 32-pounders they were smooth-bore muzzle loaders, for the rifled bore breech loader was not brought into general use in the British Navy until after the close of the Crimean War.

Within four years of her launching the *Vanguard* was serving in the Mediterranean Fleet, where Admiral Sir Robert Stopford was Commander-in-Chief. Her captain was Sir Thomas Fellowes and early in 1839 she was detached to the Levant where an "Eastern Question" was troubling the waters. It had started some seven years previously when Mehemet Ali, Pacha of Egypt, had invaded Syria in an attempted rebellion against the Sultan of Turkey. Mehemet, who was "of low origin", had begun life as a private soldier but, by a mingled policy of flattery, treachery, and deceit, had raised himself to the head of affairs in Egypt. This, however, was not enough to feed his ambition and in his more expansive moments he saw himself paramount lord of the whole of the Middle East. By 1839 he had conquered Arabia, Crete, and most of Syria, and a harassed Sultan,

anxious for the safety of Constantinople, had called for assistance
from Russia. The Czar was very ready to extend his influence to the
eastern Mediterranean and had sent a squadron of warships to the
Turkish capital and a Russian army to Anatolia.

Mehemet, marching up the Syrian coast, had met and defeated
the Turkish army at Nezib on June 29th, 1839. Two days later the
Sultan, Mahmoud, died, to be succeeded by his sixteen-year-old
son, Abdul Medjid—he looked eight years older, commented Napier,
"but it is said that his frequent visits to the harem had given him
this appearance of premature age". But while Mahmoud might have
been trusted to keep himself from being entangled in the Russian
net, the same could not be said for the inexperienced Abdul Medjid.
Neither Great Britain nor France was prepared to stand by and watch
the young Sultan fall unchallenged under the influence of Russia.
Both countries sent their fleets into the troubled waters, Britain hers
to the help of the Sultan in his struggle against Mehemet Ali, France
hers to assist Mehemet in his insurrection.

It was a tense moment, made even more dangerous by the open
and warlike preparations being carried out in France. For a week or
two the whole situation verged on a general war. Palmerston, Foreign
Secretary in London, needed all his skill to avert the danger and it
took strong diplomatic pressure and some hard bargaining to induce
France to change her mind. The best she could be persuaded to do
was to refrain from taking active steps in aid of Mehemet, but she was
not prepared to co-operate in his suppression. However, it was enough
to remove the threat of a general war and to leave the "Eastern
Question" a purely local one.

When the *Vanguard* was detached to proceed to the Levant, Fellowes
was given direct orders from Palmerston to maintain the strictest
neutrality. His instructions were to keep an eye on the Turkish fleet,
whose loyalty to the Sultan was doubtful, and to report its movements.
The *Vanguard* lay in Besika Bay, near the mouth of the Dardanelles, and
watched the Turkish fleet sail to the southward. Fellowes followed,
prevented by his orders from making any attempt to stop them, and
saw them enter Alexandria harbour, there to give themselves up
to Mehemet Ali. It was an ominous move and hardly a successful
beginning to Great Britain's self-imposed task of restraining Mehemet's
ambitions of dominating the Levant.

With the death of the old Sultan a more robust policy was considered necessary and Stopford received orders from Palmerston to take
the fleet into Syrian waters. During July the *Vanguard* was joined by
a combined fleet of 11 British sail of the line and nine French ships,
under the joint command of Stopford and Rear-Admiral Lalande.
But it was too late to stop the junction of the Turkish and Egyptian
fleets and the French and British ships wintered at Smyrna, uneasy
spectators of a situation which showed no signs of amelioration.

Early in May 1840 an ultimatum was sent on behalf of the British

and French governments to Mehemet Ali, offering to make him
hereditary viceroy of Egypt if he would evacuate the territories he
had conquered and restore the Turkish fleet to the Sultan. The
alternative was a threat to dispossess him of all his dominions, including
Egypt. He was given 20 days in which to decide, but before the
expiration of that period had proclaimed that what he had won by
the sword, he would keep by the sword. He was influenced in that
decision by his possession of the Sultan's fleet and by the knowledge
that the French ships were reluctant to act directly against him.
French sympathies, indeed, were still on his side.

The combined British and French fleet lay off Mitylene, with
the French still refusing to take any further steps towards the stopping
of Mehemet in his advance up the Syrian coast. Stopford detached a
squadron of six ships to the Syrian coast at Beyrout, placing them
under the command of Captain Charles Napier and, at the same time,
authorizing him to fly the broad pendant of a Commodore. Napier,
hot-headed, irascible, yet a brilliant commander, arrived off Beyrout
on August 12th and by his vigorous actions in harassing the flank
of the Egyptian army and cutting all its sea communications, brought
Mehemet's advance to a stop.

On September 9th Stopford arrived at Beyrout with the remainder
of the British fleet. As the ships let go their anchors Napier realized
that his independent command was at an end. He was not the type
of man to serve cheerfully as a junior officer and his brain was soon busy
in search of some method whereby he might again be his own master.
Within a day or two he had prevailed upon Stopford to land a force
of British marines to co-operate with the Turkish troops and to let
him command ashore.

Fellowes, after three years in command of the *Vanguard*, had been
relieved as captain by Sir David Dunn, and under him the ship
assisted in the landing of the marines at D'jounie Bay, nine miles
to the north of Beyrout. With them Napier carried out a number of
successful small scale actions, culminating in a lightning attack on
Sidon. It was the main depot for the southern division of the Egyptian
army and was successfully captured on September 25th.

While Napier was thus showing his skill as a general, the *Vanguard*
was back again at Beyrout, assisting in the daily bombardment of
the town. As it showed no signs of surrendering, it was decided on
October 8th to make an attempt on it from the land. Napier marched
his men round to Kornet Sherouan, south of Beyrout, with a view to
cutting the Egyptian lines of retreat, but before action could be joined,
Mehemet's army was marched out to take up a stronger position
at Boharsep, a few miles further to the southward.

On the following day Colonel Sir Charles Smith arrived to take
over the command of the forces ashore and Napier was recalled. He
had no intention, however, of going without one final fling as sole
commander. He wrote to Stopford that he was advancing on the

enemy and was too much occupied to deal with correspondence. From then on he ignored all the admiral's instructions.

"It was," he wrote, "rather a new occurrence for a British commodore to be on the top of Mount Lebanon commanding a Turkish army and preparing to fight a battle that would decide the fate of Syria; but the very novelty was exciting to a degree. I was in my glory, standing on an eminence, surrounded by the General Officers and my own staff, I fancied myself a great Commander."

The Egyptian army was in a strong position. Napier marched his men across a valley to get at them, ordered a frontal attack and was badly checked. All seemed lost when the Commodore, at the head of his staff, charged the first line of the defences. The Egyptians wavered and were driven out, to retire to their second line. But by now Napier had turned the tide. Without hesitation this extraordinary man charged again, with a "few who I was obliged to stir up with my stick". Again the Egyptians were driven out and this time they fled from the field in disorder, leaving Napier the victor of the Battle of Boharsep.

Instead of facing a court-martial on his return for his direct disobedience of orders, the soft-hearted Stopford sent Napier to reconnoitre Acre with a view to its eventual bombardment and capture. On the strength of Napier's report, orders were received on October 31st to put the plan into effect and the fleet left Beyrout the same evening. The *Vanguard*, together with the *Rodney*, *Revenge*, *Cambridge*, *Carysfort*, and *Medea* were detached to blockade Alexandria and prevent the movement of any Egyptian vessels up to the relief of Acre.

The bombardment of Acre was begun on November 3rd, and at about sunset the main magazine was hit and set on fire. It exploded shortly afterwards and blew nearly half the town into the air. Early on the 4th the Egyptians were seen to be evacuating the place, Mehemet's men being in full retreat to the southward. They were harried by the guns of the fleet as they fled along the coastal road.

After the fall of Acre, Stopford again detached Napier, this time sending him down to Alexandria, where he took the *Vanguard* and the remaining ships under his command. But the tediousness of a formal blockade was far from congenial to a man of Napier's stamp. He decided that it was time the "Eastern Question" was settled, and that he was the man to settle it. He made contact with Mehemet Ali and, after some hard bargaining, signed a convention with him on November 27th, under the terms of which Mehemet was to evacuate Syria and return the Turkish fleet to Constantinople. In exchange Napier signed a guarantee that he should retain the hereditary government of Egypt.

It was all most irregular.

"I hope," wrote Napier to the Secretary of the Admiralty, "their Lordships will approve of the steps I have taken to at once settle the Eastern Question."

Unfortunately, neither their Lordships, nor Palmerston, nor Stopford, nor Lord Ponsonby, the English Ambassador at the Porte, approved. They all denounced the convention and negotiations began anew with Mehemet Ali. Napier himself came in for a great deal of criticism and rebuke. Yet in the end, after a multitude of talk, it was Napier's original convention, with one or two minor amendments, which was finally agreed with Mehemet.

"You have seen me," wrote Napier to his wife, "a Lord High Admiral, a Commodore, and a General. I have now turned a Negotiator and have made peace with Mehemet Ali. I shall either be hung by the Government or made a bishop."

Neither of these two fates overtook him. Instead, he was knighted for his work.

With the peaceful ending of the "Eastern Question", the sixth *Vanguard* returned home. She was commissioned from time to time and in 1845 was in the Channel Fleet at the time of the Naval Review held by Queen Victoria. She remained in the Channel Fleet until 1849, when she was reduced to reserve. It was the beginning of the age of steam, and the old wooden sailing ships of the Navy had had their day. In 1859 she was paid off for good and moored in the Thames, remaining there till 1873 and being finally broken up at Chatham two years later. But she had, before that date, ceased to belong to the *Vanguard* family, as in 1867 she was re-named *Ajax*.

Her change of name was necessitated by the building of a seventh *Vanguard*, a very different type of vessel from the first six. Her career was short and unremarkable, except that she was, in a way, a link between the older, wooden *Vanguards* and the more modern ones built of steel. Although, like her predecessors, she carried masts and sails, these were only used as an auxiliary method of propulsion, for the day of the marine steam engine had come.

The new *Vanguard* was designed by Mr. (afterwards Sir) E. J. Reed, chief constructor of the Navy between 1863 and 1870. She was built at Birkenhead and was a twin-screw ironclad, fitted with reciprocating engines. She was what was known as a central battery ironclad, in distinction to the first of the iron ships, which carried their guns on the old sailing ship model, mounted along the decks and firing through ports. In the *Vanguard*, ten 9-inch guns were carried in a central battery, shut off fore and aft by armoured bulkheads. She carried 8-inch armour of iron along her waterline amidships and her displacement was 6,010 tons. Her engines of 3,500 h.p. gave her a speed on trials of 13.6 knots. She was fitted with a projecting bow below water, designed for ramming, and she carried a total complement of 450 officers and men. Her total cost was £355,000

The *Vanguard* was launched in 1869 and completed the following year. She served in the fleet at home and on September 1st, 1875, was engaged in manœuvres in the Irish Sea, being one of a squadron under the command of Admiral Tarleton. Her captain was Richard Dawkins. Astern of her in the line during the Irish Sea manœuvres was a sister ship, the *Iron Duke*. She too, like the *Vanguard*, was fitted with a ram bow.

During the exercises, a fog came down off the Wicklow coast, but not so thick as to prohibit all movement. The admiral considered that it was still safe to carry on with the manœuvres and even when the fog thickened slightly shortly before noon he still continued with the evolutions. At ten minutes before one o'clock the men on the upper deck of the *Vanguard* saw the *Iron Duke* looming up out of the fog. She was coming on apace and struck the *Vanguard* amidships, tearing a great hole in her iron plating. Within an hour the new *Vanguard* was on the bottom, though fortunately every one of her complement was saved.

As is always the case when a ship is lost at sea, there was a court-martial. Six reasons were put forward by the court to account for the disaster. First, they considered that the speed of the squadron was too great in the fog. Second, that Captain Dawkins had left the bridge before an evolution that had been ordered by the admiral was completed. Third, that the speed of the *Vanguard* had been injudiciously reduced. Fourth, that the speed of the *Iron Duke* had been needlessly increased. Fifth, that the navigation of the *Iron Duke* was at fault, and sixth, that she had made no attempt to signal her intentions. The court ordered Dawkins to be severely reprimanded and dismissed his ship. The navigating officer of the *Iron Duke* was also dismissed from his ship.

The irony of the situation was centred in the ram bow with which these two ships were fitted. The accident was held to have proved its efficacy and influenced the design of future ships for many years. Yet it was a cumbrous affair, serving no really useful purpose and making every ship fitted with it heavy on her helm and slow in manœuvring. It took a Great War, nearly 40 years later, to prove that opportunities for ramming were almost negligible and that in any case a normal bow would serve the purpose just as efficiently.

After the accident to the seventh *Vanguard*, it was over thirty years before an eighth was built. She was laid down in Barrow-in-Furness in 1908, a "Dreadnought" of 19,250 tons. Her main armament was ten 12-inch guns in five twin turrets, and she had a maximum speed of 21 knots.

When the First World War broke out in 1914, the *Vanguard* was attached to the Grand Fleet, based on Scapa Flow. For nearly two years she remained there, proceeding with the fleet on occasional sweeps at sea, but with no chance of action against an enemy who, under the command of Admiral von Pohl, obstinately refused to quit his harbours. The *Vanguard* at this time was under the command of Captain James D. Dick.

However, on January 18th, 1916, the first real hopes of naval battle emerged. On that day von Pohl was succeeded in command by Admiral Reinold Scheer, who had long been preaching a bolder strategy for the German fleet. And when, a little later, the German Emperor visited Scheer on board his flagship, the *Friedrich der Grosse*, and publicly expressed approval of his policy, the hopes of the men at Scapa Flow were raised.

Scheer's plan of action, by the time he had perfected it, was perhaps a little naive. It was to station submarines off the British East Coast bases and then, by a sweep up to the entrance of the Skagerrak with the High Seas Fleet, to entice the Grand Fleet out in the hopes of some of the ships falling a victim to the torpedoes of the German submarines. By May 23rd, 1916, he was ready. Thirteen submarines were concentrated off the British coast, while a fourteenth, *U.75*, was laying a minefield off the west coast of Orkney, which was later to claim the *Hampshire*, with Lord Kitchener on board, as an important victim.

For a few days the weather turned against Scheer and he was forced to wait with a mounting anxiety. The endurance of his submarines was limited and he knew that they would have to begin their return journey by the evening of June 1st. As day succeeded day with the weather still obstinately overcast and misty, it was going to be touch and go.

Evidence that some abnormal activity was astir in the German harbours began to build up on May 28th with the sudden increase in wireless messages. Plotters in the Admiralty watched the growth of positions on the chart from wireless direction-finding fixes, all of them pointing to a concentration of the German Fleet. The ships' call-signs used in the messages indicated that not only were the 1st and 2nd Scouting Groups involved, but also the main fleet under Scheer. As a result, at noon on the 30th, a signal was sent to Admiral Sir John Jellicoe, the Commander-in-Chief, at Scapa that there were indications of the whole German Fleet proceeding out. At the same time destroyers and minesweepers operating from Harwich were recalled in case the German ships should attempt a dash to the southern half of the English East Coast.

All that afternoon of the 30th the evidence of a large-scale movement grew. There were more and more signals from the German coast, more and more direction-finding fixes to point to a sortie in force. By early evening there could no longer be any doubt and at 5.16 p.m. the Admiralty sent messages to Jellicoe, and also to Vice-Admiral Sir David Beatty, commanding the battle-cruisers at Rosyth, to raise steam. Twenty-four minutes later, at 5.40 p.m., a further signal was sent, ordering the fleet to sea and to concentrate to the eastward of Long Forties, which lies about 60 miles east of the Scottish coast. The operations which were to lead to the Battle of Jutland had begun.

The *Vanguard* weighed with the rest of the fleet and left Scapa in the evening, one of the seven battleships which formed the 4th Battle Squadron under the command of Vice-Admiral Sir Doveton Sturdee. As the ships from Scapa and Rosyth steamed out to sea, the German submarines closed to attack, but they were so unsuccessful that it was not realized until later that they had been there. Not a single British ship was hit and, in fact, the tracks of only two torpedoes were seen during the evening.

Throughout the night the two portions of the Grand Fleet, those from Scapa and Rosyth, steamed steadily south-eastward on converging courses. By 2.0 p.m. on the 31st the battleships under Jellicoe were within 20 miles of the rendezvous given to Beatty with the battle-cruisers, and as yet there had been no sign that the enemy were at sea. Beatty's squadron was farther to the southward and was making a sweep in towards the Danish coast before altering northward on to the course which would bring his ships up to the Commander-in-Chief's position.

At ten minutes past two the *Galatea*, wing ship of Beatty's advanced cruiser line, sighted a neutral merchant vessel stopped and blowing off steam. She closed to investigate. Away to the eastward, out of sight of the British, the *Elbing*, wing ship of the German cruiser line, sighted the same vessel. She sent two destroyers to investigate. At 2.18 p.m. the *Galatea* saw the destroyers, mistook them for cruisers in the distance, and two minutes later signalled "Enemy in sight." The Battle of Jutland had begun.

The *Vanguard*, up to the northward with Jellicoe, had no part in the preliminary action in which the battle-cruisers were involved. The ships which the *Galatea* had sighted were part of the 2nd Scouting Group and, as soon as proper contact had been made between the opposing squadrons, the Germans altered course to the southward towards their main battle fleet, 57 miles behind them. The 1st Scouting Group, under Admiral Hipper, and the High Seas Fleet, under Scheer, heard the call of the German light cruisers of the 2nd Scouting Group and increased speed towards them. Beatty, intent on bringing the German cruisers to action before they could retire to the shelter of Horns Riff, was hot in chase. The two forces were closing rapidly and a general action was now imminent.

At 3.49 p.m. it began, with the German battle-cruiser *Lützow* firing the first gun. For an hour the action was heavy as both sides steamed to the south-east towards the fast-approaching High Seas Fleet. Forty-three miles to the northward Jellicoe, too, had heard the call of the British battle-cruisers and with his fleet in sub-divisions in line ahead, disposed abreast, was hurrying to the south.

At 4.40 p.m. the *Southampton*, three miles ahead of Beatty's flagship,

the *Lion*, sighted the van of the High Seas Fleet. A minute or two later
it was in sight of the *Lion* herself, and the door was opening on what
looked to be a great, and possibly decisive, naval battle. Beatty had
but one thought now, to lead Scheer's ships up to the rapidly advancing
British Grand Fleet. The signal went up to turn 16 points to starboard
and the battle-cruisers, followed by the 5th Battle Squadron, which
had been attached to Beatty's force throughout, steered north-west
towards the Commander-in-Chief.

Up to the northward, Jellicoe was anxiously awaiting news from
Beatty. For the first time since the war had begun, contact had been
made with the enemy battle fleet. The *Southampton's* signal had been
received in the *Iron Duke*, the Grand Fleet flagship, followed by others
from the *Lion*, the *Champion*, the Admiralty, giving their appreciation
of the situation, and a final one from the *Southampton*. They made it
clear that Beatty's hopes were being fulfilled and that Scheer was
steering north. At 4.50 p.m. Jellicoe signalled to the Admiralty that
a fleet action was imminent.

There was silence for the next half-hour. It was an anxious half-
hour in the battleships, for at any moment contact might be made
either with Beatty's ships or with those of the High Seas Fleet. But
all was ready as the vessels made towards the southward at their best
speed. The guns were manned and every man on board was at his
station. All knew that it was now a matter of minutes only before they
would be in action. And at half past five the mists began to come down
again, making the grey ships in their columns look a little ghostly in
the gathering gloom.

At 5.33 p.m. the *Black Prince*, on the starboard wing of Jellicoe's
cruiser screen, sighted the *Falmouth*, leading ship of the 3rd Light
Cruiser Squadron, which was ahead of Beatty in the *Lion*. It was the
contact for which Jellicoe had been waiting. As it turned out, the
Grand Fleet was in a most advantageous position, almost dead ahead
of Scheer with his big ships, who as yet had no inkling that he was
opposed to anything more than Beatty's battle-cruisers. It was not
until 14 minutes past six, when the leading German battleship, the
König, sighted the *Marlborough* that he realized that he had been led
into a well-designed trap.

With the sighting of the German battle fleet, Jellicoe decided
to deploy to port and form his line of battle on the port wing column,
led by the *King George V*. This new formation made the *Vanguard*
the 16th ship in the line, with 12 other battleships behind her. By
6.32 p.m. she was in action, opening fire on the German light cruiser
Freya at a range of 11,000 yards. Three minutes later she scored a hit
with her fourth salvo and the *Freya* stopped, disabled. At the same
time, Scheer, seeing that the effect of Jellicoe's deployment was
bringing the whole weight of the British fleet against the two leading
squadrons of his own battleships, turned away towards the south-west.
He did so under cover of a destroyer attack and a smoke screen, and

by the time Jellicoe had completed his deployment the main German fleet was out of sight.

It was not, however, long before the fleets were again engaged. Jellicoe's movements had brought the British fleet between Scheer and his bases in the Heligoland Bight and the German admiral feared the effect of his being driven further out into the open. He knew he had no chance against the superiority of the British, both in gunnery and numbers, and at 6.57 p.m. he ordered another 16-point turn with the hope of slipping past the rear of Jellicoe's ships. As it was, Jellicoe had already turned to the southward and Scheer's new move merely brought him right into the centre of the British line.

A quarter of an hour later the leading German ships were under a heavy fire from the whole of the British line. They were repeatedly hit and Scheer was in a difficult position.

"Meanwhile," wrote von Hase, gunnery officer of the *Derfflinger*, "the Commander-in-Chief [Scheer] had realised the danger to which our fleet was exposed. The van of our fleet was shut in by the semicircle of the enemy. We were in a regular death trap. There was only one way to escape from the unfavourable tactical situation; to turn the line about and withdraw on the opposite course. Before everything we must get out of the dangerous enemy envelopment. But this manoeuvre had to be carried out unnoticed and unhindered. The battle-cruisers and destroyers had to cover the movements of the fleet. At about 7.12 p.m. the Commander-in-Chief gave the fleet the signal to turn about on the opposite course, and almost at the same time sent by wireless to the battle-cruisers and destroyers the historic order: 'Close the enemy'."

Scheer's turn away was made under the cover of a smoke screen and a torpedo attack by his destroyer flotillas. As the little ships came in for their attack through the smoke the *Vanguard* opened fire on them with her 12-inch and 4-inch guns. She hit and disabled one of them with her second salvo. It was probably *S.35* which, it was discovered later, had been sunk by a 12-inch shell. Five minutes later she was again firing at the destroyers, and at 7.30 p.m. shifted her fire to a German light cruiser which made her appearance out of the smoke screens. She, too, was hit, but was saved from destruction by more smoke put up by the German destroyers.

Scheer by this time had successfully extricated his fleet, but he was a worried man. He knew that every mile he was driven to the westward increased the chance of action on the morrow, an action in which he would be doomed to almost certain annihilation. He decided to alter to the southward and to make direct for Horns Riff as soon as darkness fell, maintaining that course regardless of what attacks the British fleet might make. It was a bold course to take, but the only one which could take him out of what might become irretrievable disaster.

As Scheer turned to the south, Jellicoe altered course to south-west, and the fleets were once again on converging courses. At 8.10 p.m. contact was made again. Ten minutes later Beatty's battle-cruisers were in action and Jellicoe was hurrying towards the sound of gunfire with his battleships. Again Scheer was forced to turn away to the westward and once again the fleets lost touch. It was the last time during the whole of the war that capital ships were engaged.

Night was falling fast now and Jellicoe closed up his fleet to enable the ships to keep touch with one another during the hours of darkness. He ordered the destroyer flotillas to take station five miles astern, and in this formation he set a course of south by east for the night. The last reports he had received had put the enemy about eight miles to the westward of him and his intentions were to keep them there throughout the night until he could engage them again by daylight.

Scheer, as had been said, had decided during the night to make for Horns Riff, regardless of what trouble he might run into on the way. At about 10 p.m., an hour and a half after the last contact with the British ships, he altered course to south-east, a direction which would bring him just to the southward of the Horns Riff Light Vessel. At midnight his course brought him into the track of Jellicoe's fleet, but a difference of a knot in speed—Jellicoe's was 17, Scheer's was 16—had put the British well ahead. The German fleet encountered nothing more formidable than the destroyers which Jellicoe had stationed astern of the fleet and Scheer was able to break through to the eastward without much difficulty. By 2.30 a.m. on June 1st the Germans were within 12 miles of Horns Riff. Jellicoe in the *Iron Duke* was 33 miles to the southward.

It was the end of the battle, and Scheer's desperate move had succeeded. He had been saved from severe defeat on the evening of the 31st by the haze which had cut down visibility to a considerable extent and had made conditions for the British gunlayers extremely difficult. Thereafter, it was his own boldness and skill which had kept him safely out of a battle which he was certain to lose.

It was an unsatisfactory ending from the British side. On the evening of the 31st, when the first contact was made, hopes had been high that a decisive result would be reached. They had been raised even higher by the sight, at nightfall, of the main German fleet to the westward and cut off from its bases. But the hours of darkness had dashed those hopes and when, at 2.30 a.m. on the 1st, the fleet turned to the northward, it was obvious to all that the enemy had escaped. Throughout the action the *Vanguard* had been engaged for not more than 20 minutes, mainly because of the low visibility. She had fired 67 rounds from her guns, hit and probably disabled two light cruisers and sunk one destroyer. She herself was not hit and suffered no casualties.

The *Vanguard* returned to Scapa Flow with the fleet, there to resume the tedious watch on the German fleet movements. Scheer did, indeed, come out once more with his ships, but there was no meeting between the two fleets. After that the enemy ships remained in harbour and nothing could tempt them out to match themselves against the British Grand Fleet. Their experiences at Jutland and the narrowness of their escape had brought the consequences too vividly to their notice.

The *Vanguard* did not long survive the battle. Like her immediate predecessor, she, too, met an unhappy end. While she was lying at anchor in Scapa Flow on July 9th, 1917, one of her magazines became overheated and blew up. The ship sank within a few minutes. The loss of life was heavy, but fortunately was not so disastrous as it might have been, for part of her company was on leave at the time of the accident. For nearly ten years she lay on the bottom at Scapa before being raised and towed round to the Tyne for breaking up.

CHAPTER XVIII

BUILDING THE NEW *VANGUARD*

It was to be a quarter of a century before a ninth *Vanguard* was to figure in the lists of the Navy. Once again the nation was at war, and again the enemy was Germany. But during the 30 years which passed between the building of the eighth *Vanguard* and the ninth, the whole pattern of naval war had been changed. The development of the aeroplane was the most important factor in dictating the new tactics of naval battle, though other inventions also played their part. As a result, the new *Vanguard* reflects as great an advance in design and construction over her predecessor as did the seventh over the sixth, which marked the change from sail to steam.

This ninth *Vanguard* might well have been a very different ship from what, in fact, she has turned out to be. The name was originally allocated to the fifth ship of the projected *Lion* class, authorized before the start of the Second World War under the original re-armament programme. All these vessels were eventually cancelled before building was started, and as a result the name *Vanguard* became available for any new ship which might be built during the war. That it would be given only to a capital ship was reasonably certain, for throughout the *Vanguard* history, the ship bearing the name had been designed to fight in the line of battle.

The new ship was authorized under the 1940 war estimates and the order for her building was given on March 14th, 1941. Her keel was laid in Messrs. John Brown's yard at Clydebank on October 2nd of the same year and her building proceeded apace.

That the decision to build a new battleship was taken at that period of the war must always be counted an act of faith and vision. The country still had a long and rough road to travel before she could enjoy the fruits of victory. Yet the ordering of the *Vanguard* at the beginning of 1941 was a proof that final victory was foreseen, even at that early period of the war. It was a proof, too, that the lessons of previous wars had been thoroughly learned, lessons which have shown throughout the centuries that it is always sea-power which holds the key to final victory, no matter what new weapons may have been evolved. As soon as the seas are firmly held, and the seaborne trade of the enemy stopped, then victory is certain and inevitable. And so, no matter how black and threatening the skies might be, if the new *Vanguard* could contribute to the holding of the seas, then her building could not fail to be a natural and sensible undertaking.

There were, of course, a number of considerations to be taken into account before the final order was placed. What sort of ship was

the new *Vanguard* to be? How large should she be? What sort of armament should she carry?

There can be little doubt that this aspect of her design was influenced
by the new battleships built by Germany and Japan. The five ships
of the *King George V* class—for at that time the *Prince of Wales* had not
yet been sunk—were of 35,000 tons displacement and carried, as main
armament, ten 14-inch guns. Germany still had the *Tirpitz*, of 42,000 tons
and armed with eight 15-inch guns, and Japan had the two *Yamatos*
which, although no details were known with certainty, were reputed
to be of 42,500 tons displacement and armed with nine 16-inch guns.
There were indications, too, that both countries were building even
larger battleships. Obviously, to match the threat, the *Vanguard*
would need to be larger than the *King George V*, and also to carry a
heavier armament.

The problems facing Sir Stanley Goodall, Director of Warship
Construction, and Sir Charles Lillicrap, Director of Naval Construction,
who between them were responsible for the design and building of
the *Vanguard*, were considerable. They had to produce a ship that
could not only stand up to the biggest warships of the enemy navies,
but also one which would fit naturally into a battle fleet composed,
for the most part, of ships of the *King George V* class. The *Vanguard*
would need to make the best of two worlds. As her final shape began
to become apparent, it could be appreciated that her design had, in
fact, produced a ship that answered nearly all the requirements.

A comparison of the *Vanguard*, when she was finally built, with
similar battleships of foreign navies is of interest. It shows her to be some
50 feet shorter than the others, but of similar tonnage and of comparatively equal gunpower in primary and secondary armament.

Ship	Country	Standard Displace- ment	Length	Armament Main Secondary	
Vanguard	G.B.	42,500	814 ft. 4 in.	8 15-in.	16 5.25-in.
Iowa	U.S.	45,000	887 ft. 3 in.	9 16-in.	20 5-in.
Tirpitz	Germany	42,000	886 ft.	8 15-in.	12 5.9-in. 16 4-in.
*Yamato**	Japan	42,500	870 ft.	9 16-in.	12 5-in.

* These were the figures believed to be correct while the *Vanguard* was building. In
actual fact it was discovered after the war that the *Yamato* was of 64,000 tons and carried
nine 18-in. guns, with a host of smaller guns ranging from 6-in. to 4-in. She was sunk on
April 7th, 1945, by American carrier-borne planes in the East China Sea, about 50 miles
south-west of Kyushu.

Once the decision to carry on with the building of the *Vanguard* had been taken, her construction went ahead comparatively fast, considering the two factors which operated most in holding her back. The first of these was the natural difficulty in wartime of the allocation of materials and the competing pressure of other work, both in new building and in repair work, in the British shipyards. Throughout the whole of the war there was a perpetual cry for more ships of war of all classes; aircraft carriers, cruisers, destroyers, submarines, frigates, sloops; both to replace losses in action and to extend the field of operations as the war spread to new areas. Against this background it would be reasonable to presume that a long-term project, such as was the building of the *Vanguard*, would inevitably suffer. Yet the actual time between her laying down (October 2nd, 1941) and her launching (November 30th, 1944) compares very favourably with normal peacetime experience in the construction of battleships.

A second factor which affected the speed of her building was the result of experience gained in action. War, of course, is always the final testing ground of the design of ships built in peace, and it is experience gained there which modifies or alters the design and construction of new vessels for the Navy. While the *Vanguard* was still building these new lessons were continually being presented, and as a consequence her design had to be adapted in order to incorporate them even while her construction continued. A major alteration, for instance, which was added to her original design, was the pronounced sheer of her bows, which completely altered her silhouette during the process of building.

She had originally been designed with a bow similar to those in the ships of the *King George V* class, with very little sheer, or "lift", forward. The object of this had been to comply with a staff requirement, laid down in her specification, that her forward turret should be able to fire dead ahead with no elevation on the guns. Obviously, in the light of this requirement, it would not have been possible to give her bow much sheer, for if it were raised to any appreciable extent it would obstruct the line of fire of the forward turret guns. War experience, however, had proved this requirement to be largely unnecessary. Battleships would certainly never fight their equals at ranges which called for no elevation on the guns—about 1,000–1,500 yards—and the secondary armament would be fully adequate to deal with the smaller adversaries, such as destroyers and M.T.B.s, which would be the only ships at all likely to venture into such ranges.

It had been found, too, that the absence of a pronounced sheer in the ships of the *King George V* class made them very wet when steaming into a heavy sea, there being nothing forward to prevent the water being thrown up over the forecastle. The dropping of the requirement about the forward guns enabled a high sheer to be embodied in the new design, which in turn brought the great advantage of a drier ship, the big sheer forward throwing the water aside instead of allowing it to come inboard. So, as a result, an entirely new bow was designed for the *Vanguard*, giving her her now familiar sheer forward.

Other lessons were continually being brought to light as the war progressed, and throughout the whole of her building modifications and improvements were being made to her design. The fate of the *Prince of Wales* and the *Repulse*, and of the Japanese *Yamato*, each of which was sunk by air attack, proved the necessity of a greatly increased protection against attack from the air, and once again the *Vanguard's* original design was modified to give this maximum protection, both by the provision of a considerably heavier A.A. defensive armament and by a strengthening of the armour over decks and side.

The thickness of the *Vanguard's* armour has never been officially revealed, although it has been stated that her protection is fully equal to that of any contemporary battleship of any other nation. It is possible to get some idea of its magnitude by a comparison with that fitted in the *King George V* class. In each of these ships over 14,000 tons of armour plate was used and the thickness at the waterline is believed to be some 16 inches. It has been officially stated that the ships of this class have a considerably enhanced protection against air attack, not only through the use of a greater weight of armour on decks and side, but also through an improved distribution of the armour. They were designed and largely built before the outbreak of the last war and it would be only reasonable to presume that the *Vanguard* would be an improvement on them, not only because her increased size gives greater scope for the use of armour, but also because the trials of war were constantly revealing additional weaknesses unforeseen and unsuspected in peacetime.

One of the aspects of warship design which was greatly influenced by this wartime experience was damage control. While considerable thought had been given to it for some years, only the actual experience of war could reveal the most effective methods of incorporating it in new building. The *Vanguard* may not be unsinkable—no ship ever is, as the fate of the *Bismarck* proved in 1941—but every latest idea of localizing and dealing with damage has been brought into her design and building in order to preserve the fighting capacity of the ship as a whole in the event of her receiving damage in action. Her subdivision into watertight compartments has been carried to a much higher degree that has been usual in previous British-built battleships, so that a hit below the waterline, either by mine or torpedo, cannot have a crippling effect through the subsequent flooding of a large space. Any sign of flooding can be largely controlled by the shutting off of the affected space with watertight doors, thus limiting greatly the extent of any damage, or loss of efficiency, through this cause.

The effect of all these improvements has been to produce a battleship that is, as far as is humanly possible, the last word in naval design. During her actual construction there were four major alterations in structural design, an indication of the thoroughness with which currently learned lessons were being applied to the new ship. New weapons which made their appearance during the war—such as the wireless-controlled glider bombs, magnetic and acoustic mines and torpedoes, and the like—have all been taken into account in her building.

Only the last of the war weapons to make its appearance, the atomic bomb, remains an enigma, for its full implications in the field of naval design have yet to be studied. It would seem unlikely, in the light of present knowledge and experience, that it is yet an advantageous tactical weapon for use against a moving target like a warship. Until it can be developed and produced on a scale to justify its use at sea, the *Vanguard* will surely remain in the forefront of her class of ship. It may well be, of course, that the atomic bomb will eventually be so developed as to make it a tactical, instead of a strategic, weapon, but it may equally well be that by then an effective counter to the bomb will also be produced. All that lies in the future, on which it is idle at the moment to speculate.

During the three years in which the *Vanguard* lay on the stocks at Clydebank, her progress was steady. The repetitious clang of riveting hammers marked the gradual evolution of her hull, a slowly-growing giant, taking shape against the day when she would be ready to slide down the ways into the waters of the Clyde. The first stage of her building came to its eventual end during November 1944, and on the 30th of that month she was launched.

The launching ceremony was performed by Her Royal Highness Princess Elizabeth, heir to the British throne. It was shorn of much of its traditional pageantry by the circumstance of war, and the great ship was christened with Empire wine instead of the more usual champagne. With the country still at war, even though the end was by then in sight, reasons of security forbade the announcement of her name, and the newspapers of the following day carried only a brief report that the Princess had launched a new battleship. That it was the largest warship ever built in a British yard only became known later, when the close watch on news likely to be of value to an enemy was lifted. And it was only then also, that it became known that the new ship bore one of the most historic names in the British Navy.

As the new *Vanguard* slid into the water and the echoes of her launching died away, tugs took her in tow and manoeuvred her into the fitting-out basin, where the next stage of her building was to take place. Here she was secured alongside under the great cranes and gantries, which would be occupied during the next year or so in lifting in engines and boilers, turrets and guns, and all the hundred and one pieces of machinery which go to the making of a warship. She was not yet ready for sea by any manner of means, but the smoothness of her launching, and the proud way she lay on the water, could yet give a tangible promise of the noble vessel she was to become.

CHAPTER XIX

FITTING–OUT

THE *Vanguard* was to lie for nearly 18 months in Messrs. John Brown's yard before becoming ready to be commissioned for trials. During that period the vast mass of machinery, which had been already ordered from many hundreds of firms in every part of the country, was despatched and assembled, ready for fitting into the huge hull as it lay alongside.

During the actual building of the *Vanguard*, a new conception of the use of capital ships had come into being. No longer was the idea of a battleship fighting in a line of battle considered to be its primary task. The days of large fleets of these ships meeting one another and fighting a gun duel at a range of from 20,000 to 30,000 yards were over, and the "set battle" was a thing of the past. The advent of the new weapon at sea, in the form of aircraft operating from carriers, had changed all that, and the big engagements in the Pacific Ocean had pointed the way for the future conduct of war on the seas. Battles were now fought at ranges of anything up to four or five hundred miles, and the role of the modern battleship was to protect and strengthen the carrier task forces, whose aircraft would do the main attacking. There was still that chance, however, of a meeting of capital ships on the high seas, such as occurred at the Battles of Cape Matapan and of Guadalcanal, and in consequence the new battleships must still carry their main armament of heavy guns. But their primary duty now was to act as heavy anti-aircraft vessels, carrying a formidable armament for use against enemy aircraft attacking the carriers composing the task forces.

It was this conception of the new duties of battleships which resulted in the ninth *Vanguard* becoming the most powerful anti-aircraft ship afloat. Space had to be found, not only for the great number of anti-aircraft guns which she now carries, but also for the many control arrangements for their operation. Details of her present armament will be given later in this chapter.

The first task of the *Vanguard's* fitting-out was the installation of her engine and boiler-rooms. If a comparison is made with those embodied in the German battleships *Tirpitz* and *Bismarck*, it can be seen that the *Vanguard's* installation is immeasurably superior to the German design. The *Vanguard's* four engine-rooms each have their own independent boiler-room, so that a hit in any one boiler- or engine-room can only affect that individual set of machinery, the other three remaining in full operation. In previous design, the boilers supplied steam to a main pipe-line, from which the engines drew their supply. Thus, under the old conditions, a hit in any boiler-room automatically reduced the steam pressure to all engine-rooms, and the severing of the main pipe-line might well bring the ship to a stop until repairs could be effected.

The main propelling machinery of the *Vanguard* is composed of Parsons single reduction geared turbines, fitted on each of the four shafts. Her shaft horse-power is 130,000, which under normal conditions of wind and sea would give her a speed of at least 29 knots. The results of her speed trials have never been made public, but there can be little doubt that she has at least reached this speed and probably exceeded it, for in an emergency she could develop a good deal more than her 130,000 s.h.p. As a comparison, the shaft horse-power of the ships of the *King George V* class is 110,000, but in an emergency they can develop 125,000 when driven hard.

The boilers in the *Vanguard* are the Admiralty pattern three-drum type, but considerably improved versions of the older patterns. They were designed to embody a new system of high efficiency in oil burning, reached after four years of research and experiment at the Admiralty Fuel Experimental Station at Haslar. The first step in this development took the form of a modified furnace front, which gave a much improved performance, but something considerably better was aimed at. It was achieved after a great deal of research, and the latest naval boilers have a completely re-designed furnace front and burning equipment, which embodies radically different principles and which has proved infinitely more efficient. With this increased efficiency have also come considerably improved working conditions for the stokers in the boiler-rooms, for their work is now both easier and cleaner. The *Vanguard* is the first battleship in which this new installation has been fitted, and her experience so far has shown it to be not only a great improvement on earlier steam installations, but also much simpler in handling.

One of the drawbacks, so far as the engineering department was concerned, which was met with in all previous battleship design, was the heat generated in boiler- and engine-rooms by the furnaces and the pre-heated steam. The atmosphere was necessarily hot and humid, especially when the ship concerned was sent to a tropical station. It brought in its train a consequent reduction in the human efficiency of the engineering staff. This aspect of design, too, has been considered in the case of the *Vanguard*, and special extractors, working on a jet principle, have been fitted to all machinery spaces to reduce the humidity and to keep the temperature down to normal conditions, even in the tropics. This, again, has its repercussions on the comfort of the engine-room and boiler-room crews, giving them much more pleasant working conditions than were ever known in the past.

Every fitting used in the ship is robustly designed and has been the object of careful study, with a primary view of withstanding the shock of battle. It was not enough merely to specify standard equipment for any particular purpose, just because it had proved satisfactory in previous war vessels. This particular ship, which may well prove to be the last battleship ever to be built in this country, had to have the best of everything. No effort was spared, from the research and design point of view, to ensure that only the best was incorporated. As an instance, a new machinery mounting was evolved, which combines resilient materials with a rigid structure. This was on a principle developed by the Admiralty early in the war and brought to a new pitch of perfection by the time the *Vanguard* was fitted-out. It has proved much superior to the complicated mechanism designed by German naval architects for the same purpose and fitted in the *Bismarck* and *Tirpitz*, which consisted of a system of spring mechanisms to absorb the jarring shocks set up by a hit from bomb, shell, mine, or torpedo.

Another innovation in the engineering department was the remote control of important steam valves by hydraulic means. Indeed, throughout the whole of this department, the goal aimed at has been simplicity of operation, combined with a maximum of robustness and efficiency. It has, in a way, been surprising how far these two ideals have gone hand in hand and simplified the working of the ship while adding to her efficiency as a fighting unit.

One more improvement in past design can be seen in the siting of the pumps which deal with the possible flooding of the ship. One of the lessons learned during the war was that, when a ship was extensively holed and the consequent flooding was rapid, the pumps were often "drowned" by the rising water and so rendered useless. In the *Vanguard* special care was taken to instal these pumps as high up in the ship's structure as possible, so that they can deal with the rising water without fear of becoming submerged themselves.

The electrical supply system has been designed on much the same principle as the engine- and boiler-rooms. Here again the generating rooms have their own individual steam supply, so that a hit in one of them would have no effect on the working of the others. So much in the *Vanguard* is run by electricity that the amount generated would be sufficient to supply all the needs of a town of 50,000 inhabitants, the total output being 3,720 kilowatts. Air-conditioning plant, the galleys and bakery, the laundry, the crane for hoisting in and out the ship's boats, these are only a few of the installations run by this means, and a fair idea of the vast amount of machinery which depends on this source of power for its working can be estimated by the fact that the total quantity of electric cable used throughout the ship amounts to no less than 2,000 miles. There are 1,250 telephones installed for communication between the various compartments, and the number of electric light bulbs fitted runs into some 6,750 or more.

The water distilling plant, which turns sea water into fresh drinking water, has a daily output of over 100,000 gallons, ample for the needs of even so great a ship as the *Vanguard*. Like all the other auxiliary machinery, this, too, is the last word in efficiency.

But perhaps the most striking difference of all, especially to those with experience of the engine-rooms of older warships, is the comparative silence and complete absence of dirt in engine- and boiler-rooms when the ship is under way at sea. There is no longer the chatter of the steering engine up against the after engine-room bulkhead—in the *Vanguard* it has a compartment of its own—and aluminium paint not only saves weight, but also gives a cleaner, tidier effect in the boiler-rooms. Gone, too, are the days when a descent into engine- and boiler-rooms needed a handful of cotton waste with which to wipe away oil and dirt collected *en route*. The whole machinery lay-out now gives an impression of quiet, unhurried efficiency, and of great turbines controlled almost to a fraction of a revolution per minute by a touch of the hand on the main control valves.

The armament of the *Vanguard* can be divided into three distinct groups—main, secondary, and anti-aircraft—although the two last can work together against attack from the air. The main armament consists of eight 15-inch guns, mounted in twin turrets, two forward and two aft. It will be noticed that this is a reversion to the older practice in battleship design, where the main armament was equally divided forward and aft of the superstructure. The *Hood*, the *Royal Sovereigns*, and the *Queen Elizabeths*, all with similar main armaments, had their turrets disposed in this fashion, while the practice in ships built between the wars was to bring a preponderant proportion forward of the bridge. Thus, both the *Rodney* and the *Nelson*, each armed with nine 16-inch guns mounted in three triple turrets, had all their main armament forward, while the *King George V* class, which carry ten 14-inch guns mounted in two quadruple and one twin turret, have six guns forward of the superstructure and four aft.

The reason for this was the limitation clause in the Washington Naval Treaty, under which capital ship displacement was not to exceed a total of 35,000 tons. It meant that naval architects were forced to look in every possible direction in order to save weight, and one way that showed itself was by concentrating the main armament into as small a space as possible, so as to limit the overall length of the main armoured belt. This needed only to extend to the fore and after ends of the turrets and ammunition hoists, and so enabled a greater length of the ship near the bow and stern to be protected with lighter armour. Although it achieved its object in saving weight, it did it at the sacrifice of ease in handling the guns. The return, in the case of the *Vanguard*, to the former practice of distributing the guns equally either end of the superstructure is much more satisfactory, giving greater stability and a better concentration of gunfire.

The 15-inch guns themselves are, curiously enough, all over 30 years old. They were originally installed in the two fast cruisers *Courageous* and *Glorious*, ships of 18,600 tons, first commissioned in 1917. Both these vessels were later very largely stripped and finally converted into aircraft carriers during the years between 1924 and 1930.

Their 15-inch guns were removed and added to the reserve maintained for ships of the *Royal Sovereign* class, the *Queen Elizabeth* class, and the *Hood*, all of which mounted guns of this calibre. None of these is left now, the *Hood* having been sunk by the *Bismarck*, the *Royal Oak* and *Barham* by German U-boats, and the remainder sold for breaking up. In consequence there now exists a large stock of these 15-inch guns, and the *Vanguard* is the only British ship mounting them.

The *Vanguard's* secondary armament consists of sixteen 5.25-inch guns, mounted in twin turrets and capable of high angle as well as low angle fire. These dual purpose weapons are available either for defence against destroyers and M.T.B.s, or against aircraft. After long battle experience, this 5.25-inch gun has been proved to be one of the best of the smaller weapons ever produced for the Navy.

As a closer range defence against air attack, the *Vanguard* carries no fewer than seventy-one 40 mm. Bofors anti-aircraft guns, mounted in groups and with some of them in the six-barrelled mountings. These, being automatic weapons with a high rate of fire, can throw a great weight of shells into the sky, sufficient to make an almost impenetrable curtain of metal through which attacking aircraft would have to fly in order to press home their attack.

All the guns—main, secondary, and anti-aircraft—have had their effectiveness greatly enhanced by the installation of the latest methods of control. Included in these is what is known as "remote power control", by means of which groups of guns can be laid, trained, and aimed from a master sight. The latest radar control arrangements are also fitted, whereby ranges and bearings taken by this method are passed automatically through the Transmitting Room to the control positions. These are designed so that they can split up the guns into groups, as required, each group being separately controlled and so enabling the guns to engage a number of different targets simultaneously. The *Vanguard's* control arrangements have thus an extreme flexibility, as the various groups can be combined, if necessary, to bring a heavier defence temporarily to bear on any one target at will.

In addition to the weapons enumerated above, the *Vanguard* also carries four 3-pounder guns. These, however, are only for the giving and answering of salutes and can hardly be counted as part of her offensive or defensive armament.

As the *Vanguard* lay against the wall in the basin in the Clydebank yard and her fitting-out progressed, one could begin to see what her final shape would be and to make comparisons with the features of former designs. The high sheer of her bows has already been noticed, but her funnels, as they were being built up during this period, revealed something quite new in naval design as we knew it in this country. They are streamlined, instead of being of the more usual oval shape, and their caps are turned over towards the stern of the ship. The streamlining was the result of exhaustive wind-tunnel tests carried out with scale models at the National Physical Laboratory. The object of the caps being turned aft is to carry away the exhaust gases from the boilers and prevent them from interfering with the after gunnery control positions.

A second point which could be noticed during fitting-out was the concentration of masts, funnels, and superstructure into a comparatively small area, considering the size of the ship as a whole, a feature which has the advantage of giving considerably more space to forecastle and quarter-deck. This close grouping is strongly reminiscent of the latest United States designs, especially as regards the arrangement of masts and funnels. Combined with this one notices the much higher freeboard of the quarter-deck, which should ensure dryness at sea. In this respect, one recalls H.M.S. *Hood*, the only ship of comparable size built in this country. She was a battle-cruiser built after the First World War, but her low quarter-deck made her a very wet ship in anything of a seaway. Crossing the *Hood's* quarter-deck in rough weather was often apt to be a perilous undertaking, for the sea used to sweep across it green. Even in a moderate sea her quarter-deck was always flooded if she was steaming at high speed and everything had to be battened down. Such a state of affairs could hardly happen in the *Vanguard*, except perhaps in an exceptionally heavy sea.

Another point in her design worthy of notice is the counter-sunk hawse-pipes, which enable the bower and sheet anchors to be hove up flush with the ship's side, instead of having their flukes projecting outboard, as is the case in former warship design.

The *Vanguard* is, of course, protected against magnetic mines by degaussing gear. This is now fitted internally with automatic adjusting gear.

H.M.S. *Vanguard* was commissioned for trials on April 25th, 1946, some 17 months after the date of her launching. During this period all her machinery had been put on board and fitted into position, her superstructure finished, her typical tripod masts built up, her funnels completed, and all the thousand and one fittings which go into a battleship assembled, connected up, and put into working order. Everything had been tested, both by the representatives of all the various firms concerned in their manufacture and also by the builders who were, of course, responsible for the ship as a whole. Craftsmen had been at work in factories all over Great Britain, engaged in some fitting for the ship, and when she finally steamed down the Clyde for her trials she carried with her, in some degree or other, a contribution from almost every industry in the country.

It says a great deal for the skill and exactness of British workmanship that the trials of this great ship went off almost without a single hitch. When the main engines of the *Vanguard* were run for the first time during her basin trials in January 1946, they revolved as smoothly and with as little fuss as though the ship had been in commission for a year or more. And so it proved with almost all her machinery;

a wonderful achievement when one thinks of the many thousands of working parts which had to be fitted, and joints which had to be made, a mistake in any one of which could have resulted in a temporary breakdown. The fact that no trouble was experienced can be counted as a fine example of teamwork between her designers, her builders, and the naval engineer officers, who supervised the fitting of the machinery at every stage of its progress. By the time the *Vanguard* was ready for her trials, approximately 40,000 tons of steel had been built into her.

Before she left on her trials, she was moved down the narrow channel of the Clyde and came to an anchor at the Tail of the Bank, off Greenock. That was on May 2nd, 1946, and ten days later a Royal Standard was broken at her masthead when Princess Elizabeth, who had launched her four and a half years previously, came on board to attend the ceremony of "Blessing the Ship". The Standard worn by the ship on that day was not the usual one of the King's, but Princess Elizabeth's own personal Standard, and the day had an added significance in that it was the first occasion on which the Princess's Standard had been flown.

Princess Elizabeth was greeted by buglers of the Royal Marines sounding a Royal salute and, after inspecting the guard of honour drawn up on the quarter-deck, the officers of the ship were presented to her. The ceremony of Blessing the Ship was carried out on the quarter-deck, on which practically the whole of the ship's company was assembled, and before lunching with the captain, the Princess visited the mess-decks. She also presented Captain Agnew with a coloured print of the first *Vanguard* of 1586.

Blessing the Ship is a ceremony which has a history of many centuries. It is one of the oldest of naval customs and it was carried out on this occasion by the Chaplain of the Fleet. In it the blessing and protection of God is sought for the ship and for all those who may serve in her. A special prayer of thanks for the designers and builders ends the service:

> "... More especially at this time do we thank Thee for those by whose skill this ship has been built; for the designers, craftsmen, and all who have laboured in her building. And we pray that we may be worthy of the trust committed to our charge, that we may ever be a terror to all that is evil and bitter, and that by watchfulness and vigilance we may bear ourselves as those who serve Thee who art unseen."

At the same time the ship's chapel, which has seating accommodation for 60 people, was dedicated to St. Andrew, on which saint's day the ship was launched.

The White Ensign was hoisted on board for the first time at the ensign staff on the day of her first commissioning, April 25th. She was under the command of Captain (now Rear-Admiral Sir) William G. Agnew, C.B., C.V.O., D.S.O., R.N. The *Vanguard's* trials crew consisted of about 60 officers and 1,200 men, and the next few weeks were strenuous ones, both for ship and crew. Full speed trials, steaming trials, gunnery trials, and others to test all her complicated equipment under sea conditions, were carried out in the Irish Sea and the Firth of Clyde, and once again everything went smoothly, remarkably few faults being revealed. In so highly technical an affair as a modern battleship, this was something of a triumph.

With her trials satisfactorily concluded, the *Vanguard* left the Clyde bound for Portsmouth, which was to be her home port. And here, on August 9th, 1946, on the successful completion of her acceptance trials, she was handed over by her builders to the Admiralty and officially became a unit of the Royal Navy, the ninth, and the greatest, of all the *Vanguards*.

CHAPTER XX

INTERNAL ARRANGEMENTS

As has been seen in the previous chapters, new ideas brought forward by the experience of war had been incorporated into the building of the *Vanguard* and also into her machinery. Every small detail had been considered and a notable improvement made in almost every aspect of her design. And since a ship depends for her efficiency on her complement, an equal consideration had been given to the conditions under which both officers and men had to live their day-to-day life.

The *Vanguard* is fitted for a flagship and as such would carry a full wartime crew of approximately 100 officers and 1,900 men, and with a peacetime complement, about 100 less. To fit them all in, with some degree of comfort, into a ship of 814 feet in length and 108 feet in maximum beam, and still leave space for all her vital equipment, was certainly a considerable problem. Yet the habitability of the *Vanguard* shows a great improvement in comparison with older battleship design.

In order fully to appreciate the advances made in the new ship, a brief description of the normal facilities found in older ships would not be out of place. Those who have ever visited a warship during the time when she was thrown open to public inspection will recall the "broadside" messes, which consisted of a large space, usually on the main deck, with deal tables projecting at right angles from the ship's side, with wooden benches along each side of the tables. Here the men ate, wrote letters, played cards, and spent much of their time off duty. Above the messes were rows of hooks in the deck beams, from which hammocks were slung at night in which the men slept. Petty-Officers' messes were rather more private, being curtained off from the remainder of the mess-deck. Lockers were provided for clothes, but there was little extra space for the stowage of any personal gear.

All this has been changed in the *Vanguard*. For the first time in the history of the Navy, men no longer eat where they sleep. Proper dining-halls, seven of them, are situated on the main deck and food is supplied to serveries which communicate by lifts direct with the ship's galleys on the upper deck above. In the serveries the food is divided out on to plates, which are then taken direct into the dining halls in specially designed plate carriers, enabling eight full plates to be carried each trip. Special care is taken to ensure that all food remains hot during its short journey from galley to dining-hall. The halls themselves have cushioned benches instead of the hard wooden ones of previous days, and the tables are covered with tablecloths. After use the "mess traps"

—plates, cups, dishes, etc.—are cleaned and dried in special electric washing-machines.

The galleys, of which there are two, and the bakery are all fitted with the latest and most up-to-date machinery, and are certainly the best equipped in any of H.M. ships. The galleys contain, among other gear, potato-peeling and chipping machines, dish-washing machines, bread-slicing and buttering machines, special soup coppers, and a host of other labour-saving equipment. The bakery has an automatic dough mixer and a specially improved bread cooling room. All machinery, ovens, and stoves are run by electricity, giving maximum efficiency, ease of working, and cleanliness.

The individual messes, where the men sleep and spend their leisure hours, are no longer open broadside messes, but are all partly enclosed, giving a much greater degree of privacy and also permitting the men to sleep without all the disturbances which were so frequent in the previous open type of mess. Cheerful colour schemes have been introduced to brighten the messes, and padded seats, cushions, and tubular steel tables and chairs are provided to take the place of the old wooden benches and tables. Here there are facilities for games, such as draughts, chess, cards, darts, and so on, or for letter writing and the like.

Each mess contains about 30 men. The hammocks are stowed in "nettings" in the mess and each man has a locker for his clothes and a special shoe locker. There are cupboards for personal effects, and racks in which attaché-cases can be stowed. The individual messes are reasonably spacious and, although there is considerable crowding—as is always the case in every warship—it is much less than in all previous battleships.

Another innovation in the *Vanguard* is the provision of a special cinema. Previous practice was to rig a temporary cinema screen and projector, either on the forecastle or quarter-deck when the weather was fine, or in a recreation space when conditions were bad, bringing up benches from the messdeck for the audience. The *Vanguard's* cinema has seating for 170 and film shows are given on the average once or twice daily. The cinema is also used for the daily issue of grog to the ship's company.

Wash-places for the crew are fitted with hand-basins of stainless steel and they also have shower baths, each shower being curtained off. There are a number of these, both on the main and middle decks.

The *Vanguard's* laundry can handle the entire washing of the ship, a change from pre-war days when a ship's laundry was often inadequate to carry out all the work, the balance being left to individual enterprise. In the *Vanguard*, electric washing-machines handle the work quickly and efficiently, and large tailors' steam presses give the articles a professional finish.

An information room, where the latest newspapers and periodicals are available, is much used during leisure hours. Literature on vocational training, to help seamen in their life after retirement, is supplied, and books on current affairs can also be studied. Every encouragement is given to those who wish to study any particular subject, and also to those who wish to be well informed on what is happening throughout the world today.

The sick bay, like everything else in the ship, is fitted with all the latest appliances and embodies many improvements in comparison with older ships. A fully equipped operating theatre is available for urgent cases, there is a modern dental surgery alongside the sick bay, and X-ray apparatus is installed. There is even a waiting-room for patients. The cots in the sick bay can either be locked rigid, to facilitate treatment by the doctors, or freed to swing with the roll of the ship when at sea. A pair of headphones, connected to the ship's broadcasting system, is fitted to each cot.

The ship's canteen is run by N.A.A.F.I. and includes, among other facilities, an ice cream bar. Schoolrooms are provided for the instruction of boys and for training classes.

The ward-room, where the commissioned officers mess, is in the after superstructure on the upper deck, and the gunroom, for sub-lieutenants and midshipmen, on the starboard side of the main deck. Here again the maximum use has been made of bright colours in decoration to make them attractive, and the furniture is of tubular steel, with leather upholstery. The ward-room and gunroom are the focal points of ship's life for the officers, and are large, comfortable spaces where they can eat and relax. Both are fitted with electric stoves which add to their comfort and habitability.

Taken all in all, the general planning of the living quarters and facilities of this ship show an immense amount of careful thought and attention to detail. Nothing has been left to chance and the results show what can be done to improve living conditions in modern warships. Many of the facilities in the ship, while new to the Royal Navy, have been for some time standard practice in the United States Navy, and certainly the *Vanguard* shows that the standard of accommodation on the lower deck has been considerably influenced by American practice. It reveals a very definite advance on the arrangements in older warships and sets a standard that is likely to be followed in all new building.

Cabins for the officers are reasonably spacious and, as one would expect, extremely well fitted. The admiral's quarters for himself and his staff, when the ship is acting as a flagship, are on the shelter deck, the space used for the Royal apartments when the *Vanguard* took the King and Queen to South Africa in 1947. The captain's harbour accommodation, following normal tradition, is aft on the main deck. His sea cabin is up near the bridge.

One drawback under which the *Vanguard* suffers is that she gets very hot in a tropical climate. This, of course, applies to all ships, and especially to warships where the subdivision into compartments must be much greater than in liners and merchant vessels. The additional number of bulkheads greatly restricts a clear flow of air and prevents cooling. The *Vanguard* has air-conditioning in the important control positions, which keeps them cool in hot weather and warm in cold, but for the rest, she suffers much as all other ships suffer in extremes of temperature.

COMMUNICATIONS FOR THE ROYAL TOUR

WHEN it became known, early in 1946, that H.M.S. *Vanguard* would be selected to carry the Royal family on their tour to South Africa, a great deal of consideration had to be given to the additional radio communication facilities which would be needed to handle all the press and broadcasting requirements which so important a voyage would inevitably entail. The *Vanguard* already, of course, was fitted with a battleship's normal communication installation, consisting of transmitters and receivers for morse, both at hand speed and automatic high speed, over any distance, and also with short range radio-telephony.

This, while completely adequate for the usual communication requirements while the ship is acting in her normal role as a fighting unit of a fleet, could certainly not carry the vast increase of traffic expected during the tour, nor was it designed to undertake the many different types of transmission which would obviously be required. A number of press correspondents would be accompanying the Royal family in the *Vanguard* and would need to send many messages daily to their newspapers and to the press agencies. B.B.C. and South African broadcasting commentators required facilities for transmitting their commentaries to Great Britain and South Africa for subsequent relay over the various broadcasting systems. With a number of press photographers and newsreel cameramen on board, a means of trans-mitting photographs by wireless was also a necessary addition to the communication facilities. Above all, it could be anticipated that there would be an appreciable volume of official messages, both to and from the *Vanguard*, which would require the King's attention and would have to be dealt with without delay.

With this general picture of the main requirements in mind, the Admiralty, in conjunction with the Admiralty Signal Establishment at Haslemere, the General Post Office, the B.B.C., Messrs. Cables and Wireless, Ltd., and with the co-operation of the manufacturers of the various types of equipment employed, set about the task of providing the many sets, designing the necessary additional aerial array and other fittings, and accommodating everything into the limited space available in the *Vanguard*.

For the official messages and press reports, a system of duplex automatic telegraphy (i.e. a two-way teleprinter line) was installed in a compartment, fitted up as a radio control room, on the starboard side of the after superstructure. Three teleprinters were used, together with the necessary tape perforators and creed relays, and this made ample provision for the volume of traffic which would be handled

209   O

during the cruise. In the same compartment was a long-range radio telephone switchboard, which handled not only the broadcasting commentaries of events on board, but could also deal with direct telephone conversations from ordinary handsets in the ship to outside subscribers, or *vice versa*.

This long-range telephony made it possible to carry on an ordinary telephone conversation from ship to shore, or shore to ship, with any possessor of a telephone ashore, the *Vanguard's* circuit being connected with the G.P.O. Overseas Terminal in London or the Cape Town terminal of Cables and Wireless of South Africa. Speech privacy equipment, more commonly known, perhaps, as "scramblers", was fitted to the radio-telephony circuit to prevent any unauthorized listener picking up the conversation while on the air. For broadcasting commentaries, a disc recording outfit was also installed in case atmospheric conditions should be unsuitable at the time of the broadcast.

The facsimile apparatus, for the transmission of photographs, was also installed in this compartment. The equipment was manufactured by Messrs. Muirhead and Co., Ltd., of Beckenham, and was specially designed, built, and installed by them. It was worked by a system of photo-electric scanning of the film at the transmitter, the resulting variations in light intensity modulating the transmitting carrier wave. At the receiving end in Electra House in London, this wave similarly modulated a beam of light projected on to a photographic film, thus reproducing the picture.

For all these requirements, a special transmitter, giving a higher radiated power on short wave than any other transmitter in the ship, was installed in a compartment on the port side of the after superstructure. This transmitter was connected to a special aerial on the mainmast, cut to the requisite lengths for each of the six special wavelengths allocated to the *Vanguard* for these purposes.

One of the main difficulties found when dealing with all this additional radio equipment was that of ensuring freedom from interference to interception by all the ship's transmitters, of which there were a considerable number. To assist in this, all the receiving aerials were assembled on the foremast, with additional whip aerials, of which there were four, installed two forward on the forecastle and two aft on the quarter-deck. This was designed to give the maximum separation possible between the transmitting aerials, on the mainmast, and the receiving aerials.

While all this dealt with the main anticipated wireless traffic of the ship while at sea, another requirement that presented itself was that of providing ordinary broadcasting programmes to the Royal apartments on board and also one programme for the ship's company. This was done by the installation of three standard naval receivers, with special aerials and filters to cut out interference. Loudspeakers were fitted in each of the cabins allocated to the Royal party, with a three-way selector switch to each in order to allow a choice of three separate broadcasting programmes. In addition, radio gramophones were installed in the King's day cabin and the equerries' smoking-room, while a third was available for use on deck if required.

The whole of this additional equipment was installed in the *Vanguard* while she was undergoing conversion in Portsmouth Dockyard to fit her out for the Royal tour. It was all thoroughly tested out during the ship's preliminary shakedown cruise to Gibraltar during December 1946, and met with great success. Very few modifications were required on the *Vanguard's* return to Portsmouth before the start of the voyage to South Africa.

Quite apart from the operational requirements of the trip in this matter of communications, for which the equipment proved entirely adequate, it also provided the Navy with a magnificent opportunity for obtaining experience in the solution of the many problems involved, and also in testing out many new methods which might prove of value in future design. While warships have been fitted with short-range radio telephony for some years, very few have yet explored the possibilities of long-range speech transmission, which might well have immense operational value in time of war. Similarly, automatic telegraphy for ships is as yet in its infancy, and the experience gained in the *Vanguard* of this method of communication must be of value in the event of the process being used operationally. The tour, too, was the first occasion of a facsimile equipment being operated from sea and one can conceive occasions when its use might well prove a useful addition to naval communications.

Certainly, no ship has ever put to sea so fully equipped in this respect as when the *Vanguard* sailed from Portsmouth with the Royal party on board on January 31st, 1947. Every thought had been given to the adequate and efficient provision of every conceivable requirement and the whole complex equipment had been assembled and installed without interference with the normal naval apparatus already carried in the ship. It was a triumph of design and ingenuity, providing an all-round service unequalled by any other ship at sea.

CHAPTER XXII

SOUTH AFRICAN VISIT

THE morning of Friday, January 31st, 1947, dawned cold and grey over England. It was the beginning of that notorious cold spell, which was to last for seven weeks and to hold the country in an iron grip of frost and snow. Yet, in spite of the cold on this morning, crowds were beginning to gather in London by eleven o'clock, lining the route from the Palace to Waterloo Station and waiting for a glimpse of the Royal cars as the King and his family left England for their long visit overseas.

Down in Portsmouth, a little later in the day, a similar crowd was forming. There was a dusting of snow on the ground as the route from the station was lined with sailors and a naval guard of honour was formed up on South Railway Jetty, alongside which the *Vanguard* was secured. Snow, too, had fallen on the *Vanguard's* deck and the occasional flurry of falling flakes gave a bleak air of wintry desolation to the dockyard. Yet on board the *Vanguard* all was life and movement. The age-old ceremonial drill of welcoming a ruling monarch on board one of His Majesty's ships was about to be carried out. The *Vanguard* was manned along her port side, sailors standing shoulder to shoulder along the guard rails down the whole of her length. A Royal Marine guard of honour was drawn up on the quarter-deck and the band was there to play the national anthem at the moment of arrival. The saluting guns' crews were fallen in alongside the three-pounder guns, and the officers of the ship were mustered on the quarter-deck. Observant eyes ashore could see a tightly rolled ball of bunting at the mainmast head, two similar balls at the foremast yard-arms, waiting for the moment when the King set foot aboard the ship.

A somewhat incongruous air of gaiety in this bitter weather was given by the dressing overall of the *Vanguard* and other ships, the gay colours of the bunting, stretching from the bow up to the mastheads and down again to the stern, standing out sharply against the steely inhospitability of the wintry sky.

On board the *Vanguard* the Gunnery Officer was giving details of the Royal progress to the ship's company over the loud hailer. As he announced the arrival of the train, the first faint sounds of cheering were borne on the wind to the waiting crew. The news that the Royal cars had left the Harbour Station and were turning into the Hard was accompanied by a growing crescendo of cheering as the Royal family approached the Dockyard. Then finally the little procession of cars, the first two flying a miniature Royal Standard on their bonnets, rounded the Signal Tower and drew to a halt on the jetty. From the first stepped the King, the Queen, Princess Elizabeth, and Princess

Margaret. The second carried Queen Mary, the Princess Royal, the Duchess of Kent, and the Duke of Gloucester, who had made the journey from London to say good-bye.

The King inspected the guard of honour of seamen on the jetty and then, followed by the Royal family, walked slowly up the brow, turning at the top to help his mother down the step. As he set foot on board, those three balls of bunting were broken out into the Royal Standard at the mainmast head, and the Admiralty flag and Union Jack at the yard-arms. They would fly night and day until the King left the ship. The bosuns' pipes shrilled their immemorial salute and as they faded into silence, the Marine band played "God Save the King". The captain of the *Vanguard*—Rear-Admiral Agnew—stepped forward to greet their Majesties.

It was an early start the following morning, the ship's company being piped to stations for leaving harbour at seven o'clock. About half an hour later, led by the Trinity House yacht *Patricia*, the *Vanguard* steamed slowly out of Portsmouth Harbour into a thick, damp mist. The destroyer escort picked up the ship in Spithead and, as she made her way out into the Channel, the weather cleared. Here the *Vanguard* met the Home Fleet, steaming in two columns on an opposite course, and as the ship made her way between the two lines, each vessel fired a Royal salute and manned and cheered ship. The Home Fleet escort, consisting of the aircraft carrier *Implacable*, the cruisers *Cleopatra* and *Diadem*, and the destroyer *St. James*, took station astern. The destroyer escort increased speed, then turned 16 points on to an opposite course to pass close alongside the *Vanguard* and make their farewells.

Later that day, south of Portland Bill, the last tangible link with the home country took place. A helicopter, flying out with mails, landed on the *Vanguard's* quarter-deck, the first time in history that any aircraft had been deliberately landed onto the quarter-deck of a battleship. She was off again within five minutes, her achievement watched by many of the ship's company. Shortly afterwards the French battleship *Richelieu* was sighted. She had come up Channel to pay the respects of the French nation to the Royal family and to the *Vanguard*.

On that Saturday night, as the *Vanguard* and her escorts steamed west down Channel, they met a rising sea. The wind, too, was rising, and by midnight the ships were battling into a full gale. It lasted till the following Monday night, but after that the sea began to moderate and, although there was still a considerable swell, the ship's company could again get busy, cleaning her up and getting everything ship-shape. The escorting vessels, especially the *St. James*, had had a bad time of it, and two Portuguese sloops, which had put out from Lisbon to add their chorus of salutes to the *Vanguard* and her distinguished passengers, were slightly damaged by the seas and also suffered a few casualties in broken bones.

But as the small squadron steamed steadily to the southward, they came at last to sunny seas and tropical uniforms became the order of the day. On the Friday the royal barge was hoisted out and, although there was still a fairly big swell running, the King and Queen and the two Princesses paid a round of visits to the four escorting ships. By this time the *St. James* had been relieved by the *St. Kitts*, which had come out from Gibraltar. Their Majesties and the Princesses went first to the *Implacable*, where they watched a display of naval aircraft flying off and landing on the flight deck, and followed this with visits to the *Cleopatra* and *Diadem*, where the swell made it difficult for the barge to go alongside. By the time they arrived at the *St. Kitts*, the swell had increased considerably, and while Princess Elizabeth was descending the gangway ladder, the barge was thrown by the sea against it and smashed it. No one, however, was any the worse for the incident and the Royal party returned to the *Vanguard* without further trouble.

Deck games, parties, and a ship's company concert were organized to brighten the sea routine of the ship as the *Vanguard* approached the equator. This was the limit of the Home Fleet's escort duties and they were relieved just north of the line by the *Nigeria*, flagship of the South Atlantic Squadron, which put out from Freetown. She brought with her official mail and fresh provisions in the form of eggs and fruit. As she joined company, the Home Fleet escorts formed a column in line ahead and, led by the *Implacable*, steamed past the *Vanguard*, firing a final salute and cheering the Royal party. The carrier's air squadrons of Seafires and Fireflies took off and dipped in salute as they flew past overhead.

Out from Trinidad, away in the West Indies, had come the fleet tanker *Brown Ranger* to rendezvous with the *Vanguard*. She was met on the Sunday and the *Vanguard* refuelled from her, an operation which had been practised during the ship's previous cruise to Gibraltar. This business of fuelling at sea is not always an easy one, especially if there is anything of a sea running, but on this occasion everything went off without a hitch.

That evening, to celebrate the imminent crossing of the equator, a firework display was given in the ship. As it ended, the first acts in the old familiar naval ceremony of "Crossing the Line" were performed. Up over the bows climbed "Dolphinius, Clerk of the Court to His Most Turbulent Oceanic Majesty, King Neptune", together with his escort of police and bears. He read a proclamation convening a court on board H.M.S. *Vanguard* next morning, "to greet his fellow monarch, decorate loyal subjects, punish malefactors, and initiate novices".

The *Vanguard* crossed the line during the early hours of February 10th, in longitude 9° 30′ W., and at half past eight the ceremony started. Their Oceanic Majesties, King Neptune and Queen Amphitrite, took their places at the pool, and the captain, arriving

with the King and Queen, introduced them. And so ensued one of
the Navy's special "rags", a custom that never grows stale no matter
how many times repeated. This was rather a special occasion, as
the King and Queen, being old travellers, were welcomed by King
Neptune as the first *ruling* sovereigns ever to cross the boundaries of
his domain and were presented with equatorial season tickets.

The days passed as the *Vanguard*, escorted by the *Nigeria*, steamed
steadily south. Parties, treasure hunts, and other deck games helped
to fill up the time until, on February 16th, the *Vanguard* met the famous
Cape rollers, sweeping up out of the Antarctic Ocean. She was joined
here by the sloops *Nereide* and *Actaeon*, together with the three frigates
of the South African Naval Forces, *Transvaal*, *Good Hope*, and *Natal*, as
additional escorts for the last part of the voyage into Cape Town Bay.

On this night of February 16th, something of a transformation
scene was taking place in Cape Town. Thousands of people were
pouring into the city from the surrounding countryside, prepared
to spend a night out in the open to make sure of their positions for a
good view of the morrow's spectacle. And on the morning of the 17th
they were joined by thousands more of the city's inhabitants, till the
whole area round the Duncan Dock in Cape Town harbour, where
the *Vanguard* was to berth, was a solid mass of spectators.

The day of the 17th dawned bright and clear, one of those crystalline
South African days when the air is like a sparkling wine. Table
Mountain stood out clear and majestic against the blue of the sky.
Out in the Bay lay the great battleship which had borne their
Majesties and the Princesses from England, and as she got under way
at half past eight and steamed slowly towards the shore, the waiting
thousands could make out four figures standing on a special platform
built on the top of "B" turret. Great cheers went up from the shore
and, with the Queen waving to the immense crowd, the *Vanguard*
came gently alongside, her upper decks lined with sailors in white
tropical rig, manning ship, and with the Royal Standard still fluttering
from her mainmast head. Once again she was dressed overall and her
bunting added to the many colours of this brilliant summer day.

As soon as the *Vanguard* was secured alongside, bands ashore
played the two national anthems, "God Save the King", and "Die
Stem van Suid Afrika". The Governor-General, Meneer Brand van Zyl,
and the Prime Minister, the late General Smuts, went aboard to greet
the King and Queen. Then, for the last time on the outward trip, the
King inspected the Royal Marine guard of honour, and the two
national anthems were again played, this time by the ship's band.
As the King stepped down the gangway, the ship's guns fired their
salute of 21 guns, to be echoed by other guns ashore as, for the first
time in history, a reigning monarch set foot on South African soil.
Simultaneously the Royal Standard was lowered from the *Vanguard's*
masthead. And so ended the first chapter of the *Vanguard's* part in this
triumphal progress.

While the Royal party was ashore, the *Vanguard* spent part of her time in Cape Town, part in paying a series of visits to ports round the coast, and part in exercising with other naval units. At many places she was thrown open to visitors, and her great size and impressive armament were a permanent source of wonder and admiration to all who visited her. It was while she was in South African waters that a mishap occurred which, fortunately, had no serious consequences. Some electric cables in the computor room fused and a fire broke out which did considerable damage before it was brought under control and extinguished.

For just on two months the *Vanguard* remained in these waters, waiting for the end of the King's visit and the start of the voyage home. By April 17th the Royal party was again in Cape Province. The day fixed for departure was April 24th, a day which must be as memorable to the people of South Africa as it was to those of the ship's company of H.M.S. *Vanguard* who were on deck during that moving and dramatic leave-taking.

Once again the *Vanguard* was alongside in Duncan Dock and the stands erected around it were packed with people. They saw the Royal family come to the special platform on the dockside to say good-bye to the notabilities assembled there. They heard the two anthems played again and saw the Royal family proceed up the brow and step on board the *Vanguard*, the Royal Standard being broken out at the mast-head again. A moment or two later the King and Queen, accompanied by the two Princesses, stepped out onto the high platform above "B" turret, where they stood waving to the people who had come to watch the last moments and to say a last good-bye.

Slowly the *Vanguard* edged away from the quay, and the sound of singing came from ashore, the refrains of "Sarie Marais", of "God be with you till we meet again", of the Skye Boat song, "Will ye no' come back again?", of "Land of Hope and Glory", and finally of "Auld Lang Syne". The sound was carried across the water as the distance between ship and shore slowly widened. It was an intensely moving scene, with the songs rising from thousands of throats and with the four figures, becoming smaller and smaller as the ship moved out into the Bay, still waving good-bye from their high platform. But before the *Vanguard* was out in the harbour, the crowds broke from the stands and came streaming down to the dockside, and then, from this sea of faces and waving hands, there broke out once more the nostalgic, "Sarie Marais", and cries of "*Tot Siens*", the South African equivalent of *au revoir*.

The voyage home was uneventful, the days being enlivened in much the same way as on the outward trip, with deck games, ship's company concerts, and other amusements. And finally, when the *Vanguard* was once again berthed alongside the South Railway Jetty in Portsmouth Harbour, when the last salutes had been fired, the guard of honour inspected, and the Royal party had left the ship for their journey back to London, there were nothing but happy memories left for the ship's company, memories of a wonderful cruise and of the whole-hearted hospitality of the South African people. Thoughts began to turn towards a deferred Easter leave, and very soon the great ship lay quiet in her berth, reverting once again to the normal, everyday life of a battleship. She had steamed nearly 12,000 miles since that wintry day, some three months before, when she had left Portsmouth outward bound.

Now those days were done. As soon as leave to the crew was completed, she sailed to Devonport and was paid off, entering the dockyard for a long refit. She was, too, temporarily to sever her ties with Portsmouth, for when she recommissioned, it was as a Devonport ship, with a West Country crew. At the end of her refit she joined the Mediterranean Fleet for a short commission of six months, returning to England to take over the post of flagship of the Training Squadron, based on Portland.

It may well be that this ninth *Vanguard*, as many naval officers think, will be the last battleship to be built in this country. One hopes that she will never be called upon to add to the battle honours which are already associated with the name of *Vanguard*, for war is an ugly business, and doubly so in these days of modern weapons designed for mass destruction.

It might well be that she has another part to play. Ships of war in the past have often brought a stabilizing influence to the counsels of nations, and history shows that the White Ensign of the Royal Navy has as frequently kept the peace as it has engaged in war. The presence of a British warship on a troubled scene used to bring confidence and a guarantee that justice would be upheld. "Grey ambassadors" they were called, and this, perhaps, would be the proudest role of all for the new *Vanguard* to play, an ambassador of peace.

REFERENCES

CHAPTER I

1. Corbett, *Drake and the Tudor Navy.* Appendix C, Elizabethan tonnage measurements, ii, 421.
2. Monson, *Naval Tracts,* i, 321. A similar statement by the Duke of Stettin when taken to Chatham to inspect the Navy bears out this method of construction. "I found them all built very low at the head, but very high at the stern, so that it made me shudder to look down." Transactions of the Royal Hist. Soc., New Series, iv, 65.
3. Pipe Office accounts, 1588–1589. *Armada Papers,* N.R.S., ii, 319, 323.
4. Walsyngham to Stafford. C. S. Misc., v, 29.
5. Hakluyt, *Principal Voyages.*
6. Wynter to The Principal Officers. *Armada Papers,* N.R.S., i, 81.
7. Note on Ships in the Queen's Pay. *Armada Papers,* N.R.S., ii, 180. Foljambe Papers, Hist. MSS. Comm., XV, v, 117.
8. *The English Mercurie,* July 23, 1588.
9. Seymour to Walsyngham. *Armada Papers,* N.R.S., i, 300.
10. Wynter to Walsyngham. Ibid, i, 214.
11. Seymour to the Council. Ibid, i, 330; Wynter to Walsyngham. Ibid, i, 332.
12. Wynter to Walsyngham, Ibid, ii, 7.
13. Ibid, p. 8.
14. Ibid, p. 10.
15. *Una Carta del Padre Geronimo de la Torre.* Duro, *Armada Española,* ii, 405.
16. Wynter to Walsyngham. *Armada Papers,* N.R.S., ii, 11.
17. Don Luis de Miranda. Duro, ii, 271.
18. Seymour to Walsyngham. *Armada Papers,* N.R.S., ii, 4.

CHAPTER II

1. Monson, *Naval Tracts.*
2. Corbett, *The Successors of Drake,* p. 46.
3. Carew to Cecil. Add. MSS. 6177.
4. Dr. Roger Marbecke, *A brief and true discourse of the late honourable voyage into Spain, and of the winning, sacking and burning of the famous town of Cadiz there, and of the overthrow of the Spanish Navy at that time, with a report of all other accidents appertaining, by Dr. Marbecke, attending upon the person of the right honourable the Lord High Admiral of England all the time of the said action.* B.M. Sloane MSS, 229.
5. Corbett, *The Successors of Drake,* p. 75.
6. Marbecke, *A brief and true discourse, etc.*
7. Sir Francis Vere, *Commentaries.*
8. Edwardes, *Life of Raleigh,* ii, 139.
9. Ibid.
10. Hatfield Papers, vi, 379.
11. Hans Williamson, Letter of Intelligence. S. P. Spain, xxxii, fol. 58.

12. Monson, *Naval Tracts.*
13. S. P. Dom., James I. lxv, 16.
14. Lediard, *Naval History*, p. 440. Walsyngham, who was pardoned on his return to England, later attempted to sieze the *Dreadnought* and set up again with her as a pirate. He was sent to the Tower and, presumably, later hanged. S.P. Dom. April 17, 1622.
15. Foedera vii, iii, 165.
16. Mansell to Buckingham. Cabala i, 140.
17. Monson, *Naval Tracts.*
18. S.P. Dom., James I, clxxxv, 99.
19. S.P. Dom., Charles I, iv, 136, 137.
20. Gardiner, *History of England.* vi, 40.

CHAPTER III

1. Thomas Buck to Sir R. Cotton. Pepysian MSS. *Miscellanies*, x, 380.
2. Churchill, *Voyages*, iii, 372. (Naval Tracts.)
3. S.P. Dom., Charles I, cccxxxvi, 76.
4. Ibid, 13, 14, 15, 21, 74, 75, 77.
5. Hollond, *Discourses*. N.R.S., p. 268.
6. S.P. Dom., Charles I, cxlix, 92.
7. Clowes, *The Royal Navy*, ii, 19.
8. Pepysian MSS. *Naval Minutes*, p. 274.
9. Hollond, *The Navy Ript and Ransackt*. N.R.S., p. 178, 179.
10. Ibid, p. 153.
11. S.P. Dom., xcviii, 26.
12. *The Diary of Henry Teonge, chaplain on board his Majesty's ships Assistance, Bristol, and Royal Oak, anno* 1675 *to* 1679. (London, 1825.)
13. *Diologicall Discourse of Marine Affaires*. Harl. MSS., 1341.
14. For confirmation of date see S.P. Dom., lvi, 101.
15. Oppenheim, *Administration of the Royal Navy*, 239.
16. S.P. Dom., v, 6, 24, 36.
17. Ibid, cccclix, 8, 60.
18. Ibid, xxxiv, 85; lvi, 66.

CHAPTER IV

1. Gardiner, *History of England*, i, 200.
2. *The First Dutch War*, 1552–1554. N.R.S. i, 48.
3. *An Exact and Perfect Relation of the Terrible and Bloody Fight*, etc. B.M. Press, Mark E, 665, 11. (Printed in *The First Dutch War*, N.R.S. i, 204.)
4. Hist. MSS. Com. Rep 13, App. 1, p. 636.
5. B.M. Add. MSS. 17677, U, fol. 146. (In Latin, translated in *The First Dutch War*, N.R.S. i, 231.)
6. *The Answer of the Parliament of the Commonwealth of England to three papers presented to them by the Ambassadors Extraordinary of the Lords the States-General of the United Provinces, the first whereof is dated May* 24, *the second May* 27, *and the third June* 3, *upon occasion of the late fight between the fleets.* Bodl. Lib., Tanner MSS. liii, fol. 55.

7. Clowes, *The Royal Navy*, ii, 149.
8. Cal. S.P. Dom, May 24, 1652.
9. Clarendon S.P., Cal. ii, 743; C.O.S. to Blake, 10th June, 1652.
10. Cal. S.P. Dom., July 11.
11. Cal. S.P. Dom., July 19, 335, 339 *et seq.*
12. *The First Dutch War*, N.R.S., ii, 105.
13. *A Great and Bloody Fight at Sea*. B.M. Press, Mark E, 674, 7.
14. *The First Dutch War*, N.R.S., ii, 117, 118.
15. Ibid.
16. Ibid, ii, 266.
17. Ibid, ii, 272. Blake to the Council of State.
18. Granville Penn, *Memorials of Sir W. Penn* i, 446.
19. *The First Dutch War*, N.R.S., ii, 282. A letter from General Blake's Fleet.
20. Ibid. ii, 313. Letter from Amsterdam.

CHAPTER V

1. See Cal. S.P. Dom., 1652, 541, sending Blake intelligence from Holland of their impending departure.
2. Bodl. Lib., Tanner MSS. liii, fol. 152. Blake to C.O.S.
3. *The First Dutch War*, N.R.S., iii, 81. Orders of C.O.S.
4. Ibid., iii, 89. Letter to C.O.S.
5. *Mercurius Politicus*, B.M. Press, Mark E, 638, 18. News from the Fleet.
6. Ibid, p. 22. Letter from the Fleet.
7. *The First Dutch War*, N.R.S., iii, 92. Blake to the Admiralty Commissioners.
8. *A Perfect Account*, B.M. Press, Mark E, 683, 21, p. 805.
9. *The First Dutch War*, N.R.S., iii, 418. Orders of C.O.S.
10. Hist. MSS. Com., Rep. 13, App. 2, p. 85.
11. *The First Dutch War*, N.R.S., iii, 393. Major N. Bourne to the Admiralty Committee.
12. *A Perfect Account*, B.M. Press, Mark E, 689, 14, p. 899. Letter from aboard the *Nonsuch*.
13. *The First Dutch War*, N.R.S., iv, 79.
14. Ibid, iv, 101. A letter from the *Eagle*.
15. Ibid.
16. See Preface to *The First Dutch War*, N.R.S., iv, pp. 15, 16, 17.
17. Duke of Portland MSS. Navy Papers, 1640–1696, fol. 171.
18. Ibid, fol. 180.
19. Clar. MSS. 45, fol. 269. News from London.
20. Ibid.

CHAPTER VI

1. S.P. Dom. Commonwealth, xxxv, 144. Deane to Salwey and Carew.
2. Log of the *Vanguard*. (Printed in G. Penn, *Memorials of Sir Wm. Penn*, i, 526–532.)
3. Archives of The Hague, De Ruijter's Journals, May 4. (Printed in *The First Dutch War*, N.R.S., v, 127.)

4. Log of the *Vanguard*.
5. Archives of The Hague. M. H. Tromp to States-General, May 21.
6. Ibid, May 28.
7. Log of the *Vanguard*.
8. G. Penn, i, pp. 496–498. R. Lyons to President of C.O.S.
9. Ibid.
10. Log of the *Vanguard*.
11. G. Penn, i, pp. 496–498. R. Lyons to President of C.O.S.
12. Ibid.
13. Thurloe State Papers, i, 277. A Letter from The Hague.
14. G. Penn, i, pp. 496–498. R. Lyons to President of C.O.S.
15. Log of the *Vanguard*.
16. See Preface to Part XII, *The First Dutch War*, N.R.S., v, 147.
17. Thurloe State Papers, i, 340. A Letter of Intelligence.
18. Ibid, i, 298. A Letter of Intelligence from Middleburg.
19. S.P. Dom. Interregnum, xxxviii, 22. Blackborne to Admiralty Commissioners.
20. Ibid, xxxviii, 14. Monck to Admiralty Commissioners.
21. Ibid, xxxviii, 40. Taylor to Admiralty Commissioners.
22. Log of the *Vanguard*.
23. S.P. Dom. Interregnum, xxxiv, 10. O. Cox to Cromwell.
24. Log of the *Vanguard*.
25. Ibid.
26. S.P. Dom. Interregnum, xxxix, 11. Cubitt to Blackborne.
27. Ibid, xxxix, 10. O. Cox to Cromwell.
28. Thurloe State Papers, i, 406–411. Letters of Intelligence from the Hague.
29. Ibid.
30. Log of the *Vanguard*.

CHAPTER VII

1. J. R. Green, *A Short History of the English People*, iii, 1270.
2. John Evelyn, *Diary*, October 17, 1660.
3. See A. T. Mahan, *The Influence of Sea Power upon History*, p. 107
4. S. Pepys, *Diary*, March 6, 1665.
5. Clowes, *The Royal Navy*, ii, 256.
6. Campbell, *Lives of the British Admirals*, ii, 145.
7. List in the Rijks Archief.
8. Grant, *British Battles*, i, 317.
9. Ibid.
10. Brandt, *Life of De Ruijter*.
11. Grant, *British Battles*, i, 317.
12. Campbell, *Lives of the British Admirals*, ii, 148.
13. Grant, *British Battles*, i, 320.
14. Clowes, *The Royal Navy*, ii, 265.
15. Roxburghe Ballads, vi, 435.
16. Earl of Clarendon, *Memoirs*.
17. S. Pepys, *Diary*, August 8, 1665.

CHAPTER VIII

1. See *Poems on State Affairs*, vol. i, p. 253, on the fall of Clarendon.

   "Pride, Lust, Ambition, and the People's Hate,
   The Kingdom's broker, ruin of the State,
   Dunkirk's sad loss, *divider of the fleet*,
   Tangier's compounder for a barren sheet,
   This shrub of gentry, married to the crown,
   His daughter to the Heir, is tumbled down."

2. Campbell, *Lives of the British Admirals*, ii, 365, 366.
3. *Revue Maritime et Coloniale*, Vol. lxxxii, 137, which prints the letter in full.
4. A. T. Mahan, *The Influence of Sea Power upon History*, p. 122.
5. S. Pepys, *Diary*, June 2, 1666.
6. *Revue Maritime et Coloniale*, lxxxii, 137.
7. Ibid.
8. Grant, *British Battles*, i, 324.
9. Ibid, i, 325.
10. *Revue Maritime et Coloniale*.
11. Campbell, *Lives of the British Admirals*, ii, 162.
12. Lefèvre-Pontalis, *Jean de Witt*.
13. S. Pepys, *Diary*, June 7, 1666.
14. Sir W. Temple, *Observations*.
15. J. Evelyn, *Diary*, June 17, 1666.
16. *England's Tryumph and Holland's Downfall*. From the Euing collection, No. 93. *Songs and Ballads*, N.R.S., 63.
17. de Guiche, *Mémoires*, pp. 249 *et seq.*
18. Chabaud-Arnault, *Revue Maritime et Coloniale*, 1885.
19. S. Pepys, *Diary*, July 10, 1666.
20. Ibid., June 13, 1666.
21. Duke of Buckingham, *Memoirs*. (London, 1723.)
22. Bodl. Lib., Ward E, 25, fol. 55. Printed in *Songs and Ballads*, N.R.S., 66.
23. S. Pepys, *Diary*, July 27, 1666.
24. Ibid. June 8, 1667.
25. Ibid. June 10, 1667.
26. Ibid.
27. Clowes, *The Royal Navy*, ii, 291.
28. S. Pepys. *Diary*, June 14, 1667.
29. Sir W. Temple to Lord Lisle, Temple's *Observations*, ii, 40.
30. S. Pepys, *Diary*, June 13, 1667.
31. Cal. S.P. Dom, 1667, p. 196.
32. Ibid, p. 200.

CHAPTER IX

1. S. Pepys, *Memoirs relating to the State of the Royal Navy for Ten Years determined December*, 1688. Printed in Rev. J. Smith, *The Life and Correspondence of Samuel Pepys*, 1841.

2. D. Hannay, *A Short History of the Royal Navy*, i, 449.
3. S. Pepys, *Memoirs relating to the State of the Royal Navy, &c.*
4. Campbell, *Naval History of King James II*, ii, 387.
5. S. Pepys to Capt. Rooth. Pepysian Library, No. 2850, p. 61.
6. R. G. Howarth, *Letters and the Second Diary of Samuel Pepys*, pp. 67–69.
7. Hornby, *A Caveat against the Whigs*, ii, 50.
8. Lord Hervey, *Memoirs*.
9. D. Hannay, *A Short History of the Royal Navy*, i, 461.
10. Grant, *British Battles*, i, 425.
11. Josiah Burchett, *Memoirs of Transactions at Sea during the War with France* (London, 1703), p. 137.
12. *London Gazette*.
13. Grant, *British Battles*, i, 429.
14. Ibid.
15. Josiah Burchett, *Memoirs of Transactions at Sea during the War with France*, p. 150.
16. *The Life and Glorious Actions of the Right Honourable Sir George Rook, Kt., Sometime Admiral of the English Fleet.* (London 1707.)
17. Minutes of Council of War called on July 28 on board the *Bredah*.
18. Clowes, *The Royal Navy*, ii, 359.
19. G. M. Trevelyan, *England under Queen Anne*, i, 308.

CHAPTER X

1. Captain Edward Thompson, *Seamen's Letters*, i, 147.
2. Ibid, i, 140.
3. *The Gentleman's Magazine*, 1740, pp. 183–184.
4. William Thompson, *An Appeal to the Public to prevent the Navy of England being supplied with pernicious Provisions, etc.* (1761.)
5. Boscawen to Clevland, P.R.O. Admiralty Secretary In-Letters, 1–160.
6. Edward Thompson, *Seaman's Letters*.
7. Ibid, ii, 24.

CHAPTER XI

1. P.R.O. Admiralty Secretary In-Letters (Intelligence), 3941.
2. Newcastle Papers (Cabinet Memoranda) B.M. Add. MSS., 32,996.
3. Admirals Journals. P.R.O., Adm., 50/95. June 3, 1758.
4. Ibid. June 6, 1758.
5. Ibid, June 8, 1758.
6. Ibid, July 22, 1758.
7. Wolfe to Sackville, May 12. Hist. MSS. Com. Rep. IX, iii, 746.
8. S.P. Colonial (America and West Indies), 76.
9. Durell's despatch, March 19. P.R.O. Admiralty Secretary, In-Letters, 481.
10. Gibson to Governor Lawrence, Doughty, *Journal of Particular Transactions*, v, 65. James Gibson was an officer in the *Vanguard* during the expedition against Quebec.

11. Remigny to Bougainville, Sept. 11, 1759. Printed in Doughty, iv, 121.
12. Townshend to Pitt. Doughty iv, 112.
13. Sir Julian S. Corbett, *England in the Seven Years' War*, i, 476.
14. Saunders to Pitt, November 19, 1759. B.M. Chatham MSS. 79.
15. Newcastle Papers, 32,899.
16. Horace Walpole, *Memoirs of the Reign of King George II*, iii, 231.
17. Walpole to Sir Horace Mann, December 13, 1759. *The Letters of Horace Walpole*, iv, 7.
18. Murray to Amherst, April 30, 1760. Thackeray, *History of Lord Chatham*, i, 472.
19. Pitt to Lady Hester Pitt, Chatham Corr., ii, 45.
20. *The Gentleman's Magazine*, 1762, 130.
21. Ibid, 131.
22. "A Society of Naval Gentlemen", *Britannia Triumphant*, p. 275. (London, 1777.)

CHAPTER XII

1. Clowes, *The Royal Navy*, iv, 73; J. Ralfe, *The Naval Biography of Great Britain*, ii, 35.
2. *Napoleon's Correspondence*, ii, 76.
3. *Victoires et Conquêtes*, x, 375.
4. St. Vincent to Nelson, Jan. 8, 1798.

CHAPTER XIII

1. St. Vincent to Spencer, May 1, 1798. N.R.S., *The Spencer Papers*, ii, 441, 442.
2. Spencer to St. Vincent, April 29. Ibid, ii, 438.
3. Dundas to Spencer, June 9. Ibid, ii, 448.
4. Log of the *Vanguard*. She was a polacre corvette, with six guns and two swivels.
5. Berry to the Rev. Dr. Foster, May 29, 1798. Printed in Sir H. Nicolas, *Despatches and Letters of Vice-Admiral Lord Viscount Nelson*, iii, 17, note.
6. Nelson to Lady Nelson, Nicolas, iii, 17.
7. These figures are given in *Histoire Scientifique et Militaire de l'Expedition à l'Egypte*, but differ from those given by Napoleon in his memoirs, which are considerably less, and those given by M. Thiers, which are considerably more. Some confirmation can be found in an intercepted letter from a French officer at Cairo (Intercepted Letters, II, 144)—*Je me suis demandé à moi-même, comment le gouvernement Francois avoit fait tant d'efforts, et exposé une Armée de quarante mille hommes, pour venir soumettre un peuple si féroce et si abruti.*
8. St. Vincent to Nelson, May 21, 1798. Nicolas, iii, 26.
9. Nelson to Spencer, June 15. Nicolas, iii, 31.
10. Log of the *Vanguard*.
11. A. T. Mahan, *The Life of Nelson*, p. 287.
12. Nelson to Lady Nelson, July 20, 1798. Nicolas, iii, 45.

13. Nelson to St. Vincent, June 29, 1798, Nicolas, iii, 38–41.
14. Log of the *Vanguard*.
15. Signal log of the *Vanguard*, N.R.S. *Great Sea Fights*, 1794–1805, ii, 56.

CHAPTER XIV

1. Sir Edward Berry, *An Authentic Narrative of the proceedings of His Majesty's Squadron under the Command of Rear-Admiral Sir Horatio Nelson, from its sailing from Gibraltar to the conclusion of the Glorious Battle of the Nile, drawn up from the Minutes of an Officer of Rank in the Squadron.* Printed in Nicolas, *Letters and Despatches*, iii, 48.
2. J. M. Tucker, *The Life and Naval Memoirs of Lord Nelson*, p. 267.
3. Sir E. Berry, *An Authentic Narrative, etc.*
4. Signal log of the *Vanguard*.
5. Memorandum by Captain Webley, N.R.S., *Great Sea Fights*, ii, 26.
6. Clowes, *The Royal Navy*, iv, 360.
7. Clarke and M'Arthur, *Life of Admiral Lord Nelson, K.B.*, ii, 78.
8. Log of the *Goliath*.
9. Ibid.
10. Sir E. Berry, *An Authentic Narrative, etc.*
11. Log of the *Bellerophon*.
12. Sir E. Berry, *An Authentic Narrative, etc.*
13. Ibid.
14. Ibid.
15. Hood to Viscount Hood, N.R.S., *Great Sea Fights*, ii, 24.
16. Nelson's Despatch to St. Vincent, August 3, 1798. Nicolas, *Letters and Despatches*, iii, 59. Nelson did not include himself in the list of wounded.
17. Ibid.
18. Hallowell to Nelson, Nicolas, iii, 89.
19. Clarke and M'Arthur, *Life of Nelson*, App. 5, ii, 480.
20. Spencer to Nelson, Oct. 7, 1798. Nicolas, iii, 75.

CHAPTER XV

1. Nelson to Lady Nelson, about Sept. 25, 1798. Nicolas, *Letters and Despatches*, iii, 130.
2. Nelson to St. Vincent, Nov. 7, 1798. Nicolas, iii, 166.
3. Nelson to Troubridge, Dec. 15, 1798. Nicolas, iii, 202.
4. R. Southey, *Life of Nelson* (Everyman Edn.), p. 141.
5. Nelson to St. Vincent. Nicolas, iii, 212–213.
6. Nelson to Keith, June 27, 1799. Nicolas, iii, 391.

CHAPTER XVI

1. *Victoires et Conquêtes*, tome xiv, 18.
2. James, *The Naval History of Great Britain*, iii, 164.

3. Sir W. Clowes, *The Royal Navy*, v, 82.
4. Log of the *Vanguard*.
5. James, *The Naval History*, iv, 297.
6. Dundonald, *Observations on Naval Affairs*, p. 6.
7. Sloane-Stanley, *Reminiscences*, p. 283.
8. From the Madden Collection (Country Printers, vii, 163). See N.R.S., *Naval Songs and Ballads*, p. 320.
9. Clowes, *The Royal Navy*, v, 1–2.

CHAPTER XVII

1. Commodore Sir C. Napier, *The War in Syria*, i, 9.
2. Ibid, i, 139.
3. Ibid, i, 280.
4. Napier to Mrs. Napier, November 26, 1840. See Clowes, *The Royal Navy*, vi, 332.
5. Commander Georg von Hase, *Die Zwei Weissen Volken*, p. 196. von Hase was Gunnery Officer of the *Derfflinger* during the Battle of Jutland.

INDEX